A STANDARD RELIGIOUSLY IRRELEVANT VERSION (S.R.I.V.)

TWIST OF FATE EDITION

Steve Morgan

(LIKELY) FIRST & ONLY
PAPERWEIGHT,
DOORSTOP, BOOKEND EDITION.

Copyright © 2021-2023 by Steve Morgan

 A catalogue record for this book is available from the National Library of Australia

All Rights Reserved.
ISBN: 978-0-6459105-1-3 (ebk)
ISBN: 978-0-6459105-0-6 (pbk)

Cover image: SimoneN © (shutterstock)

Typesetting and design by Publicious Book Publishing.

Published with the assistance of
Publicious Book Publishing
www.publicious.com.au

Including the right of reproduction in any form, or part. Unless; in brief, & with acknowledgment of this work & author. All clipart used with permission & disclaimer:
https://creativecommons.org/publicdomain/zero/1.0/licence.

A STANDARD RELIGIOUSLY IRRELEVANT VERSION (S.R.I.V.)

TWIST OF FATE EDITION

DISSIMILAR TO PSALMS

LEAD NOT ANY TO TEMPTATION. THEY ARE QUITE CAPABLE OF FINDING THEIR OWN WAY.

A LOWN DISPOSITION = MINDFULNESS. MUCH LOTUS POSITIONING FOR MEDITATION IS MOST BENEFICIAL FOR BRINGING CALMNESS, & MINDFULNESS.

IT HAS BECOME WIDELY ACCEPTED THAT SOME PEOPLE INSIST ON ADOPTING THE IDENTIFICATION OF A CAT, OR OTHERKIN. BETTER, IS TO ADOPT THE LIKENESS OF A TREE, NOURISHED BY CLEAR, FRESH WATERS, ALL MANNERS OF FRUITS WILL YIELD, IN THEIR DUE TIME, & SEASON.

IF SOMEONE ASKS, "WHO TAUGHT YOU? WHO WAS YOUR TEACHER?" THE WISE WOULD ANSWER, "NOBODY. I ONCE WITNESSED THE FOLLY, & INEPTITUDE OF THE IGNORANT, & SELF-RIGHTEOUS. IT WAS THEN THAT I DECIDED TO AVOID BOTH."

STEVE MORGAN

Satire, hyperbole, lampooning, mockery, taunting, comical, ridiculous. Call the scriptures what you will, just don't call it a holy adytum. A sanctuary of the soul, unless that soul wish to be amused to the point of 'holy' risibility. A gelastic disposition, this should be a mandated staple of all who read, study, or swoon over the scriptures. If one observes the plain translated English text as it has been offered by scholars. Time & again numerously places, & occasions read in the Judaeo-Christian Bible transmogrify, causing a scratching of the head, & quizzical thoughts. Much of the world today has forsaken, & forgotten how to laugh at itself. Let alone some praised notional religious anecdotes. This is a storybook offering readers a harmless, & jocose account of several Standard Bible anecdotes to help remedy this. Those that are too often read, & believed as only topics of homiletics. Like, what is with the 'idea' of our innate basophobia? According to the churches own ipse dixit explaining (Genesis 3:1). Believers are taught to be most terrified of tripping over. Falling over themselves in a mad rush to be somewhere better than here & accepted the offer & redemption of a redeemer.

The Religiously Irrelevant Version is an aniconic motley collection of Judaeo-Christian Bible folktales highlighting several extraordinary modern oddities, beliefs homogenised with the folklore of the Christian religion. Tales that are entertaining & easily relatable to modern people. In celebration of the stories, & Promethean human ingenuity.

ABOUT THE AUTHOR:

Born into a Christian family, in 1971, Steve applied himself to an extensive study of Christianity through the 1990's. Leading to a departure from the faith in the mid 2000's. In 2012 Steve was forced into retirement with a disability. Since, his life has grown with several interests emerging. An amateur parrot breeder, amateur Colour Pencil artist, writer, reader & avid lawn Bowler. Is a fan of quality film, documentaries, & intelligent comedy: "Fluffy", & Bill Bailey. He has an ever widening assortment of interests; Stoicism, philosophy, & Egyptian History. Never married, he lives with himself in Echuca, a border town on the Murray River in regional Victoria, Australia, with adopted children, his beloved flock of parrots. Interest in paronomasia, & neologisms began in earnest during the worlds longest lockdown in Victoria, Australia during the recent Covid-19 pandemic, 2021. Producing The Standard Religiously Irrelevant Version, a parodied edition of several Christian folklore, & The Punisher's Dictionary (TBP). A dictionary of puns to standard English phrases.

DEDICATED TO:

ALL NEMO, PILULOUS* (NOBODY) TYPES &
ALL GNOMES OF INSIGNIFICANCE. TO THE FACELESS
NEVER MENTIONED IN A PUBLICATION.

STEVE MORGAN

CONTENTS

NOTE ABOUT THE AUTHOR: viii
ABBREVIATIONS & SYMBOLS: ix
GLOSSARY* xi
    A: xi
    B: xiii
    C: xvi
    D: xvii
    E: xix
    F: xx
    G: xxi
    H: xxiii
    I: xxiv
    J: xxv
    K: xxv
    L: xxvi
    M: xxvii
    N: xxix
    O: xxx
    P: xxxi
    Q: xxxiii
    R: xxxiii
    S: xxxiii
    T: xxxvi
    U: xxxviii
    V: xxxviii
    W,X,Y,Z: xxxix
FRONT MATTER: xlii
Introduction to the Newest Bit: 1
    A QUESTIONABLE PARTHENOGENESIS: 1
Then there were actors: 18
    SOME OTHER ACTORS: 18
A tired Pastoral Paul 29
    TIGHT-AS: 29

A STANDARD RELIGIOUSLY IRRELEVANT VERSION (S.R.I.V.)

One-se please!..32
    PHILLY:...32
'Cleanliness - is Godliness'...33
    JUDAS:...33
To be forewarned..35
    A JOAN CITIZEN:..35
Reminder..38
    CITIZEN JOAN II:...38
Hospitality..40
    CITIZEN JOAN III:...40
Reexamining the tales of the Revelation to John.............................41
    A REEVALUATION OF JOAN:...41
A BIG BANG!..53
    THE ACTIVATION:..53
Exit stage Right, & left if you must!..94
    EUDOXUS:..94
As Instructed...119
    LEAVE-IT-TO-GUS:...119
More than a lot of people..121
    CENSUS:..121
Prophet...128
    PROPHECIES OF CHAMELEON:.....................................128
Wisdoms...130
    PROVERBS OF DRU:...130
Exactly!...136
    DISSIMILAR TO PSALMS:...136
For commercial good..141
    REAL ESTHER TATE:..141
POSTSCRIPT:..151
    Reevaluation of Paul:..152
    Paul's acting with Thecla:...155
    The Petrine Reevaluation:..160
    The Reevaluation of Pete (Stoner):..163
AFTER THOUGHT:..166
BIBLIOGRAPHY:...169

NOTE ABOUT THE AUTHOR:

Born into a Christian family, in 1971, Steve applied himself to an extensive study of Christianity through the 1990's. Leading to a departure from the faith in the mid 2000's. In 2012 Steve was forced into retirement with a disability. Since, his life has grown with several interests emerging. An amateur parrot breeder, amateur Colour Pencil artist, writer, reader & avid lawn Bowler. Is a fan of quality film, documentaries, & intelligent comedy: "Fluffy", & Bill Bailey. He has an ever widening assortment of interests; Current affairs, quirky history, Stoicism, philosophy, & Egyptian History. Never married, he lives alone in regional Victoria, Australia, with his beloved parrots. Interest in paronomasia, & neologisms began in earnest during the worlds longest lockdown in Victoria, Australia during the recent Covid-19 pandemic, 2021. Producing The Standard Religiously Irrelevant Version, a parodied edition of several Christian folklore, & The Punisher's Dictionary (TBP). A dictionary of puns to standard English phrases.

A STANDARD RELIGIOUSLY IRRELEVANT VERSION (S.R.I.V.)

ABBREVIATIONS & SYMBOLS:

†. obsolete.
(*). Asterisk (*) words/phrases, see the Glossary.
arch. Archaic.
OE. Old English.
c. circa., 'approximately'.
i.e. id est, 'that is'.
esp. Especially.
n. Noun.
v. Verb.
adj. adjective.
Slan. Slang. Frances Grose - Bibliography.
f. from.
Lex. Lexicophilia (website).
Od. Dict. Odford Dictionary.
OCD. Oxford Concise Dictionary.
Barr. Grant Barrett, Dictionary.
Brist. Joy Bristow. Bibliography.
Fowl. Fowler's Concise Dict.
Aust. Australian.
Auth. Neo. Author's neologism.
DFS. Dept. Family Services.
E.B.A.. Enterprise Bargaining Agreement.
(Agreed conditions of 'Fair work, fair pay').
Fr. French.
Fors. Forsyth. Bibliography.
Ger. German.
Gk. Greek.
Heb. Hebrew.
Hin. Hindi.
Ital. Italian.
Jn. (Apostle) John.

J. Folk. Jewish Folktale/lore.
J. Jewish.
Jap. Japanese.
Lat. Latin.
Lit. Literal.
Koenig. John Koenig. Bibliography.
Matt. (Apostle) Matthew.
Meltz. Peter. E. Meltzer. Bibliography.
NHO. Neurotic Homogenous Obedience. Uniform Mental Obedience, i.e., Christianity.
Paul. A. Jon. Paul Anthony Jones Bibliography.
Sco. Scots/Scottish.
Span. Spanish.
Vulg. Vulgar. (Frances Grose).
W. Drop. Word Drops. Bibliography.
Yidd. Yiddish.

A STANDARD RELIGIOUSLY IRRELEVANT VERSION (S.R.I.V.)

GLOSSARY*

This glossary is an A-Z of all underline* words/phrases found in commentary as an explanation assisting a reader's comprehension.

A:
- Ab aeterno - (Lat.) (ab eye-TER-no) Since time began.
- Adamitism - To practice nudity.
- Abcedarian - Teacher of/to learn the alphabet.
- Abracadabrant - Marvellous, Stunning.
- ASBO - Anti-Social-Behaviour-Order
  (As a fine, punishment for breach).
- Absquatulate - (ab-skwat-choo-leyt) - To abscond.
- Abstracted - Lost in thought. Lost elsewhere in mind.
- Acerebral - Without a brain.
- Acumen - Quick, & accurate decision making. (Auth. Neo.) a queue of men (context prevailing).
- Adonis - Footer/Endnote #62.
- Advenae - (Lat.) Stranger, new arrival, visitor, newcomer.
- Admiral's watch - High quality, restful sleep.
- Adrantomy - Dissection of the male body.
- Affinity - (OE) The attendants, companions, groupies of a big shot. Brist.
- Afflatus - Divine creative inspiration, or compulsion.
- Agitophasia - Hysterical condition causing rapid (confused/bewildering) speech. To the god-mythologist, speaking in tongues.
- Agelast - (aj-elist) Those who have lost a sense of humour.
- Agrestic - Primitive, uncivilised; belonging to the field, pasture.
- Aggiornamento - (Ital.) Meaning to bring up-to-date.
- Agminate - (AG-me-nit) (f. Lat) agmen, means "army, troop on the march".
- Aichmopobia - Intense fear of sharp-pointed instruments.
- Anchorite - Religious recluse.

- Anywhen - Any time. Commonly used by peasants (South England). Not in dictionaries.
- Alcaide - Jailer.
- Alibosh - Obvious false, or, exaggeration.
- Almery - A storage recess, with shelving. Brist.
- Allotriophagy - (al-uh-tree-oh-fuh-gee) Urge to consume abnormal, & unhealthy foods.
- All Holiday - "It's all over", completely finished.
- Ambosexan - Both Male, & Female.
- âme damnée - (Fr. Lit. Damned soul). A servant, tool of another person, group.
- Abmosquious - Author's neologism. A delightful non word, describing someone with a blood type that is not attractive to mosquitos.
- Anabiosis - To revive, bring back to life. (f. Gk.) for again, ana, & life, bios.
- Androgynous - Of indeterminate sex. Part male/female appearance.
- Anguilla - Eel.
- Aniconic - Symbolic rather than literal representation (of the Judaeo-Christian Bible narratives.)
- Anserous - Absurd, stupid.
- Answer-jobber - A skilled trade of writing answers.
- Antre - A cave, cavern, grotto, dugout, pothole.
- Antanagoge - Countercharge in retort of an accusation.
- Apanthropy - (uh-pan-throh-pee) - A desire to remain alone.
- Apologibe - Insincere apology.
- Apple Dumplin' shop - (Slan.) Woman's bosom.
- Aprosexia - (ap-roh-sehx-ee-h) - Inability to concentrate for a distracted, wandering mind.
- Arbiter elengantiae - An authority on style, fashion, tastes, protocol, etc.
- Ariston - (Gk.) Breakfast/brekkie.
- Arriviste - (ah-ree-vist) Ambitious, ruthless, self-seeking.
- Asceticism - Severe self-discipline. Avoiding indulgence on religious grounds.
- Asseveration - A solemn or emphatic declaration or statement about something.

A STANDARD RELIGIOUSLY IRRELEVANT VERSION (S.R.I.V.)

- Asteroids - Painful haemorrhoid like swellings plants suffer. Od. Dict.
- Asque - (Ass-Queue) (Auth. Neo.) A queue of donkey's. [Donkeys in original quote].
- Astrophe - (as-truh-fee) The feeling of being stuck on earth. The sense is briefly broken when gazing into the night sky, wondering 'what's out there?' Only to be reminded of our bond to the ground we tread. See also onism. Koenig.
- Ataraxia - (at-ah-rax-siah) Serenity, calmness.
- Ataxy. - (Not a Taxicab) Disturbance in bodily function.
- Atelier - An artist, designer's studio/workshop.
- Amen - "We are in fierce agreement. This should End - Now"!
- Asplode - Uncouth expression, representation of explode. Uneducated speech. (Vulg.) To fart!
- Aubadoir - (n. Oh-bah-dwah) the otherworldly atmosphere just prior to 5 a.m. Koenig.
- Auld Lang Syne - (Scot. folk New Years tune, 1778) auld lang syne means, 'Times gone by'… a distant past. Syne means 'Since, subsequently, moreover, furthermore'.
- Aureate - Golden.
- Auripotence - Dominance, power, Influence.
- Avifauna - Birds.
- Avatar - An icon/figure representing someone. Release of the soul from the body. A manifestation of a deity.
- Awkward - The word awk signifies Left as opposed to Dexter = Right. Things done awkwardly are sinister. Done from the Left. Dexter, (Lat. 16th Century) = from the Right.

B:

- Babalog - The 'young' irrational, easily influenced westerner concerned with social issues, fads, & superficialities.
- Bacchanalia - Drunken Roman festival in honor of the Greek god of wine, Bakkhos/Bacchus. Privately funded, & renowned for licentious behaviour.
- Bacon - See, Turkey bacon.
- Baptism - To 'Christianise' bread rolls.
- Balaamite - Religiously greedy, for financial gain.

- Barcode - The code-of-practice-&-conduct for all Bar patrons/publicans.
- Barman/barnman - Farmyard Impressionist. See barman - Od. Dict.
- Barometer - (Auth. Neo.) A devise to check the alcoholic content of a grogged-up bar/pub patron.
- Bass - Vegetable fibre. Bristow.
- Bedewed - Drunk. In this context, well-satiated by morning dew.
- Bell, book & candle - The religious variant of cancelling someone. To excommunicate from the congregation.
- Bel esprit (belespree) - (Fr. lit. beautiful mind) gifted/witty person.
- Belue - Sea monsters, whale.
- Betwixt/(Betweenity) - Between two things/people.
- Bibliomancy - Form of divination by opening the bible to a random passage, & interpreting said passage in relation to a circumstance.
- Bien pensant - (Fr.) Rational, right-thinking.
- Bigotry - Unrestrained, unchecked conceit. A conceited try-hard/wannabe.
- Biking - (f. Jap.) All-you-can-eat buffet.
- Bilboes - (Not an extra in "Lord of the Rings") Sliding shackling bar to detain prisoners ankles.
- Bio - Biological.
- Bioluminescent - Organism that glows in the dark.
- Bishop - A drink of 'wine & water' with a roasted orange, (instead of a wedge of lime).
- Blandiose - Appearing impressive, having pretensions of grandeur.
- Bleeding deacon - Those who believe themselves indispensable, & the font of wisdom, but is also morally, ethically pernicious.
- Blocked at both ends - Finished.
- Blin Fou - Blind (full) Drunk. Sixteenth Century (Sco. word).
- Blurb. - (v.) As a verb. To flatter, & compliment oneself from self interest.
- Boi - (boy) Feminine male, masculine lesbian.
- Boondocking - Living without modern amenities, & other luxuries of convenience.
- Bosh - Crazy, foolish. c. mid 1800's.
- Boulevard Journalist - Journalists who are exploitative, unscrupulous.

A STANDARD RELIGIOUSLY IRRELEVANT VERSION (S.R.I.V.)

- Blutterbunged - Overcome by surprise. See also, gloppened, pixilated.
- Braggart - 1. Boaster of achievements/possessions. 2. (Auth. Neo.) Appraiser of Artwork.
- Braaivleis - Open fire barbecue.
- Brangle - 1. To squabble. 'War of words'; dust-up… potentially causing, 2. Bent angles.
- Breast Fleet - (Slan.) Roman Catholic, on account of beating their breasts during confessional.
- Breastsummer - (Not nude sunbathing) The supporting beam to an entrance, or portico.
- Breviloquent (breviloquence) - Succinct in speech.
- Brobdingnagain - ENORMOUS! Opposite to lilliputian.
- Brownstudy - Melancholic meditation.
- Buddha - An ascetic.
- Bug - Originally, & the oldest meaning of 'bug' is an object of fear, i.e., a goblin, vampire, 'evil' entity. In the so-named 'The Bug Bible' (c.1551) translation of Psalm 91:5, the (Heb.) term for 'the terror' in this passage was rendered bug, reading: "…not fear the (bug) of the night." Likely meaning an external night-terror, than an emotional experience of alarm, fear, panic (terror). See, - BUG: Edwards.
- Bukateria - Cafe, eatery, insignificant place to eat.
- Bulldozer - A pretentious, boring politician.
- Bumbershoot - Umbrella.
- Bush Oyster - Mucous, snot.
- Bush Telly - Camp fire.
- But & Ben - Two room dwelling. BUT = kitchen, inner room. BEN, outer room. Bristow.
- Butter-print - A child that noticeably resembles parents.
- Buttock-mail - (Sco.) Tax levied on persons who practiced 'Interconnectedness' (see below) out of wedlock.

C:

- Cabobble - Mystified, confused.
- Cackling Cheats - Fowls, chicken.
- Cachinnate - Laugh loudly, in an unrestrained manner.

- Cacoethes Loquendi - (Lat.) Verbal diarrhoea, gift of the gab, flowing tongue.
- Caller - (OE) meaning 'fresh, & cool', as in 'caller waters'. Not in modern dict. Edwards.
- Cancel - Public boycott. To withdraw support. Regard as socially unacceptable. (Auth. Neo.) If cancelled, the punishment is placing the perpetrator in a very small jail cell.
- Candid - (Modal v. + v. Contraction) 'Can+Did'. The deity can, & did do…
- Captain Cook - To take a 'look', to peer at something.
- Carp - (v. Not the Fish) To fuss over, be picky, object to trivial matters. Never pleased.
- Caravanserai - See xenodocium. Strictly a Middle-Eastern Caravan park.
- Caterwaul - Howl with an appalling noise. (As mating cats, or, singing out of tune).
- Centralia - Desert, like the centre of Australia.
- Change one's life - Die. Face death.
- Chevroleg (Toyotoe) - Jocular reference to legs.
- Circumambulate - Walk around as a ritual.
- Clack Box - See 'Garrulous'.
- Clamberskull - Very strong drink. Overpowering liquor.
- Clancularious - (†.1656) Secret, shrouded, private, clandestine.
- Clinomania - Urge to remain lying down. (A sleep disorder).
- Clay resident - Die. (Put to clay; to kill).
- Clericus pacis - (Lat.) Cleric of the peace, principal legal officer of authorities. Brist.
- Cobweb Morning - A Norfolk term for morning. Describing the gleaming of cobwebs in the early morn dew shimmers.
- Codpiece - Man's breeches, for modesty.
- Collywobbles - Stomachache.
- Comfoozled - Spent, exhausted.
- Compos mentis - (Lat.) Sane, balanced mental state.
- Compurgator. - Sworn witness to good character.

A STANDARD RELIGIOUSLY IRRELEVANT VERSION (S.R.I.V.)

- Concordat - A mutual interest agreement between the secular & 'Holy See'. Ol' El standing here for the Holy See, Dru as the secular party.
- Condiddle - Steal, pilfer, 'borrow'.
- Confarreation - (Lex.) Roman Marriage.
- Contraband - A musical ensemble of bootleggers.
- Contaminotion - Those viral, spurious projections oppressing debate, & reality.
- Continually - Real long passageway, tunnel, maze. See Od. Dict.
- Controver - (c.1721) Trafficker of false gossip. See also effutiation.
- Corvée - Unpaid labourer.
- Coronal - Crown of the head.
- Crapulence - Feeling's of sickness after much indulgence in drinking, eating.
- Coxa-commissure - (coxa) Hip-(commissure) joint. Thus, Hip-joint.
- Chance the poker - To exaggerate a story.
- Chilth - (Cornwall dialect, United Kingdom) Describing an attempt to escape a chilled atmosphere.
- Chrestomathy - Select (Bible) narratives.
- Churchyard Cough - A cough that terminates in death.
- Cypher - 1. A coded message. 2. (Auth. Neo.) a little noise made by upset people (often women) when frustrated.
- Cryptozoology - Study of imaginary, or unproven creatures, monsters, entities.
- Chuck a U-ie - (Aust. Slan.) Perform a U-turn.
- Cuff & Stuff - Arrested.
- Culp - A fond delusion. Imaginary attribute.
- Cup-shotted - Sloshed, bent over ale…as drunk.
- Cunctation - Procrastinate.
- Curate's egg - (British idiom) of something containing both good, & bad elements.

D:

- Daedalic - Creative, innovative. Shrewdness.
- Damascene moment - Like the alleged apostle Paul. A 'conversion'/change in mind.
- Dandiprat - As described. Obliging.

- Dansey-headed - Staggering, clumsy, stumble.
- Day-raw - Early morning. As the sun rises over the horizon.
- Defenestrate: Throw from a window.
- Deluge - The first experiment in baptism, where one's lustration's, those imagined, or actual harmful res gestae (Lat. lit. Things done) are suddenly believed to become impeccant (faultless/pure).
- Dephlogistication - Fireproofing. To make something fireproof.
- Desanté - (n. day-suhn-tey) The brooding delirium of sickness, where time near stops, & menial tasks are difficult to complete. Koenig.
- Dekna - (Hin.) meaning to see. English, to take a dekko (look) at something.
- Dendranthropology - Theory that mankind evolved from trees.
- Derby - New Testament city.
- De profundis - (Lat.) for "Out of the depths" (First line Psalm 130.) Showing deep misery, sorrow.
- De trop - (Fr. - də tro) Unwanted, superfluous, undesirable.
- Deve - 'Protection' Levi. (Development Levi).
- Diablerie - Originally connected to an 'evil deed.' (Diabolic) Has morphed to mean recklessness.
- Dictionary - (Three bonuses of a...) (Auth. Neo.) 1. Used as an aide to better elocution, 2. and much betterer word knowing, 3. A breed of canary trained to assist to execute correct elocution.
- Diktat - Orders/decrees imposed without popular consent.
- Ding dongs - Songs.
- Discept - Absolute nonconformity. Disagreement.
- Discreetly - (adj.) i.e., dorgone - dohr-gon.) Acting in a dorgone manner, describes the wish to separate oneself from something, people without being noticed.
- Disguised - († c.1600) Drunk.
- Distinguisher - (Auth. Neo) an Upper Middle Bogan fire retardant.
- Doch-an-dorris - Last drinks.
- Dog (cat)- Latin - Senseless, rubbish writing/speech.
- Donnée. - A basic fact or assumption.
- Dragon's teeth - Actions that bring extinction. From Greek mythology of Cadmus & Jason's quest for the golden fleece.

A STANDARD RELIGIOUSLY IRRELEVANT VERSION (S.R.I.V.)

- Droit du seigneur - (Lit.) "Right of the Lord." Though often referencing sexual right. In this context, representing a 'Sense of entitlement.' An appropriate concept describing the modern elite.
- Dybbuk - (J. Folk.) Spiteful wandering spirits, demons.
- DYKWIA - (Acronym) Do You Know Who I Am?
- Dysania - Difficulty in waking, or getting out of bed.

E:

- Eco-roof - Rooftop vegetation's/garden.
- Ecozoic - (Imaginary period of a) harmonic balance between Human & environment.
- Effutiation - (†) Catastrophonical nonsense.
- Egalitarianism - Of equal right, & opportunity.
- 'Egg on your (his) chin' - A polite euphemism to draw attention to an unzipped, unbuttoned fly in hopes to save the 'offender' from embarrassment.
- Ego ramp - Rostrum, dais.
- Either-still - Anyway!
- Elbow Crooker - Excessive drinker.
- Electro-plasm - Otherworldly.
- Elfin - Mischievous. Naughty, High-spirited, boisterous.
- Eloquence - The artful (often oral) concealment of a 'lower falsehood' by persuasion of fools, that a 'higher truth' awaits.
- Elp - Sly, trickster. One who evades responsibility.
- Emodox - (n.) Those who present a mood that is out of sync with the rest (or majority) of society. They panic, quibble, or show a pensiveness about a certain topic.
- Emotion - A disease in determination between the heart & the head. Oftentimes, causing a discharge of Sodom Chloride from the eyes.
- Ensconced - To settle comfortably.
- Entomic - Related to creepy-crawly's.
- Entomophagous - Eating creepy-crawly's.
- Epexegesis - Interpretation Rationale, observation, justification.
- Essoinment - An excuse of absence.
- Eternal Box - Death/dead. Coffin.
- Etymology - Study of word origins, & meaning changes through history.

- Ethereal - Dainty, elegant, beautiful.
- Euroclydon - (you-rok-li-don) Fierce tempest, huge storm.
- Eugonic - Existing on artificial foodstuffs.
- Everton toffee - Coffee.
- Exeshoetion - The (accidental) destruction of footwear.
- Exhort(ion) - In religious affairs, to harangue the conscience of another upon a spit & roast it till a golden-brown discomfort is achieved.
- Exile - Forced to serve the homeland abroad without having an official ambassadorship appointment.
- Exordium - Beginning, introduction (Front matter).
- Expergefactor - To do with waking. An alarm system is an expergefactor.
- Extinct(ion) - The raw material & condition that theology uses to create a future position.
- Extraneous - Irrelevant, unrelated to the subject.
- Extraforaneous - Outdoor.
- Extolment - Enthusiastic praise.

F:

- Fabulosity - Exaggerated statements/stories (often made up).
- Facetiae - (arch.) Comical, witty sayings/commentary.
- Faffle - Useless work. No satisfactory result for the time spent.
- Falsetto - Inexact Ice-cream. Od. Dict.
- Famelicose - Persistent hunger.
- Fandango - Foolishness in argument or act, esp. politically, in public affairs, or serious topics.
- Fantod - State of unease, discomfort, anxiety.
- Fry - (Pl. Noun) Newly hatched fish.
- Fatidical - Gifted in prophesy.
- Fatuous - Large posterior.
- Fedifragous - To break an agreement, oath.
- Femtosecond - One quadrillionth of a second. 10 to the 15th power.
- Fell - (Adjective literary) Evil, as in cruel, terrible.
- Feresy - (f. Middle English fere, partner + heresy.) A fear that your partner has, or is changing in ways not

A STANDARD RELIGIOUSLY IRRELEVANT VERSION (S.R.I.V.)

understood. Whether anything could be done, despite the former person in essence no longer existing. Koenig.
- Forbye (also Forby) - In addition, besides, as well.
- Forgetfulness - A gift of the deity bestowed upon an individual in compensation for their insolvency of conscience.
- Fomes - Anything that infects with disease.
- Fogo - Overpowering stench.
- Fie - Expression of passioned outrage.
- Fire - in a metaphysical sense fire represents the beginnings of 'humankind's' determination, & strength of character. After-which, the vibrant energy of 'fire' was eventually domesticated.
- Firkytoodle - To cuddle/fondle.
- Finagle - To use devious means to achieve an end. To cheat.
- Fisticuffs - Manacles, hand-cuffs.
- FibbertyJibbet - A Sexually provocative woman. A better word than promiscuous.
- Fons et origo - (Lat.) Basis, cause, source, origin. The epicentre.
- Flabergudgion - Threadbare state.
- Flaneur - Idle about aimlessly. See also perambulate.
- Flarting - To mock, jeer.
- Flatuosity - Windiness.
- Flummery - Insincerity. Empty compliment. Foolish talk.
- Flux-ale - Poor quality drink.
- Fly-speck - A prototype of punctuation. Performed in great service by flies of all regions to the works of literature.
- Freedom Lawn - Uncultivated lands.
- Fubsey - Plump.
- Fudgel - Pretend to work, or do anything significant, productive.
- Fukubukuro - Gift bag of unknown & varied merchandise.

G:
- Gadabout - Wanderer, rambler, pleasure-seeker.
- Galagog - (n.) the state of being simultaneously awed, & unsettled by the vastness of the universe. Koenig.

- Gamme - (gam) Realising moving timepieces forward/backward an hour makes no difference to the day. There are still 12hrs of light. Twelve hours of After-Light.
- Gasconade - Extravagant boasting.
- Garbanzo - Chickpea.
- Garrulous -Excessively talkative.
- Gedunk - Snaks, easily consumed foodstuff.
- Gentes - Family/group related by paternity.
- Geep - Cross between a goat & sheep.
- Ghough - (n. hawkh, drawing air sharply in through mouth) the bottomless pit in the psyche for more; praise, food, money, life, more daylight, more sleep. Caused by the panic that all these & more will be stripped from you too early. Koenig.
- Gladiola - (n. or v.) The excited expression of a happy soon-to-be-bride. (Particularly, of Italian, Mexican, or Spanish bloodline).
- Glóssa (language) - Ecstatic/foreign/unknown speech. Requiring an 'inspired' interpreter for understanding.
- Glossary - Explanation of words that shine (throughout this book).
- Gloppened - Surprised!
- Gnosis/Gnostic - Spiritual (mysterious) knowledge.
- Goat-drunk - (c.1592) Lecherously drunk.
- Goig - Someone (thing) instinctively distrusted. Having an inexplicable bias & aversion.
- Golgotha - A hat. (Victorian Slan.) Taken from the New Testament gospels where Golgotha is called 'Place of the skull.' (Matt 27:33; Jn 19:17).
- Gollohix - An annoying, untimely audible nuisance.
- Goonda tax - Bribe, extortion taxes.
- Gormid - Individualistic, & selfish.
- Granmarian - (Auth. Neo.) Well educated grandparent. Specifically versed in semantics.
- Grammar-folk - Well educated.
- Green answers to blue questions - Answers unrelated to the question.
- Grimgribber - Lawyer.
- Grinnow - A stain earlier unnoticed.
- Growlery - A retreat when ill, or in a bad mood. First coined by Charles Dickens, Bleak House.

A STANDARD RELIGIOUSLY IRRELEVANT VERSION (S.R.I.V.)

- Grundyism - Intolerant conventionality. Purism.
- Gyromancer - Practice of divination by spinning in circles until the performer's dizziness caused them to fall.

H:

- Haeccity (also, Haecceity) - the individuality, or what differentiates one from another.
- Harold (Holt) - To disappear without a known cause, reason. Like former Australian Prime Minister who simply vanished after going for a swim. He was never found, seen again.
- Hamlet - Piglets. Od. Dict.
- Hammurabi - Sixth king of the first dynasty BC of Babylon. Instigated the first known collection of laws.
- Hamster Healthcare - High volume healthcare with no specialised attention.
- Hanker sore - (adj.) finding someone so attractive, but unattainable it actually becomes extremely annoying. Koenig.
- Hand & Pocket Shop - Eating establishment where monies are exchanged for foodstuffs.
- Heartspur - (n.) An unexpected surge of emotion that has a cause that is difficult to explain. Koenig.
- Hebrew - A male Jew, expressly distinguished from a Shebrew.
- Hedonism - Pursuit of pleasure, self-indulgence.
- Helmet - (adj.) died & gone to sup with Zabalus (below) & his minions.
- Here & Thereian - To be of no established or permanent residence.
- Heteroclite - Abnormal, irregular. Departing from the standard norm.
- Hibernaculum - A shelter fit for hibernation.
- Hickering - (f. Heb hikrín) to protect an image + hankering, craving. Is the habit of falling hard for an acquaintance, imagining an entire future of togetherness. Koenig.
- Hobble-de-hoy - i.e, a Youth. Sometime between boyhood, & manhood.
- Hobson's choice - (No choice at all!) Accept an offer, there is no other.
- Hocker - An (aggressive) criticiser, nagger.

- Horsefeathers - Moronic, silly, made-up.
- Horticulturalist - A specialist in the customs, traditions, lifestyle of the promiscuous.
- Hosiery - (n.) Firefighting equipment; buckets, spades, hoses etc.
- Hooverise - To be sparing/stingy (esp., with foods).
- Homegoing - Funeral, death.
- Honeyfuggle - To flatter, or express admiration for someone/thing for gain.
- Homerkin - A beer. In this context, a wine (or, several more).
- Honorificabilitudinitas - (Lat.) Meaning 'honourableness'. Dating to the Thirteenth Century. The English equivalent, honorificabilitudinity used since the sixteenth Century. See, W. Drop.
- Humbuggery - Deceitful, crap ideas, & proposals. Nonsense prose.
- Hum Durgeon - A deadly fabricated disease.
- Humgruffin - A repulsive, hideous person.
- Humpie - (Aus. f. an extinct Aboriginal language) A makeshift hut/dwelling. See also antre.
- Hutzpah (also chutzpah) - Extreme self-confidence.
- Hypnopompic - Half dream state. From the Greek hypno (sleep), pompic (sending).

I:
- Idea pot - Head. Also Knowledge box below.
- Idlewild - the thankful feeling of being stranded some place where little, or nothing can be done. The place that frees imaginations to run wild, without the prospect of material activity.
- IDP - Internally Displaced Person.
- Infans - (Lat.) Child.
- Infantulus - (Lat.) Infant boy.
- Ilius - (Lat.) Son.
- Ignis Fatuus - (Lat.) Luminescence.
- Incertitude - To have an attitude of forcefully making known qualifications.
- Indagate - To seek, or search out (as sufficient causes to, answers for…).
- Indread - Inward shamefulness. Often secretively held.

A STANDARD RELIGIOUSLY IRRELEVANT VERSION (S.R.I.V.)

- Inkyo - (Jap.) referring to the custom of stepping down or resigning a position. A more interesting word than abdicate.
- Inquilinate - (Lex. †. v.1623) To sojourn, dwell in strange places.
- Interconnectedness - (Auth. Neo.) Sex. To copulate, sleep together.
- Interview without coffee - A dressing down, disciplinary meeting.
- Italian hands - politically clever, subtle in business & life choices.
- Itinerate - A 'religious' travelling salesman.
- Impavid - Fearless. Antonym - pavidus.
- Intemperance - Lack in moderation/restraint.
- Ipse dixit - (Lat.) Literally, "he said it himself". Implying, doubt of truth. Further evidence is required.

J:

- Jenticulate - (posh) Greek way to say 'eat breakfast'.
- Jobation - Severe berating. Taken from Jób's reproofs by the deity. See book of Jób.
- Jocoserious - The melding together of 'jocular', & 'serious'.
- Jouska - (n.) The hypothetical, but very satisfying conversation that compulsively play out in your head - the cathartic heart-to-heart, analysis etc., of an event… Koenig.
- Jug-Bitten - See Blin Fou.
- Juice Bar - Pub.
- Jurgy - (Nothing to do with a jury) Means 'inclined to be argumentative'. Disappearing Dict.
- Justing - (n.) the tendency of telling yourself that it takes only one tiny tweak to solve an issue. Koenig.

K:

- Kadot - (n.) 1. f. Finnish kadotus. Once meant loss, or perdition. Now eternally damned. The sense, dread that we will all face the wall, be non-existent one day. Koenig. 2. (Auth. Neo. In grammar) The sound a period makes when marking the end of a sentence.
- Keak - Twisted injury. As a spinal deformity. I.e., the Keel becomes mangled.

- Keep - (n.) The innermost personality trait rarely let out to play with, or be exposed to another (often an embarrassing experience). f. The innermost sanctuary of a fortress. Koenig.
- Kettle of fish - In a muddle, confused.
- Kick-drop - (n.) to recalibrate former ideas to align with real-world expectations.
- Knight-errantry - Idealistic without regard for practicality.
- Knocker up - (NOT a sexual euphemism). Rather, 19th Century employee who went about knocking on windows waking people. Before the invention of affordable alarm systems.
- Knowledge box - Head, intelligence.
- Kosher - 1. Jewish laws of purity/properness. DeKosher, against purity. 2. (Auth. Neo.) A Female co-op. Opposite to Koshim - male co-op.
- Kvetch - (Yidd.) Complain, or criticise.

L:

- Laniate - (v.) Tear to pieces, lacerate, maim, maul.
- Lapidate - To stone. To pelt, throw stones. Stone to death.
- Latrocinium - A meeting/office conference. Religious parlance, a synod.
- Lay down Knife & Fork - The apocalypse.
- LeitKultur - (Ger.) Leit, 'Leading' (adj.) + Kultur, 'Culture'; "Leading Culture". Barr.
- Levanton - (n.) Euphoric emotional lift. Barr.
- Levee - Defined in the OCD. (2) as receiving guests after waking.
- Lex Talionis - Eye for an eye. (Could also be a Mafia boss.)
- Locupletative - (Lex. c.1827) Enriching.
- Lookism - Discrimination on grounds of appearance.
- Longevity - The unusual, insane ideology that allows for the extension of one's fear of death.
- Lord of Misrule - (No relation to misconduct.) Master of Christmas pageants.
- Lown - Calm, quiet sea.
- Liberosis - (n. f. Ital. libero - free) To free oneself from unnecessary worries. To live playfully & carefree. Unburdened from silly stresses, but remaining balanced. Koenig.

A STANDARD RELIGIOUSLY IRRELEVANT VERSION (S.R.I.V.)

- Lick-for-leather - Rush at speed.
- Licksome - Agreeable, pleasant, amiable. The Disappearing Dict.
- Lilliputian - Very small.
- Living Impaired - Dead.
- Lucifungous - Fleeing or hiding from light.
- Ludic - Undirected playfulness.
- Lucullan - Luxurious meals.
- Luftmensch - (Ger.) Contemplative, but impracticable persons, with no clear occupation, or income.

M:

- Mail - gender-neutral dude, chap, geezer, lad, guy, gent, fellow (you get the leitmotif). Babcock.
- Maffle - To stammer, stutter, blunder as a fool in speech.
- Magsman - Swindler. One who looks for the easily cheated. A scammer.
- Mariology - Study of the Virgin Mary.
- Maritality - Excessive affection of a wife for her husband. The correlative - uxoriousness. Affection of a Husband for his wife.
- Masculara - The application of mascara by hipster priests, & other genteel males of Kamit.
- Masculus infantulus - (Lat.) Masculine child.
- Malaise - Discomfort, unhappiness, angst, trouble.
- Mataeotechny - A pointless study discipline (particularly of a science).
- Matchbook University - Higher learning institute with low academic standards. Barr.
- Matterocracist - New power structure where meritocracy is replaced by what is deemed to matter in importance. The current Eco-activist, eco-warrior are two examples.
- Matutolypea - Early morning bad mood.
- Mauritania - West African country.
- Mamamouchi - Someone of self-appointed importance. Believing they are more important than they likely are. Fitting for a Politician, Environmentalist activist, & even the Environmental ideology of Climate Change. The ultimate modern mamamouchi cause.
- Mater - (Lat.) Mother.

- Mater meretrix (Lat.) A mother by foricatrix (fornication).
- Meander - (Auth. Neo). Contraction of 'Me, & her ('er).
- Meretrix - (Lat.) Harlot.
- Messianic (adj.) A messy manic teenager.
- Metabolic clinic - cafe.
- Metamorphic - Rock transformed by heat/pressure.
- Memento Mori -'Remember Death'. Socrates said we should 'practice death'. To know, what is really important.
- Modus vivendi - Way of life, conduct, behaviour, activities.
- Mores - Characteristics, customs of a society/community.
- Mortaville - Balad Air Base, Iraq. Which was under constant attack. So, describes continuous attack. Used here describing persistent, drip-fed brainwashing propaganda.
- Moment - A moment is precisely a fortieth of an hour. W. Drop.
- Monkey - (Auth. Neo). Set of keys to use on Monday's.
- Monadnock - Isolated hill, mountain.
- More's the pity - (Idiom) Expression of regret for the immediately stated comments.
- Mot juste - (MOE zshoost) Most suitable phrase, or word for precise communication.
- Mountebank - An Itinerate quack. A performer. Teller of stories using sleight of hand techniques.
- Micawber - The eternally optimistic, despite contrary evidence, & little justification. Based on a character in Dickens' David Copperfield. Used here defining the Green, Climate change, 'renewable' lobby who persistently advocate for the Socialist rearrangement of society.
- Micturate - Urinate.
- Mingy - See Sting-bum.
- Misandry - Dislike of, prejudice for, contempt of men/male gender.
- Misqueme - (c.1000) To dissatisfy, to offend, to disgruntle, to anger, to 'hurt' feeling.
- Mugwumpery - Stupid. Mad. Idiotic.
- Muliebrity - Womanliness. Womanhood.
- Mumblenym (Mum-bul-nim) - Words a reader likely has no idea how to pronounce, having not encountered them before.

A STANDARD RELIGIOUSLY IRRELEVANT VERSION (S.R.I.V.)

N:

- Naches - (Yidd.) Pleasure, amusement, enjoyment.
- Nail - a neutered Mail. Babcock.
- Natalis - (Lat.) of Birth. Brist.
- Nature - (n. Auth. Neo.) A mature naturalist.
- Natus et renatus - (Lat.) Born, & reborn (as in baptised). Brist.
- Naughty-Pack - (n.) 1. Person of tawdry character; 2. Promiscuous woman; 3. Wicked male; 4. Defiant, unruly, wayward child.
- Necessitarian - Someone believing there is only one way for the world to behave, live. Human conduct is dictated by force, as opposed to libertarianism.
- Necrology - Worship of the dead.
- Needle & thread - Bread.
- Neologies - New word/expressions. Invented words.
- Ne'er-be-gone - Someone who has no clue where their home is. They haphazardly move as a wanderer freely, taking them everywhere & nowhere all at once. Koenig.
- Nicotine - To cuff 'n stuff teenagers.
- Nighthawk - (n.) Recurring, nagging, (guilt ridden) thoughts that plague the mind only during AfterLight hours. Koenig.
- Ninja - As maestro Alfa geek, hotshot, doyen.
- Nisan - Seventh-month Jewish civil calendar. First month of religious year. Pun on the automobile of Nissan Motors Co.
- No Afternoon Farmer - Quick, no hesitation to act.
- Nocent - Harmful, or hurtful.
- Noceur - A late night reveller.
- Nofungelical - (Auth. Neo.) to describe the ultra/fundamentalist evangelical Christian. Or, anybody with no sense of punish, fun.
- No Longer requiring a ventilator - Having died.
- Nomothetic - Legislative.
- Nosopoetic - Anything producing unhygienic infection, disease.
- Notekin - Little notes.
- Noyade - Mass execution by drowning.
- Nudnik - A pestering, boring person.

O:

- Obloquy - Slander, 'evil-speak', abusive speech or utterance of another.
- Odeon - (f. Gk, odeon meaning a building for musical performances (amphitheatre)).
- Omnify - Enlarge. Merriam Webster Dictionary (Online) To make universal.
- Omnicide - The destruction of everything.
- Omniparity - Omnipresent, all-embracing equality.
- One-se - One piece full-length garment.
- Onism - the realised frustration that all life is essentially restricted. The conscious registering that we are all stuck in solitary confinement; of one place at any given moment in time. That our physical body inhabits a lone place at any point in space. Koenig.
- Onogata - Soubrette - Actor, actress.
- Open this (the/your) Kimono - (v. phrase) To expose, spill, reveal information. Barr.
- Open your lunch - To expel gas, to fart.
- Ophidian - Reptile/a snake.
- Opia - The intense, but ambiguous sensation of eye contact. As described. Koenig.
- Opitulate - (†. v.1582) To assist, ease, support.
- Opsony - Food of any type with bread.
- Oscitancy - Gaping drowsiness. As with a boring sermon.
- Ossifrage - Lit., "Bone-Breaker."
- Otiose - Serving no practical purpose. Indolent, idol. Leisurely.
- Outré - Unorthodox, irregular.
- Ovolactarian - Diet excluding all meats, fish, & dairy. Eggs permitted.
- Ouroboros - Though meant to be, & often is a positive symbol of spirituality, regeneration, & unity. Used here as a negative.
- Owl-light - Dusk.
- Ozurie - the state & feeling had between desiring the life you think is deserved, & the life you currently have. Koenig.

A STANDARD RELIGIOUSLY IRRELEVANT VERSION (S.R.I.V.)

P:

- Pabulum - Sustenance for animal's & plant alike.
- Palingenesis - A 'new' or second birth to a higher form. Not quite a resurrection. But, theologically close enough to cabobble others.
- Parev/parve - (J.) Meat, & dairy free meals.
- Parrot-top - Fashionable hairstyle of multi-coloured pastel colouring.
- Pater - (Lat.) Father. Brist.
- Pamphagous - Omnivorous. To eat everything.
- Pandiculate - To yawn, & stretch arms, & body mournfully.
- Parthenogenesis - Reproduction without fertilisation.
- Pantophagic - See Pamphagous.
- Parochial - Narrow-minded.
- Paronomasia - Play on words. Also pasquinade.
- Painite - 1. Borate mineral. 2. (Auth. Neo.) A painful night.
- Pauperum supervisor - (Lat.) Overseer of the poor. Brist.
- Peccable - Prone to sinning.
- Perambulate - Roam, wander about.
- Periapt - A charm, bracelet worn about the person.
- Pereginus - (Lat.) Wanderer, like the so-called pilgrim falcon.
- Peeve - Irritates, annoy.
- Phallus - (Vulg.) Male sex organ (erect).
- Phatic - Instead of speech, noises are made; i.e., incomprehensible (Baby talk).
- Phratries - Kinship group, tribal society.
- Philodox - Someone who loves fame, glory, prestige/title.
- Politesse - (pah-lih-TESS) Formal politeness, etiquette.
- Ponder - (Auth. Neo). An act similar to woolgathering, allowing the mind to travel way beyond the viewing of a pond.
- Polymicrian - Cramped, confined, poky, tight.
- Preach - A type of religious fruit. Preaching, to hand out the fruit.
- Predictus - (Lat) Above-stated, previously mentioned.
- Procellous - Stormy.
- Procuratores ecclesiae - (Lat.) Churchwardens. Brist.
- Pridie - (Lat.) The previous day. Brist.
- Primogeniture - First born.
- Primo Waters - First class water. The best in quality.

- Prostibule - A harlot, prostitute. Brist.
- Phylactery - Small (leather/vellum) box containing Hebrew law texts worn on the brow at morning prayer by Jewish men as a reminder.
- Phytoplasmas - Bacteria causing plant disease.
- Piaffer (piaffe) - Advanced dressage display. A slowly elevated trot without moving forward.
- Pilulous - Small, insignificant. As a pill in size. (Just as described).
- Pipers bidding - Last minute invitation.
- Pipestone - Hard red clay of the America's. Used by American Indians for tobacco pipes.
- Pixilated - Lead astray, as if by pixies; disoriented, drunk.
- Planet-ruler - Astrologers.
- Pleep - To express yourself with a whining, moaning tone. Disappearing Dict.
- Plums in his mouth - Is to be well-spoken.
- Plonker - (Vulg) 'Birthday suit'. Male sex organ (Also modern British slang-idiot.)
- Prandicle - Small (portions). Small meal.
- Proficuous - (Pro 'fic' u 'ous) Profitable, beneficial, advantageous. Useful.
- Promethean - Rebelliously innovative, & creative.
- Psychomachia - (psycho-MACH-ia) The struggle in the soul between good & evil.
- Puella - (Lat.) Maiden, single.
- Puella lacorum - (Lat.) Maiden of the place.
- Pumpkinification - The reckless, or unworthy, inconsistent, degrading praise of something. W. Drop.
- Punish - (puh-nish) To 'pun' Paronomasia (& pasquinade above). Slightly amusing, silly, funny, ridiculous. Od. Dict.
- Purse-proud - Ostentatious, pride in one's wealth.
- Puritanism - "The haunting fear that someone, somewhere, may be happy." H. L. Mencken. See, Botham.
- Puzzomful - Toxic, poisonous, harmful, damaging, infectious, filthy. Disappearing Dict.

Q:

A STANDARD RELIGIOUSLY IRRELEVANT VERSION (S.R.I.V.)

- Quaresimal - (Often used as describing a meagre/ skimpy meal). Used here as a description of skimpiness in attitude. See also Mingy, Sting-bum.
- Querencia - (Span.) A safe haven. To feel secure & able to be true to self.
- Quotidian (ly) - Daily, run-of-the-mill.
- Quaquaversal - (Kway- Kwe- VER- sel) Turning everywhere. No nook or cranny was safe from it.
- Quisquous - (Kwis- Kwuss) (Not to be confused with Quizcuss: inquisitive) Perplexing, confusing.

R:

- R.B.S. - Rather be sleeping.
- Rabbit-proof fence - (Aust. Slan.) Very distant, or remote from civilisation, or area.
- Ramfeezled - Exhausted.
- Raw-gabbit - To speak confidently on topics from ignorance.
- Reciprocity - The practice of exchange for mutual benefit.
- Reciplay - As it sounds. Playing with ingredients for a recipe. Od. Dict.
- Reconigibe - (Auth. Neo.) Insincere recognition.
- REM - Rapid eye movement.
- Remittance-man - Tax-man.
- Ruricolist - People of the rural regions.

S:

- Sacreligious - A sack, (marsupium) that houses, & protects religious icons & other precious paraphernalia for safe-keeping.
- Sanguisugent - Blood sucking.
- Several - (Determiner & pronoun) of more than two, but not extended to many.
- Scabulous - A tattoo, or scar on a body region that is treated & adored like an autograph. Koenig.
- Schmegeggy - Idiotic, foolish, jackass.
- Scandal Broth - Gossip over a cuppa.

- Scuddler - Dish-maid/domestic servant.
- Scudways - (Sco. dialect) Hidden, ulterior, cloaked, concealed purpose & motive.
- Shikse (shik-seh) [(J) derogatory] non-Jewish, or Jewish girl not adhering Jewish tradition.
- Schmuck (Schnook) - (J.) Fool.
- Sentiency - The ability to feel, perceive things.
- Sinistrodextral - From Left Right.
- Singularity - A state, fact, quality of being 'singular'; in mind, action, belief.
- Skranky - wrinkled, thin, lean, scrawny. See Disappearing Dict.
- Sempiternal - Semper- (Lat. always). Eternal, -a really, really, really long time.
- Shadrach - Unaffected by flame/heat. Taken from the Bible tale recorded in the Old Testament, Daniel 3:26-7.
- Shickered - (Sh-eye-kerd) - (Yidd.) for drunk. This word is not part of the original quotation.
- Side-slip - Illegitimate child.
- Sine prole - (Lat.) Without issue.
- Siolist - Anyone claiming knowledge of a topic unknown.
- Sleeke - (Auth. Neo. f. Taoist thought) Opposite to Woke. If 'woke' determines alertness to perceived injustices, real, or (most likely) imagined, Sleeke is Yin (light) to Woke yang (dark), Neither Sleeke, nor Woke can exist harmoniously without its compliment. Day chases Night, a chase to restore harmonious existence.
- Smittlish - Contagious, infectious (diseases).
- Smoking it up - (can refer to drug taking/sharing). To 'chat' someone up for romance or sexual play. Barr.
- Snool - Submissive, & obedient to authority figures.
- Snollygoster - Corrupt, dishonest. Person of ill-repute.
- Snuff - Offence, to be offended.
- Socialism - (Not 'socialising' with friends). A system of government with utopian ideological intents. Marxism-Leninism. Is anti-individualism, & pro-welfarist. Entails ever encroaching government intervention/control of individual lives.

A STANDARD RELIGIOUSLY IRRELEVANT VERSION (S.R.I.V.)

- Solysium - (n. Soh-lee- zee-uhm) The unhinged delirium of extended aloneness, where mythical creatures playfully form inside your head to make a social life all the more ambivalent. f. Solitary, existing alone, + asylum, sanctuary, + Elysium the (ancient Gk.) of heaven. Koenig.
- Somewhen - At some time.
- Snuggery - Small, cosy place.
- Soapedy (n) A television program combining drama, comedy, & soap-opera elements.
- Sockdolager - (n. sok-dol ə-jer) a decisive, conclusive remark. Kind to a 'knock-out' blow (to the woke).
- Solastalgia - Coined in 2003 by Australian Academic/ Philosopher Glen Albrecht to describe mental, or existential anxiety, despair, discomfort caused by environmental issues.
- Solooksist - To act in vanity, never passing the opportunity to admire the self.
- Sonrock - A fireside seat.
- Sophocles - Fifth Century (BC) Greek playwright. His works are best known for the examination & relations between the morals, & order of the divine, & humans.
- Sorrowful tale - Three months in jail.
- Spavined - Over the hill, old, run-down, ancient, elderly.
- Spel - According to (Richard) Verstegan (c.1550-1641) means mystical speech, oracle, hidden knowledge. See Gospel entry, Edwards.
- Spike-bozzle - To sabotage, ruin, make ineffective.
- Spilus - Skin marks, & spots. Adjustment of Greek spilos.
- Steam-packet - A Jacket.
- Stooshie - (Sco.) also stashie since 1824. Commotion, fuss, fight... Barr.
- Straddle-bug - (n.1831) A long legged bug/insect.
- Stale-drunk. - Still drunk from the previous night. Having to pump oneself with stimulants.
- Sting-Bum - Stingy, mean.
- Stockholm Syndrome - A psychological bond to someone/something/rule/order.

- Stomachichus - (Lat.) for upset stomach. See Wamble cropped below.
- Stone tavern - Jail.
- Sturm und Drang - (Ger.) A State of unpleasant emotional turmoil.
- Suerza - (n. soo-wair-zuh) Spanish suerte luck + fuerza, force. The sensation, impression, amazement with the miracle that you exist at all. Despite all odds to the contrary, your life emerged, winning the lottery of distinct reality. Koenig.
- Supermarionation - (n.) Puppet show of semi-animated marionettes. Barr.
- Supernatural - Greatest organic. Od. Dict.
- Swale - Windy, cold, bleak.
- Swankienda - (n.) Mansion, impressive dwelling. Barr.
- Swine-drunk - So drunk he became sleepy. Sixteenth Century drunk.
- Swivet - A state of panic, fluster, confusion, agitation.
- Swoly/Swolten - More interesting terms of description. In reference to hot, or sweltering.
- Sybaris - Greek colony of southern Italy notorious for their hedonistic lifestyles.
- Sibyllistai - A term coined by Celsus for the 'early church folk' who had belief in the Sibylline predictions of the Sibyl of Tarquin.

T:

- Talmud - Jewish ceremonial Law, & legend.
- Tatterdemalion - Tattered cloths.
- Teemful - Pregnant.
- Tergiversate - Abandon a principal, belief, & change loyalties.
- Terminological inexactitude - Coined in 1906 by Winston Churchill. Euphemism for an untruth, or something likely essentially correct, but technically inaccurate.
- Tête-à-tête - (TeT-ah-tet) Face to face meeting.
- Thaumaturge - Someone claiming to work miracles.
- Theanthropic - Embodying a deity in human form. Having both divine, & human attributes.
- Thenadays - In those days.
- Theology - Study of the 'nature' of a deity, & religious belief.

A STANDARD RELIGIOUSLY IRRELEVANT VERSION (S.R.I.V.)

- Theolobotonologia - A Herbalist compendium of cures of ailment & sickness. Authored by said herbalist (1694).
- the Til - the felt assured knowing that there is a vast reservoir of achievements, places to explore, & other possibilities yet available to you in life. Koenig.
- Thwankin - Scottish word describing the clouds as mentioned.
- Tight-laced - Rigid, or according to modern puritanical standards.
- Tope - Drink too excessively.
- Tourbillion - Dust-devil, twister, vortex.
- Transcribbler - To transcribe with scribble.
- Transhumanism - Theory of human evolution. Esp., through technology, & science merger.
- Transmarine - To cross or extend over an ocean, sea.
- Trans-Stygian - located in Hell. (Lit.) the far side of the mythic Greek river Styx which divides the Underworld, & terra firma.
- Transfluvial - Located on the other side of a river.
- Traveltainted - Travel wearily.
- Tref - (J.) Foods considered not aligning with dietary law.
- Triglot - (f. Lat.) Written in three languages.
- Trumpery - (Has nothing to do with former American President Trump.) Describes attractive, yet useless, valueless articles.
- Turkey bacon (Bacon) - Hired security.
- Turophile - Cheese fancier, connoisseur.
- Tuff - Volcanic ash/rock. (Light) porous rock.
- Twiddle Diddles - (Vulg.) Testicles.
- Tu quoque - (TOO-TWOH-kwee.) Accusations by someone for (an offence) that the accuser is also guilty of committing. For instance, the Socialist/'progressive' Left in politics accuse the opposition for a 'crime' the Left often commits, while verbalising an accusation. Noticed often regarding the current hysteria surrounding 'Global Warming/climate change elitist advocates.
- Twarvlment - Long-winded (speech).
- Twitler - Users of social media to (often anonymously) bully, harass someone else (into submission, or admission of a perceived guilt).
- Tyromancy - Cheese divination.

U:

- Uglyography - Meaning bad, or poor spelling.
- Uhtceare - (OOT-key-are-a) restless wakefulness before dawn (in worry). (OE). Fors.
- Unfortunate - (adj.) Poor, ill-fated, unproductive.
- Unky - Lonesome. (Unked) - lonely.
- Unsex - To 'change' gender. To make other than the originating gender.
- Unsoulclogged - Free from spirit & burden.
- Urchin - A Child.
- Urf - stunted, ill-formed (child) person.
- Ut dicitur - (Lat.) As is said.

V:

- Vacomacation - A holiday spent in bed doing nothing extraneous.
- Varmint - Troublesome, mischievous person.
- Valgus - Bow-legged.
- Vanishing-day - Resurrection.
- Vaucasy - (n.) the fear that life is but the product of circumstances, stimuli, & is therefore reflexive. Causing feelings of powerlessness. Koenig.
- Vertiginous - Dizzy, giddy, woozi.
- Vicus - (Lat.) Town, village, district.
- Vocating - Idling about.
- Volander - the ethereal feeling of floating through the air, able to see, witness peoples, & places. Wondering, or imagining what those places were like, or what people were feeling. Koenig.
- Volapük. (VOLA-puke) - An artificial language concocted in 1879. Originally proposed to be an international tongue based on extremely modified words from both English, & Romance languages. Thankfully its metaphysical processes are now history.
- Vomitory - (Vulg.) A passageway of an amphitheatre type stadium which allows movement, exit, & entryway.

W,X,Y,Z:

A STANDARD RELIGIOUSLY IRRELEVANT VERSION (S.R.I.V.)

- Waggish - Humorous, facetiously silly.
- Walpurgis night - Nightmare. The experience of…rather than the emotion of being terrified. See, nightmare. Meltz.
- Waps - (n. Plural. British Slan.) Woman's breasts.
- Weathercock - 'Capricious', fickle person who changes their mind according to popular, current trends.
- Weather-spy - Stargazers.
- Weequash(ing) - Spear fishing.
- Welkin - (OE)- sky. Paul. A. Jon.
- Wheeze - Joke.
- Whindle - Feigning sickness (groaning).
- Whipping-cheer - 'banquet of lashes'. Flogging, punishment by whip.
- Will-o'-the-wisp - Fanciful desires.
- Wamble cropped - Nauseated.
- Wambliness - Unease of the stomach.
- Wisenheimer - Smart ass.
- Witworm - Someone who likes wit.
- Woke (ness) - Alertness to perceive injustice in society.
- Wimmin (Womyn) - Phonetic & Non-standard spellings for women. Invented by feminists to dispense with the element - men. Fowl.
- Word-pecker - A player with words.
- Wyrd - (Word) Of Anglo-Saxon origin, roughly pertaining to fate, & destiny.
- Xenodocium - Superior person's fancy word for motel/hotel. I have used this word to mean hospital. See also caravanserai.
- Xenotransplantation - Transplanting non-human materials into human beings.
- Xeric - Extremely arid, torrefied.
- Yám; Mayim - (Heb. -imm; MY-im) Sea; Waters.
- Yemeless - Negligent!
- Ylem - The substance early philosophers thought created & formed the universe.

- Yestreen - (No endorsement of Listerine!) Meaning yesterday evening.
- Zabalus - (Lat.) The devil. Brist.
- Zielschmerz - (zeel schmerts) f. Two (Ger.) words, Ziel - goal + schmerz, pain. The dread felt when pursuing a life-long dream, knowing that former protections are no longer valid. Koenig.
- Zoological (Marvel) - A logical fixture for housing animals. Od. Dict.
- Zythepsary - Brewery.
- Zwodder - Drowsy curse of a new day.

A STANDARD RELIGIOUSLY IRRELEVANT VERSION (S.R.I.V.)

THE CHURCH CLAIMS TO BE A HEALER, WHILE BEING RIDDLED WITH SORES.

STEVE MORGAN

FRONT MATTER:

Satire, hyperbole, lampooning, mockery, taunting, comical, ridiculous. Call the scriptures what you will, just don't call it a holy adytum. A sanctuary of the soul, unless that soul wish to be amused to the point of 'holy' risibility. A gelastic disposition, this should be a mandated staple of all who read, study, or swoon over the scriptures. If one observes the plain translated English text as it has been offered by scholars. Time & again numerously places, & occasions read in the Judaeo-Christian Bible transmogrify, causing a scratching of the head, & quizzical thoughts. The world that birthed the Judaeo-Christian sacred books were steeped in, & surrounded, & influenced by the tales of other ancient deities. Many were coupled with a concubine. Did the Hebrew Bible deity have a wife? Assuming an alleged Son is lauded to have spontaneously arrived. A conception espoused by an emerging off-shoot religion. Was the New Testament's Mary the latest dalliance of the Jewish deity? Might you sceptically snort, well duh. Yet, that autoschediastic insemination of a maiden surprised everyone. Including the maiden who should have been abruptly dumped by her betrothed, according to Bible lore. Chancing the poker*, it sounds like spiritual adultery was committed by the deity. Did a Heavenly litigation proceed, & did it take place in the Celestial courtroom? Who was the presiding judge; another regional deity? Maybe, the Archangel Lucifer; now Satan? Perhaps, such an episode had Luci formally kicked from the Celestial realms? The Bible, nobody should be able to evade upon observation the root & branch of its ventriloquism, its quisquous bumfuzzling antics.

Who was, is this dramatis persona three, to one Unitarian? Male, Female, or trans as observed & believed these days by the modern left 'progressive' God-mythologist. What caused the deity to think to begin & fashion people? What were those 'people' like? What is it with the 'idea' of our innate basophobia? According to the churches

A STANDARD RELIGIOUSLY IRRELEVANT VERSION (S.R.I.V.)

own ipse dixit explaining (Genesis 3:1). Believers are taught to be ever mindful of a lurking 'sin'. So, are most terrified of tripping over. Falling over ourselves in a mad rush to be somewhere better than here. The place humanity offered by the deity as redemption.

Do not think The New Testament escapes, & is devoid of a multitude of weird encounters. There are ample mare's nests here also. Such as, when a fellow Paul, after an abduction episode by an alien figure sporting way bright vestments, forced a reversal in attitude. Instead of Paul's usual rampaging about some rival clique, he did a No-ah (See The Activation Flood episode) & began championing what was earlier despised. Several people were reported to have shrugged off their wooden (stone to the ancients), overcoat & rejoined society as if nothing unusual had transpired, while the one the commentators called 'messianic*', leaped into the clouds; to reappear to a few mates a little later. In the wake of this episode, members of a gang began thinking earnestly that, bugger it. The reality, the sting of our own mortality was kinda bumpkin. Was not the final curtain for that had been mysteriously torn asunder in their Great Cynic-Gog. One fellow was reportedly at an R' n' R resort. When during an assumed Walpurgis night* he suddenly awoke to scribble thoughts about the nightmare just witnessed. Swarming with even more idiosyncratic, surreal things that nobody was to ever know.

Without remorse, or fear of viewing Christian tenets & believed proclamations as irrational. This book offers the reader an enlivening observation through ridiculous words & phrases describing the impossible, the fanciful episodes of the Judaeo-Christian books. While also appreciating that some of its beliefs may not present as outrageously inimical. The issue is that the assumed 'light' of this religion hides as much truth as it may reveal. Light, possesses two properties, on the one hand it 'reveals' hidden things. But, it also tends to 'blind' people, just as an animal is blinded by headlamps. Tending to lull people into a sense of reverence, & hysteria. Not unlike the hysterical religious reverence of modern times. Of the climate change zealot who has an assumed & impending doomsday clock speedily running to the obliteration of planet Earth.

Concession must be made there are disturbing parallel's with the argumentum ex silentio of Christian speculations & the insidiousness of the 'new' religion of the 'eco-warrior' so prevalent in our modern times. This storybook is an <u>aniconic</u>* motley collection of Judaeo-Christian Bible folktales highlighting several extraordinary oddities of the eco-warrior woke, homogenised with the folklore of the Christian religion. There is no attempt to familiar separation of the text as would otherwise likely be expected. The text could be called a desultory diegesis as there are no verses, & no titles within a new parodied Bible book indicating a separating of certain themes, episodes of the narrative. The only indicator of a new chapter, or new tale under comment is its title at the beginning of a 'new' Bible book. A saving grace might be the supplied proem for each chapter. These were written to offer a context for the future narrative. Esp., for those who may not be familiar with the <u>haeccity</u>* of a Bible book.

This book then, is my meagre effort at counteracting the numerous deafening harsh scenarios voiced by many gloom-masters with a religious, & secular persuasion & conviction. I wanted this book to essentially offer an altered reading experience to other amphigory Bible publications. As already witnessed, to highlight, & assist with this are scattered about varieties of wonderfully <u>mumblenym</u>* words; to pique & persuade. But, there is no need to be funky, & be alarmed. If befuddled with occasional rhetoric, rest assured. Not all atypical expressions to come are abstruse. The context & your aptitude will not fail you. Even if the term, or phrase is unfamiliar. The general gist will likely prevail. Withal, realise each of us is equipped with an astoundingly vibrant mental onomasticon; a word list & personal lexicon built up over the years. Nonetheless, to assist a reader navigate & make a better connection with the definientia, & to <u>omnify</u>* your personal built-in lexicon, a Glossary is supplied. Specifically, this is to help dilate your personal onboard thesaurus with terms & expression knowledge. All <u>underlined</u> words & phrases with an asterisk (*) beside them can be found in the glossary. For terms, & phrases not found in this brief <u>dictionary</u>*, a modern lexicon, &/or electronic definition search should meet your requirements. Might the nettle be grasped

A STANDARD RELIGIOUSLY IRRELEVANT VERSION (S.R.I.V.)

with a continuance in reading. Rest assured all is exoteric with rib-tickling delights awaiting the reader joining the journey when you do.

Far from a philologist, or true wordsmith. Far be it that the author is considered a true modern <u>bel-esprit</u>*. Rather, he has a fascination with <u>paronomasia</u>*, & <u>neologisms</u>*. So, will delight in the moniker <u>witworm</u>* or <u>word-pecker</u>*. Moreover, the prose blatantly ignores the idea that non 'specialised' publications like this burlesque title should avoid alternative, sophisticated wordish expressions. Confirming that the many really only read at an uncomplicated, menial level. What is called advertorial language should then be used in near all publications.[1] The well-worn motto is 'keep it simple stupid'. In protest, where's the fun in oversimplification? Esp., with such a galumptious, mirific, & frabjous text as the god-mythologists & bible itself claims. Near every standard Bible reads as artless as the next. Rarely differentiating it from established, dated mores. British philosopher Ludwig Wittgenstein (1889-1951), maybe channelling an apostle speaking about language, once opined that we should: "Leave childish acts, thoughts, & language to children, & grow up."[2] Why then are these Judaeo-Christian texts afraid to be purposefully intelligent, or sharp-witted, if not a little recondite? Obscurity abounds in all tales, yet they are always simplified to a point of childlike sameyness. How does that make the reading of such texts remotely <u>ludic</u>*? Let alone <u>proficuous</u>*? Why remain nescient, or be circumlocutory when a pellucid opportunity presents itself to advance in maturity? Syne, the wonderful, strangeness on offer would be missed, if you remain sclerotic & were to baulk at a neologism that isn't known.[3]

There are several goals to have been achieved by this publication, aside the obvious of being a gelastic, eupeptic title; (1) to jar a reader to viewing the tales, & themes in commentary differently. It is difficult to escape the strangeness of Standard Bible texts. (2) to have readers also cerebrate modern <u>fandangos</u>* plaguing us currently. Finally, the underlining expectation: (3) this is an offering of <u>punishing</u>* accounts using a written arsenal, & showing off the remarkable depth of the English language. That the tales offer a colourful; a playful,

---

1. Advertorial - a melding of Advertisement+editorial = simple, easily understood. Taggart.
2. See, 1 Corinthians 13:11.
3. Syne means 'Since, subsequently, moreover, furthermore'. See, Auld Lang Syne - glossary.

& linguistically sharp, & enlightening reading experience for an audience. The intent is to bring to a reader a narrative that is highly expressive. A string of narratives manipulated, & retold from Standard Bible tales that are entertaining & easily relatable to modern people. In celebration of the stories, & Promethean human ingenuity.

Influenced by Samuel Langhorne Clemens (Mark Twain) who produced the title, The Diaries of Adam, & Eve. A most poetic, & humorous piece of literature that was published posthumously. Aspiring in this title, to have written this chapbook with alterity to Standard Bible texts. Employing some delights of forgotten, little used or cognisable phrases, teasing slang, & other oddities are spattered about the narratives. All which are sure to leave your eyes rolling about the floor.

The following title, is a burlesque production of familiar Biblical apologues. Pasquinading several familiar, but recognised terminological inexactitudes* of the holey Judaeo-Christian Bible that is likely something of a curate's egg* to readers. Highlighting chrestomathy* of both the Bible story, & fragile modern convictions. Employing several mot juste* foreign, Jewish, Greek, & Latin Bible locutions, & several suitably placed notices & instruction manuals. Many of these are adapted from genuine notices from around the modern world. All which add spice to the narrative. Why this approach? Why consider writing 'another' parodied Bible. Why choose to ignore the befuddling potential of audiences with terms, phrases that may discourage? Simply, because I can.

Offered in these pages is a string of narratives that likely appeals as they were inspired by the intrinsic neophilia of paronomasia. Considering, it is still clearly believed, potentially out of a sense of fear of reality that followers of religions can sneer at death; that there may be an extension to a life; that death is effectively ruled out. To postulate such a concept, as the ancient second Century philosopher Celsus argued in his criticism of the emerging Christian belief, is it really worth the time & expense of finding out, or wasting time believing? Despite the fancied notion espoused in scriptures, not one person has ever been reanimated from a state of continued clinomania, resting with their wooden overcoat. Only to reappear & begin conversing with former colleagues or close kin. Not one. Yet, such is espoused by the religious

A STANDARD RELIGIOUSLY IRRELEVANT VERSION (S.R.I.V.)

believer.[4] Still, the religious notion of a 'virgin birth' - parthenogenesis* is equally nonsensical, & a beloved doctrine. Both doctrines are satirised in this book. Besides, why is the vagueness of 'god' an accepted idea? To many modern believers, a deity, god, is the ultimate guiltwright*; the one who has a ledger of all your deeds. Both good, & bad. At the 'closing' of time. Whether at your death, or the assumed demise & rebirthing of planet Earth to a presupposed utopia, deeds will be weighed, & the unworthy will be sent into perdition. While, the worthy, the accepted 'righteous' relax mockingly in Utopia.[5] The concept of a god who would willingly do this, is ridiculous. Howbeit, the very conception of 'a god', is as diverse as there are people on planet Earth. A presumed entity that by definition, cannot be defined!

It is often argued that 'god exists.' Yet, when asked how this is known, the believer often resorts to some 'faith' based explanation. This, does never explain what god is, or, which god is espoused. But, does hint of the willingness to be convinced without knowledge. Because it is quite the 'lace-curtain'; the virtuous expectation. Just as any modern Generation 'E' devotee (see below) with their eco-warrior pretences. God, can only prevail as much as an orange-striped nineteen eyed Startle-batter blurplegalgre does. Completely chimerical. Belonging to the realm of cryptozoology* & imagination. Theology*, should perhaps be a branch of cryptozoological study? The concept of a god, supreme being overlooking all creation surely should be consigned as cryptobiont; a fictional entity 'existing' wholly out of sight.

This book was written to indulge my curiosity about what might emerge if purposefully, an irreligious viewpoint of its texts was chosen. The narratives are secularised, & intermingled with modern themes, & ideologies. Specifically, this project began during the outrageously draconian 263day Victorian 'lockdown' of 2021. Where ordinary life in this Australian State forcibly ceased. When government was effectively little but political cavalier; faineant Lotus-eater's. A faustian government unaware & unconcerned with the destructive entelechy of their diktat's*, or the moral obligations they have to the population.

---

4. See, 1 Thessalonians 4:13-17; Matthew 9:24; 2 Corinthians 5:15.
5. Such a concept permeates all religions. The Christian/Jewish concept seems to have been doctored from the Egyptian Book of the Dead.

Forbye*, much of the world today has forsaken, & forgotten how to laugh at itself. Let alone some of its religious concepts, & interpretations. Including the ideas, theories of the twenty-first century modern religion of the eco-warrior. Not without using offensive, or obnoxious, disparaging language. Unlike much of society who seem to only use a stream of billingsgate, attacking the jugular of belief, & the religious ideologies they undoubtedly disrespect, misunderstand. The trust is this project lives in the parodied words of R. W. Emerson, "Religion to a modern is entertainment." That this book is successful in offering readers a harmless, & jocose account of several Standard Bible anecdotes. Those that are read, & believed as only topics of homiletics.

Withal, there is a strange, & disturbing phenomenon shaping our communities. An intensified new form of religion; a myopic 'Solastalgia'* destructively sweeping through Western cultures; with high priestesses, priesthoods of 'Wokeness'* subverting human reciprocity with their constant contaminotion* poisoning debate, & standard logical, biological knowledge. Surely, others can also see this is Environmental Socialism* dressed in Wokeness garb. The new 'Social democracy' has become the twenty-first Century 'Inquisition'. With a religious fervour, this 'new' cross-examination has cultivated an unheard-of loathing; cultural, of national sovereignty, & of the self. Near every aspect of our modern lives; our thoughts, style of clothing; long past speeches, & actions are all by the puritan*. Labelled reprehensible, & impure, & condemned as insensitive to the 'snowflake' babalog* brigade. Generation 'E'; the luftmensch*, & progressively idiotic weathercock* environmentalist; entitled, electronic & ever eggy, & exasperated. The often prolifiely cavil Twitler*. Freedom to exercise individual expression invokes fierce scrutiny from this 'new' breed of 'E's'. Eventually, being hounded into atoning the obloquy*. To show genuine indread*, & steps are made proving. They are on the sawdust trail; an apologetic retraction for the misqueme* is offered but rarely accepted. The donnée* of the self appointed 'illuminati' is unfortunately, true for many. Seldom are there any who can expostulate by agonistical exchange. Seems, many are hesitant to engage with these mumpsimus, hidebound misologist's eristically. Modern parochialism* has a bellicosity that has diminished the ingenuity, sovereignty & playfulness of

A STANDARD RELIGIOUSLY IRRELEVANT VERSION (S.R.I.V.)

individuals. Turning countless people to a mind-numbing dullness of automatism. Society is full of apologetic crowds, & a 'yellow press' full of <u>boulevard journalists</u>* afraid of their own silhouette who would rather shadow ban any contrary, conflicting discussion. Than attempt eristic conversations with opponents. The apologetic 'collective' is filled with senseless quibblers bent on displaying a puerile <u>pumpkinification</u>* of all things deemed '<u>ecozoic</u>'*.

Clear is the pursuit these days, just as the emerging Christian belief system adopted by intending to force a change to all expressions of Pagan life. Another 'religious' minority has assumed the right to pressure all people into the servitude of the unelected. These are the faceless 'elite class'. Presuming to impose diktats upon the majority. Insisting a total <u>modus vivendi</u>* be accepted. Theirs is a puritanical 'wokeness'. The collective is aswarm with the fatuities of haughtiness, & sanctimony. Modern clerisy is cant. Much of our society presenting now as <u>schmegeggy</u>*, & more <u>jurgy</u>* carping by the day having received their indoctrinations (qualifications), & conclusions, opinions from a <u>matchbook University</u>*. Forsaking the lessons of <u>Sophocles</u>*; the unbearable woke show no knowledge of human tragedy. Or, of our humanness. While modern religion assumes some knowledge, seen in Bible books like Psalms. Yet, the religious often display a lack of the endless struggle with our own fallibility, lack in erudition, & our susceptibility to consequences whenever we violate a cosmic order.

The cost to the rise of this puritan 'wokeness' is a deep cynicism that has lead many followers of both established religion, & the new environmental religions into a cyclical miserableness. Stridulous & scrannel remarks abound. Where they assume the right of stewardship, & mastery of others, but are never 'lords' of themselves. The most ideological & faustian are the <u>elp</u>* & <u>bleeding deacon</u>*. The <u>mamamouchi</u>* who have adopted the virtual moral high ground of self-appointed importance, while abnegating all responsibilities. They assume a posture <u>droit du seigeur</u>*; the right & stewardship of <u>arbiter elengantiae</u>* over the rest of us. Elp's are the unelected, self-appointed procrustean <u>emodox</u>*, whose proclivity is dictating how society is to conduct itself. While evading responsibility, & ignoring their own <u>tu quoque</u>*. With a persistent use of argumentum ad baculum, they beat the psyche of our younger generation with all manners of fear-porn threatenings, & emotional blackmail of a hapless, or <u>extinct</u>* future.⁶ It is as if the elite pedlars, & other true believers of such ideologies have suddenly become autistic. Where, only complete compliance to 'Greenwashed ideologies' & utopian desires is accepted. All Western societies must forsake established realpolitik in favour of transition. Our lifestyles, long-held traditions, & principles. Our personal sovereignty; i.e., particularly any religious (read Christian) beliefs, & opinions. Basic freedoms of conscious; of association, & other basic rights. Liberties, & rudimental ethical standards must all be reproached, & abandoned. Feeding habits also must have a 180degree turn about. The mamamouchi would like nothing more than the complete abstinence by most of the consumption of livestock. Convinced these must be abandoned to the whims of a new, & emerging food oligopoly. <u>Eugonic</u>* foods are by the <u>necessitarian</u>* said to be advantageous & more sanative than the consuming of those <u>fell</u>* & amoral esculent animal products. Which are poo pooed as enhancing & necessary for life. Using propaganda such products is advertised as great benefit for world stability, & sustainability. Pushing for the consumption of what are essentially bird foods. Unnatural things for human consumption, like <u>entomic</u>*, & <u>entomophagous</u>*, & 'Frankenfoods'. In short, a complete reversal of society, & our conduct is required 'to save the planet', &; therefore, humanity from its self destruction. If the Roman lyric poet Horace had been still with us he would have called such proposals cobbled together by Abnormis sapiens; the wise without learning.⁷ The 'jet-setter,' political classes of the world comprise many abnormis sapiens. Believing adamantly every other citizen is hoi polloi patsies. So, must accept <u>Hobson's choice</u>* with the push to lower the standards of modern living for everyone, but the elp. The elites who deny their ideologies are nothing but untested, & proven illogical belief's. A myopic delusion of saving the planet' from an impending doom. The more these elp's push their infantile,

---

6. *argumentum ad baculum*, (Lat.) To threaten by beating until the opponent agrees. Our modern society is 'beaten' persistently to believe the notion of a dire Global-Warming event that can, or will only be reversed when the demonisation of natural, efficient energy sources is completed, & the elite grow in wealth, & power, & self-sufficient stability in life at the expense of the 'little people'.
7. See Wood, (A - 7 / 91). Horace - (65 B.C. - 8 B.C.).

A STANDARD RELIGIOUSLY IRRELEVANT VERSION (S.R.I.V.)

& anserine nonsense. Including the looming 'climate' catastrophe. The more internecine as mere effutiation* they become. The desire of these elp's would lead to a total transformation. The delegitimisation of our species & how our lives are conducted individually. There must be a comprehensive 'resetting' of Western societies, hailed as 'The Fourth Industrial Revolution'. To bring about the desired but imaginary 'ecozoic balance' to a world apparently in climatic upheaval.

All people subscribing to capitalism are increasingly becoming punished. Harangued by hockers* to believe there is a worthlessness to individualism; its known benefits, & the liberty, freedoms it offers to a free people. So, all societies must be prepared for complete tergiversation* toward omniparity*. All must abandon current individualistic freedoms, thought's, belief's & become subservient. The elite, the elp are however, exempt. For them, the reversal & a return to a 'healthy planet state' can only be made when the Mortaville* 'little people' persistently suffer brainwashing attacks to believe. They should be gracious to be the âme damnée* of the elite class. 'Happy' in subservience. Accommodating the standards that are accepted by the few. Jettisoning of long-held dietary, & societal norms. Many being given legitimacy, & being established throughout the wider world because of a religious premise. Those premisses now being slowly abolished. Encouraging this 'metamorphosis' while persistently verbalising individuals & corporations alike to 'transition', & metanoia in recognition of their will-o'-the-wisp* are world leaders, & those captivated by the new world of 'politically correct' language, & belief. Those insisting that the majority must at all costs, revere & pay homage to beliefs, & other virtues of a senseless minority. Who's rhetoric often resembles the fear of Chicken Little; "The Earth is melting. The Seas are rising. You can't misgender me. There's only … years left before we're all dead." The planet is faced with an imminent dies irae unless all follow the 'cock of the walk', the elp with deference. More's the pity* of the woke. Is there a wonder why our younger generation suffers acute nemotia; the dolorous fear & despair that the world is mired with an Iliad of terminally life-threatening woes? Such persons must be assured all these frightening opinions are peddled by controver's*. Our communities must recover the understanding that mankind is but imprudent blockheads. The current state of education has birthed the dullness of, particularly the young being all too ready to digest & feel more than use their given idea pot, & knowledge boxes*. Sadly, modern topics like 'Critical Race-Theory' & the other prejudiced social reengineering assessments has replaced critical thinking. In the following narratives; my intent is to counter this delirium, & feared opinion. As Goethe once announced: "Man is born not to solve the problems of the universe, but find where the problem begins. Then restrain himself in the constraints of the comprehensible."[8] Along with presenting something; optimistically chucklesome, I am asking a reader to cogitate, anatomise, & ratiocinate some of the topics, & themes of the narrative, esp., those questioning some modernisms. We are all in need of reminding of the Monty Python song: "Always look on the Bright side of Life." Life is meant to be lived. Not irritably like the woke seem to celebrate. But, in wonder of our surrounds, with a sense of awe for the daedal* of our being.

All this is not the inspiration for this publication. But, is only mentioned as information that highlights our modern leitkultur*. Rather, this oeuvre sets out to highlight some of the weirdness of the current 'Solastalgia'* interwoven into religious tales in an imaginary, & humorous manner. Employing donnybrook odd, archaic, & 'bookish' terms to also liven those Bible tales.

Although oddly sounding, or seeming mad, & absolute bosh*. The strangest words scattered throughout the text likely have fallen out of fashion, or, been unknown for their antiquity, & bookishness. Several, are terms describing the emotions that we all encounter as part of our human experience. Terms for responses to life situations, occurrences that you have, but didn't know there was a word to describe it. Where it was felt suitable, the attempt was to describe accurately these reactions, gut feelings, sensations by introducing the words assigned to those states. Assorted words & phrases offered in this book have an absolute fabricated, double-meaning. Liberty has been taken with actual meanings. For instance, the name Cain is punned. In the Bible he was the primogeniture* of prime transient sentiency. Trusting each facetiae* in the narrative is found fitting. English, because it is not strictly corseted by rules as others, like several other languages, allow

---

8. See Wood, (M - page 64 / 102).

A STANDARD RELIGIOUSLY IRRELEVANT VERSION (S.R.I.V.)

such inventing & play on words for their sound. Other words were completely invented. Many of these are now collecting much lexical dust; like Volapük*. Which thankfully never really saw any serious light of day. From a fascination with words comes an interpretation of the Bible narrative that I am convinced is delightfully amusing. Statements that vivify the over all reading experience for an audience. The additions of strange phrases throughout this book add charm, & humour to the text, as they often replace contemporary jejune, & banausic words & phrases. If not accompanied by an asterisk (*), it is trusted the context allows easy recognition to a meaning.

This irreligious edition, is an unorthodox compilation that does not play the gender, identity, sexist victimhood game. Nor do I pit these against the other. This book is written as neutrally as possible. Despite mentioning several modern identities related, marginalised topics. Some readers might tag my inclusion of these as politically incorrect, racist, or other dismissive label. I have nonetheless, penned this book to lard those Judaeo-Christian tales of commentary. The pharisaic, the numinous, & woke. Using punishes & rhetorical expression as the propulsion. Any adverse snuff* felt, or that may arise while reading some of the controversial topics scattered throughout this tome, is the inquietude of the reader alone. Esp., of any mental or physical disturbance of those who will never read this book if they catch wind of that material. The author takes no responsibility for how an audience interprets any narrative. All were composed of a clear conscious, devoid of malice. Readers are encouraged: "Opinion does never equate to fact. Perspectives offer deception, not truth. To become distressed by another's external perspective, written, or verbal, is not the fault of that perspective offered. Distress is only your estimated understanding. At any point, you have always the ability to revoke all distressing moments." "… Why should we be hagridden in this life with piffling matters? Rather, our focus would be better served by cerebrating our own (miracle of life/existence)." "Just as sure as facing the wall ourselves, changing, or revising opinions are part of life. If you have not done this in a while, please have your pulse checked, - you might have expired already." (From 'Dissimilar to Psalms').

Just as our mental dictionary morphs, & expands, so our lives forever change. Much as the weather. So does language. Everyday words, thoughts, phrases morph, shape-shift, & evolve.

Except it would seem the expressions of religious texts, i.e., of the Judaeo-Christian books. So, why not bring a slight alternative to conventional declarations of religious Bibles? Here, on offer are interpretations of some favoured, well-known Bible stories with an unseen comedic twist; by using some archaic & modern words & phrases. Neologisms that are intended to <u>aggiornamento</u>*, & cause the reader to reconsider the Standard Bible text. By their use, it is unintended the reader gets cold feet. Rather they recognise in this book a <u>daedalic</u>* characteristic that brings a little <u>naches</u>* to the soul.

Assumed unexpected. The body of this book launches first into The New Testament, The Newest Bit. Moving through to A Reevaluation of 'a' Joan. Only then, The Activation episode of Genesis, & several well-perceived tales. Following with a Postscript are added several other authoring's from some reports that are of <u>gnostic</u>* tradition. Such as further Reevaluations by Peter, & Paul. Before a 'Final Thought' as a farewell. Assumed still by a collective of religious activist persons sometime near, or post The Activation (i.e., the birthing of the whole universe thing, & everything else). A very gifted entity at some point is said to have tricked, & exploited an ignorant soul into what is considered real bad. To many religious folk, this 'entity,' might be recognised as the ultimate expression of an 'elp'. The one from whom our elpness was learned? According to assumptions of this Bible episode, humankind all turned to pot. Did our primogenitors really <u>'smoke it up</u>*'? Or, as Caroline Taggart suggests in 'New Words for Old', 'pot' may be a corruption of a 'cup (drink) of grief'? When humankind had engaged & 'swallowed' what is apparent, & so taught in commentary. A most egregious conclusion to draw. That a tale as this in the Genesis narrative has been characterised, & taught as the 'Fall-of mankind'. An ineluctable truth following such an agonistic encounter. That the collective conscious of humanity still now chooses to view the deposed entity with unexplainable <u>goig</u>*. But, why treat with opprobrium & much contempt, this personality, or the actions of the first Humankind's of this tale? Why has subtlety, or craftiness become synonymous with deception, deceit, & contempt in this narrative? Why should the presumed anguine personality of Genesis 3:1 be assumed to harbour misrepresentative intents? Esp., when in some modern circumstances, subtlety & shrewdness is not necessarily deceitful. Is it really apposite

A STANDARD RELIGIOUSLY IRRELEVANT VERSION (S.R.I.V.)

to always assume the worse, or a defeated result for Humankind's from this tale? Seeing, this is the churches own ipse dixit*. That this episode was the epicentre, the fons et origo* of our choplogic peccable* nature. Ever since, humankind has wrestled psychomachia*.

One of the greatest gifts of modern humankind howbeit, is our ability to view things with relative neutrality. Though we do still tend to view near everything through rose-coloured lenses of our life experiences, we have a cognitive ability to choose what is principled, & realistic. Or, what is proof-less, & indefinite? Only a few these days are bold enough to rightly draw a non-identical conclusion to the madness of woke, & religious projections about life on this blue marble. Having woken themselves from slumber to the realism that there has been a 'religion' that is divisive, & alienating. They call out the idiocy, foolishness, & illogicality of another's perspective when necessary. Noticing it has insidiously emerged alongside accepted societal norms. Steadily marching unawares through much of our society, & religious, & other established institutions.

This book is my attempt at calling out the Machiavellian nature of the woke, & environmentalist, & conventional awkward themes of the Christian religion. With its often irrationalities, inconsistencies, bigotry*. It makes little sense that conventional, established religion (Christianity particularly), can be censured. But, the new religion of wokeness is sacred; untouchable. Groupthink preaching is 'off limits'. Discepting*, or being critical of the 'group' is not tolerated. Here, with impavid* resolve, the trend is forsaken. Acknowledging many modern ideas might have noble undertones. They nonetheless are, when used by the impetuous, mugwumpery*. Particularly, of the ideologies of modern terrain worship, the virtuously 'inclusive.' The 'intolerant,' 'anti-everything modern' religion of the woke. With the narratives commented on in these pages. It was realised earlier, humanity is wired to conceptualise or postulate a variety of ideas. But, according to the collective woke. None, but their own ideas are acceptable.

Throughout this book, is used as much impartial language as individuality allows. There is no malice directed to any 'controversially' modern belief, individual, aspirant espoused. In a sense, the narrative serves to slam the collective agelast* of society. Those who take offence, or presume a hurt for its own sake & polemic parti pris.

These are they who have replaced many common sensibilities with an intolerant discriminatory alertness; to a perceived injustice. That ultimately demands an aseptic life, & an elimination to all references of a Promethean* history, & instil a humourless subservient living. In an amusing effort, to expose some questionable woke, & religious ideas, Standard Bible tales were employed as the platform. Purposefully playing with, & manipulating those rumoured exploits with a clear conscious. Understanding that many of my non-identical reckoning in these pages are harmless. If anything, it will likely be the strangeness of some of the rhetoric used that might sound too irksome, or laborious. Too different to be recognised Bible prose for refusing to follow slavishly doctrinaire expectations. This is a transmogrified fictional send-up of the Judaeo-Christian books & the tales they contain. Submitting now this playful imitation of the Judaeo-Christian Bible.

Bible book personalities; their titles & occupations, & thoughts have all been manipulated playfully, often chancing the poker* for hyperbole purposes. For instance, readers will come across characters with strange sounding names. Beginning our jaunt shortly with renditions of the tales of Matt-Hue ('apostle' Matthew); Iesous (Jesus); Tight-as (Titus); Citizen Joan (John). Are likely familiar New Testament characters. Moving to: El Neberdjer (God/deity/divinity.)[9] Mo-she (Moses); Ah-Ron (Aaron); Mir-I-am (Miriam); Ben-jamin (Benjamin); No-ah (Noah); A-Sue (Ahasuerus/Xerxes).[10] These are some Old Testament personalities to be met in the Old Testament. As the New, Old Testament personalities have also been played with; their presumed occupations, desires, thoughts of these & other characters. Including, but not least the principal deity. Much manipulation of chapter themes was conducted for hyperbole purposes also. As with an obvious reversed order to standard bibles.

Much word 'play' was engaged in this storytelling. Intending to bring the narrative to life. Though diverging from an assumed familiarity, a reader should still recognise many themes, & stories parodied in the coming pages. Added for clarity, are several Bible references, & several historical truths, & regional tidbits. Trusting

---

9. (el-neber-jer) Egyptian.
10. Persian King mentioned in Ezra 4.

A STANDARD RELIGIOUSLY IRRELEVANT VERSION (S.R.I.V.)

further interest is secured in the story's told. Footnotes explain & offer reference to these where they occur in the text. Each chapter is largely a self-contained unit. Containing narratives & themes that follow, but irreligiously, the order of those found in Standard Christian Bibles.

The composition of this S.R.I.V. (Standard Religiously Irrelevant Version) contrasts the N.I.V. (New International Version) E.S.V. (English Standard Version) N.R.S.V. ('New' Revised Standard Version, which are honestly the latest 'modernised' instalments of the 1611, King James Bible) or any other modern 'standard' popular bible interpretation. The order is backward, beginning with New Testament tales. The following standard bible books compromised are; unusually beginning with, A Questionable Parthenogenesis* = (mostly) Gospel of Matthew; Some Other Actors = The Book of Acts; Tight-as = Titus… Through to A Reevaluation of 'a' Joan = Revelation. These are the Newer Bits. The New Testament, & strangely begin this "Standard Religiously Irrelevant Version" (S.R.I.V.). Then, The Activation = Genesis; Eudoxus = Exodus; Leave -it-to-Gus = Leviticus; Census = Numbers; Prophesies of Chameleon = The Prophetic books; Proverbs of Druid = Proverbs; Dissimilar to Psalms; Real Esther Tate = Esther. These comprise the Olden Parts, The Old Testament. Moving to concluding with several parodied stories from non-canonical, Apocryphal books. Those not recognised as part of scripture, & a Final Thought.

Regarding the structure of the testaments in commentary, the coming tales of the Old Testament (Olden Bits) are printed awkwardly*. Appearing upside down because, the Old Testament was originally aligned to the Right, & written in Semitic languages (Hebrew*). Just to confuse everyone but their native readers. Familiarity to English readers nonetheless, demands the Olden bit, pretending to represent the Oldest Testament although should be aligned left still reads as any English magazine, sinistrodextral*. Tales, of The New Testament books, came to us from ancient Greek. So, is written & read in the familiar fashion.

There is great confidence the following commentaries & interviews will not be dull, rather enjoyable to read. A delightful narrative that is waggish* for the ribs for the ridiculousness of conclusions drawn. If by reading, chuckling, & digesting, & deriving even the minutest message from this book, a reader walks away with the resolve to think about some of the themes commented on, or even change the world just a little for the betterment of others. If so, my job is done. Maybe, some of the silliness you read in the following commentary somehow sparks a licence for you to explore more areas that deserve liberosis* during your remaining days.

Inspired by several religious, & non-religious books, my awareness, & knowledge of Bible narratives. Fabricating them into what is a comical form of Bible events. Having no longer a belief in any 'Bible' tale as sacred does not mean there is an attempt to delegitimise or denigrate the faith of millions. Or Christian heritage. Rather, seeking to leave readers gelastic & eupeptic for the spirited ludic prose of the coming pages. In full acknowledgment that for believers sacred beliefs these tales & characters & the 'past' they allegedly tell. Is often seen as factually sound & so, cannot truely be made redundant. This Religiously Irrelevant collection of Standard Bible stories is a cynical propaganda device. Knowing well as its creator I might have been taken in by my own ruse. I now offer my sincere thanks & gratitude to the authors of the books of all words, & phrases employed. Trusting the prose does those works justice. Finally, readers are not obligated to imbibe this book in the usual fashion. How it is arranged, & printed. The text could legitimately be read just as any standard Bible if desired. As any standard Bible is printed, the Old Testament begins the book. If chosen, a reader could just as well begin in the middle of the book, & read first the Olden Bits (Old Testament) tales. Only then, moving back to the Newest Bits. Either way, readers are now encouraged to join the author. Let us now inquilinate*. Taking a parodied sojourn through an assortment of familiar Bible folklore as told by using delightfully expressive words, & phrases. For no other reason, than a ludic wish to bring about a little boffo in describing several tales of the Judaeo-Christian Bible in manners that are as different as fine fettle is to plague. That being so, this book is penned as a risible relief to the current corybantic nonsense of the woke/environmentalists religion. Trusting therefore a reading of this little nonsensical interpretation of several loved Christian tales is found locupletative*. Enjoy this Religiously Irrelevant parody of the Judaeo-Christian Bible.

Steve Morgan, Echuca, Australia, November 2021.

A STANDARD RELIGIOUSLY IRRELEVANT VERSION (S.R.I.V.)

FABLE, & MYTH SHOULD REMAIN FABLE, & MYTH. MIRACLES MUST BE SEEN AS POETIC IMAGINATION. TO INDOCTRINATE, THESE AS EMPIRICAL TRUTH SHOULD TERRIFY. ONLY THE CHILDISH ACCEPT THEM. ONLY THROUGH INTELLECTUAL ACUITY CAN THE CHILDISH MIND BE RELIEVED OF THEM.

ADAPTED FROM SIMILAR BY HYPATIA OF ALEXANDER (375-415)

LAUGHTER SHOULD FLOOD THE EYE, NOT WRINKLE THE BROW.

AN ODDITY: A REVERSED NEWEST, & OLDEN BIT BIBLE.

SHUSH... IT'S MYTHIC TO BELIEVE NEW TESTAMENT TEXTS PRECEDE THE TWELFTH CENTURY.[11]

---

11. Adapted from - The Christ Scandal, (H) p353. Tony Bushby.

THE NEWEST BITS:

Introduction to the Newest Bit:

The New Testament (Newest Bit) would ordinarily follow the Old Testament. But, this edition begins in this fashion for the simple reason the fabricated, parodied mix of tales below would likely be widely known to most people. The 'New Testament' of standard Bibles being also the most often read by believers. Aside, there was a desire to do something different to other parodied, & standard Bibles. The gospel of Matthew is the first gospel of The New Testament, & like the three other gospel accounts, allegedly depicts the birth, & teaching, as with several other exploits of a God-man Jesus. Most of the following spiced narrative is a parody to the gospel of Matthew, with several choice Latin terms (see Glossary). Opening with Logos (the 'alleged Word of the deity), 'Divine Conviction' being asked how many generations had proceeded the present. Moving to the birth of a child, some of the sermons on the mount, before closing remarks of another similar person.

A QUESTIONABLE PARTHENOGENESIS:
There came an indefinitely continued progress of events formerly, present, & future regarded as a whole. It was not much different from the before of The Olden Bits in comparison with the now, being The Present. At that stage, in a region there was hardly any Legos about. Only being birthed in another province as a base sauce for mealtime. There was no Lego. That other wondrous brick of play, being fitted together as all manners of objects, & landscapes. Telling stories while playing. This came decades after a someone became so inventive.

Of the then-time before this moment, there were Logos, Divine Convictions. Philosophical questions were asked of 'Divine Convictions'. What, when, how, & why is everything? How many ages had been? In answer, 'Divine Convictions' did reply after consulting the latest enchiridion edition: 'Hitchhiker's Guide to the Galaxy'. Sussing, "The answer to the questions of everything & of all the ages preceding this age, is: 42." By divine convictions did forty-two generations be deduced to have passed prior to the present.

How-when, & why, sometime after, Divine Convictions decided a time to not cavort with a naughty-pack* native; a maiden shikse*. Despite being the vicus* meretrix* she was completing her doctorate studies in Mariology*. Awaking one morn, she was much relieved to find she was not with a infantulus* side-slip*. Neither was there a cause to conjecture 'bout spontaneous Parthenogenesis. With much adulation, after this awareness did she bang out an 'Identifier triptych'. She did have multiple scribal copies. These were hastily sent to her entire 'communications' list. Scribed on the tablet was:

(Insert scribal address)

Dear ...,

Just thought to write you. The most joyous realisation happened to yours truly. I did awake just this morn to my psyche in magnifico. I am autonomous. Still, I am not mater meretrix*! For this I shall forever be lucky, that I did not receive a spontaneous parthenogenetic ally. Unsurprised, I did after consuming short eats of pastries, dim sums & other varieties suffer a slight eruption of borborygmic* noises. With much wambliness* I saw our resident mohel. Who said it was minor collywobbles* & had nothing to do with his profession. Can you believe it, he had the 'foreskin, oh, the stones' to retort,: "Heal thyself" while handing me his notes on the matter that did read: "The patient left my practice feeling much better except for her original complaint." To add insult to the infliction I was handed a small gourd containing several pilulous* objects & told abruptly: "Take two until passing away." At that, the Mohel promptly took flight for a circumcision conference.[12] I was only asking him about the probability of spontaneous Parthenogenesis. Which I had heard is unprecedented in humankind. It cannot be established without the fusion of gametes, forming a zygote? Surely, you all can see in my line of work, this would not be as fun, or lucrative if such was to occur. To my mind forever the clericus pacis*

---

12. Mohel - Jewish Circumcision doctor. Reference to Luke 4:23.

A STANDARD RELIGIOUSLY IRRELEVANT VERSION (S.R.I.V.)

has been toppled proleptically. I do henceforth, this morn liberate all sisters who announce that Political Correctness & papal miracles are equally soft-headed. I have also sought instructions from my Almanac of Oddities Manuel, but none answers are offered. Not even the local horticulturalist* is much help. Predictus*, no sorrow does come to these breasts this day; however. Ut dicitur*, I've been hanging around a few times with an odd fellow, Joseph…& I trust that you will ne'er inform my kin… ah, must be off, there is an advenae* at my door. Regards.

Now, pridie* there was a new mater* who did claim to have bore a masculus* ilius* by spontaneous parthenogenesis. Round & square Stars were there, one night of celestial phenomenon. That they did light up a whole province. Their brightness did disturb all sleep patterns. So, many weather-spy* ruricolists* was out ogling, & casting their votes for who would become this year's 'Lord of Misrule'*. Thus, no one really took that much notice of the new born as they were too busy gasping at the light show on display.[13]

The natalis* event, on account of the festivities was pretty low key. Except for a few planet-rulers* who did come to profess fortunes of stargazers. They happened to drop in to the xenodocium* to ask directions, & to see who was the best cicerone (guide) of the events taking place. Noticing the infans* & new mater recovering their strength. The travellers did ask quietly the front desk, where the most opportune spot in town was. That they too could best observe the Christmas window display, & from where announcements of fortune could be offered regards the current light show. They did depart leaving several gifts; boxes of chocolate, flowers, an embroidered blanket & bassinet set. In a suggestion box they did leave a congratulatory divine conviction & thank-you. Upon making a slight recovery, the new mother could hardly wait to write a note revealing her joy at finally having the opportunity of becoming a mater. She too, did have correspondence upon several triptych scribed. In it, she expressed:

"My autonomy is certainly a special individualism. With levanton* praises - Gladiola*! I have written this today with much rapture. The strangest occurrence did happen. I awoke this morn to my body doing a wondrous thing; by spontaneous Parthenogenesis, I have

---

13. Round & square - rhyming: 'Everywhere.'

given a masculus infantulus* reality. Though much sore still, he's a perfect example to show off to those who disparage that spontaneous parthenogenesis by humankind is even possible. Here; however, I suppose is the proof to all naysayers. I will surely become a celebrity. It's as if I have been natus et renatus*. I now say to all procuratores ecclesiae*; I shall be forever lauded as the only of wimmin* kind to have been so fortunate. My votive is still intact. How fortunate am I? There was only minimal male involvement too. Oh, don't stress, he's not the pater*. That's all a mystery. Sine prole* I am the boring puella lacorum*. But, rest assured this situation is about to change. Anywho, a kindly juvenis* assisted during the birthing contractions. With some encouragement, & panting assistance. It was he who did require the oxygen mask however. Thanks a lot Joe! The only regret, was that the birthing suites in other xenodocium offered only hamster healthcare* & are not very well fitted out. This place is riotously noisy. It's also drafty, & lacking in privacy from the main street. Unluckily, nobody has seemed to notice. This caravanserai* was the only place I could afford. Was close to home. Every other in the district is booked out by those bloody star-gazers, & other revellers.

Now, what do you think about the name Immanuel? I don't particularly like it. It's a bit too exotic for an infans, don't you think? I did though have a dream-state consultation with a famous eidolon apparition. After, we both decided the snapper's name shall be Joshua. Plain, I know. But, it does remind me of one of our forebears. That can't be a bad thing? The usual soon to be in-laws complained. But they forget, I'm a modern womyn with modern social, religious, & political views. Everyone knows, Joshua is fitting. Out of interest, does Joshua translate to the Bethlemite name Iesous? A cousin suggested it. Looking forward to showing this masculine orientated fellow off when I return in a couple of days. Regards all the well-wishes. But, stop with the flowers. The perfume is overwhelming."

On completion, she did promptly have the Barn concierge scribe Cu-nei-form copies & sent to the local wailing corner.[14] That it might be broadcast widely to have people know she is a good breast fleet*, & will be partaking of the required confarreation* ceremony.

---

14. Cuneiform - see, Fig. 1.

A STANDARD RELIGIOUSLY IRRELEVANT VERSION (S.R.I.V.)

So, refrain readying the <u>buttock-mail</u>*, & labelling of a <u>prostibule</u>*. Only by divine conviction, if one does believe it, can any spontaneous parthenogenesis see reality. Reality of this type had finally occurred.

Around this time, there was a Cabinet meeting taking place of all the Federal Government. Invited were all manners of regional officials in heated discourse regards the celestial phenomenon. Much back & forth bantering negotiations occurred about all manners of things. At the closing of the barbecue, parley was recommended; and a delegation of government officials, & several thousand Corrections Officers should be sent to the Bethlemite regions to survey. If needs arise detain & place residence under virtual house-arrest indefinitely. There had recently been notification of a government issued curfew. Because of the strangeness of the celestial phenomenon, currently underway in that region. Some government appointed bureaucrats had begun prancing that there would be a midscale outbreak of blindness if something weren't done to curtail movements. Since the commotion about the places surrounding the celestial happenings, the enforcement of all government 'rules' became order of the After-Light.

By sheer chance, the meretrix & new mater & infantulus was all able to escape scrutiny of their 'identity tablets'. They did have to festinate <u>continually</u>* through a labyrinthine. A Series of real long rat-lines that had been calved out directly under their house, & the Birthing Barn. These tunnels fortunately lead directly to the Kamit i.e., Egypt (See Eudoxus). To where all did escape those government officials.

Several hundred government officials, & corrections personnel did get really annoyed. <u>Peeved</u>* at the lack of record keeping skills of the public staff. Specifically, at the Birthing Barn. For although a womyn in labour was recently admitted, & having given life successfully to a tyke, she & the newborn had simply vanished through their symbiotic relationship. Neither of their whereabouts could be accounted for when staffs were asked. Such ineptitude enraged greatly Correction Officers much, that they did begin to <u>nicotine</u>* indiscriminately. Numbers however escaped <u>fisticuffs</u>* by hiding in baskets, under bed mats, & caliginous corners, & staircases of their dwellings. Particularly, toddlers, & esp., those in their early Tweenies. The ruse the authorities told everyone & their parents cuff 'n stuffed, was the kids were being taken in for a medical eye exam. The government had to assess potential eye damages after staring too long at the heavenly display. It fortunately happened to the escapees that there was a Joan who had entered the darkened passages quite awhile before them. Having been the Superintendent of the regional mazes under the cityscape. Now, Joan was an odd one. Clothed in tatterdemalion* camel's hair kilt & sporran, every time Joan did open the choppers, there was much twarvlment*, & blustering. Seeking to bugger off expediently from Joan's blustering the three did seek the speediest direction through. Directions were promptly sort after & given! At least Joan knew every corner of the maze, & which direction was the fastest way to Kamit.

Months of Sundays passed since escaping into the Kamit. It dawned on a Joshua's mother to have him officially trained to swim. Now is it common knowledge that the earlier a tyke is taught survival skills at Deluge* classes. The greater the chances & willingness & ability to pass those skills to another. An Iesous was shortly signed up to the local Deluge classes. After noting well the signage: Warning! "In the absence of a saviour, swimming is prohibited." Whereto he passed with honours, medallions & many other certificates of merit. Roundabout, several Iesous, & other Joshua's, did begin new ventures.

Somewhen, another Iesous had grown into a fine dandiprat*. He was most certainly dissimilar to others of his age, & those in the androgyny classes he engaged. Most others were unfortunately, still callow, as green about life as grass. Showing little maturity they were the usual Messianic* types. But, one Iesous was the rare nature*, having plums in his mouth*, he did show great eloquence* that did further his entrepreneurial skillset. Despite being mainly a home-tutored, & self-taught lad. He was confident, & an outstanding community oriented young fellow. Showing great politesse*, he was a well-natured, considerate youngling, oozing integrity. He did show a level headedness not often seen in persons of his age, of around 30years. Although still living at home, this wasn't considered all that surprising. He was a Millennial after all! Was about this time a sense of self-consciousness began to play many tricks upon his mind. Esp., during those long nights when alone in the house. During a vivid REM* dream-state, that an Iesous did have many visionary third-eye

A STANDARD RELIGIOUSLY IRRELEVANT VERSION (S.R.I.V.)

encounters. Prompting a few maxims burned onto his mind. He did when he had awoken, scribe these onto his Cu-nei-form journal for later reference. Assuring that he shall not have these ideas passes to the oblivion of the short memory only, & so be lost & forgotten.[15]

- Not long after waking from a night of rest & slumber, no matter how much was consumed the previous day. The waker always suffers ghough*, having awoken with a grumbling stomach region. The rightness of a saying heard is; "Mankind can't just survive & be productive the following day properly without further meal times. Esp., in the mornings." This was probably the most important time for the consumption of foods of great nutritional value; Needle & thread* alone just doesn't cut it. Neither is it of worth to try thy hand & milk chocolate. Such will only cause cows to peanuts in protest. Leave these tricks to Bacchanalia*. Some people may show a tendency to stertorous. Others, may become cadaverous-looking after excessive drinking from the river Lethe which often has an apnoeas reaction.
- Wherever anyone does preside, no matter their station in life, or in what city region, or country they live. The people will always have a sense of reverence for a special person or thing. They will cherish above something else, their favourite personality, place, & object. Society does have lots of individuals after all! Each comes to their lives with a different set of circumstances, values, & mores unique to those peoples & places. Treat others like individuals. Listen, & disagree. Fine. But, do not neglect being civil to them.
- The taking of a Census, as well as the odd Ballot, & Electoral cycles of authority figures to positions of Government; local, regional, State, & Federal are a usual. Some say this is a basic, & must practice of a 'Free' democratic society. Prague Spring allows citizens to at least keep the muse of a possibility of gaining assistance with the help of a kindly, but often autocratic bulldozer*, member of a Parliament. Most often an autocrat offers you a turkey during their fabulist lobbying. Sometimes, those elected or reelected officials do what they promise for the people during their campaigns. But, this is so rare; hens will likely grow teeth before anyone realises.

---

15. See Fig. 1.

- A viry unco bulldozer being is a politician. Always redy & promising our meliority, but not at there own expense.
- From his copy of 'Dissimilar to Psalms' was recalled:
"Do not lead another into temptation. They are
quite capable of finding their own way."

It was one particular morning, upon waking that Iesous did <u>open his lunch</u>* & let go a zephyr breeze. Being over bloated from the previous night's meal. Suddenly, he did receive an unexpected Tweeter notification from his avifauna companions. It was also plastered across the morning broadsheets; having made headline news. A Joan, who he did recall might have been the same who had been of great assistance in fleeing to the Kamit sometime in his early years, had been arrested. Authorities had finally been able to uncover the tunnels to Kamit under the Bethlemite Birthing Barn when someone tipped authorities off during another smuggling operation. A Joan was caught up in the following struggle. Upon hearing this Iesous was quite surprised, for he did think that Joan must have retired. Being near the elderly. It did bemuse him therefore that Joan had been arrested. Not long after, it finally dawned on Iesous; he did not have to spend all his time at home. So along with his mate Gali-lee the two did properly rent a two bedroom villa on the sea near Cape-nermum. On the outskirts of the <u>swankienda</u>* burb of Naza-et. Was a lovely villa, nestled among a town of trees. A grove of citrus & stone fruit owned & operated by the Zeb-U-Lan. With Naph-tali neighbours, who were descended from wrestlers.[16]

Beginning a life for himself here that Iesous, after much impromptu practicing, his <u>zielschmerz</u>* was finally realised. Scoring an itinerant teaching position with the College of Independent <u>Itinerants</u>*. The sea shore inspiring the following day's lessons while taking a stroll one afternoon in a state of <u>ponder</u>*. An Iesous did come across a couple of fellers mucking about with their favoured pronoun, <u>several</u>*. <u>Fry</u>* were let to exercise for a while in a net in the ocean. Simon, a relative of the 'Olden Bit's' (Peat), an' Drew his stepbrother. Iesous, did begin a conversation with them. As he was really interested in what type of fish they had? How esculent were such fry. Were they the best of the region for a nosh up with

---

16. See, Census.

A STANDARD RELIGIOUSLY IRRELEVANT VERSION (S.R.I.V.)

chips? It was after all, approaching Sabbath & it were his turn this week to organise dinner. But, as usual he'd left the shopping, & preparation too late. So, the household would have to settle for a few nan loaves, & fish n' chips that night. During the conversation, both Simon an' Drew asked what he was doing with his life; i.e., vocationally? Iesous' know-how & charisma was awoken; for soon after both men were recruited as co-itinerant research assistants. The exclusive affinity* to Iesous; however, for all the others had research sidekicks already. Was not long hence till Iesous & his aides did score several 'teaching' posts at various Cynic-Gogues throughout the region. Where he mainly taught a newish philosophy: "How wokeness is demolished." In his spare time. He also taught healing practices, both pagans, & modern styles so as to not cause consternation betwixt either camp. On one occasion, he was required to banish a gang of dybbuk* to another room. They did become really unruly during lessons. More & more of his lessons became well received, & his reputation did precede him that students came from as far as ten cities away, as well as locals, & a few from across the road from Jordan's place.

It did come by happenstance that the popularity of Iesous's teaching methods was such, that he & is entourage did secure a lucrative plein air venue for future lectures. An outdoor amphitheater. Wasn't really an amphitheater per se, rather, just the vestibule frequented often by a cosmopolis of men, womyn, & infans with an estimated capacity for about 5000persons audience (10,000 if kids, wives, or girlfriends were counted). Admittedly, this vestibule was not even as spacious, or in famous standing as those in the regions of Greece, or Rome. But, still a pretty special, loved venue by locals. It seated about only one Hundred souls nearest the peak of the mound. The rest of the 5,000+ audience was unfortunately standing room only. By the vicus pauperum supervisor's* did the lectures be relayed to them. One of these attendees did happen to be a well-versed transcribbler*. An amanuensis hastily transcribed the lessons & gave them to the assigned repporteur. Iesous's lesson to his new adult students included the following.

- "There was to be made no discriminatory opinions regards the 'poor of spirit' who was obviously suffering depression. For, they have run dry of drink. They too, are afforded the right to study my other course, "How the wokeness is to be demolished. Is their right, even more so than someone else to be able to take this course."

Iesous did also announce in the hearing of all who regularly cleared out, & did clean their eye tear ducts. As was recommended by old Dru the Wise-Craft.[17]
- "It is quite healthy to release & clear thy eyes every now & again. Mourning, & thy brightens which it doest again bring to thy darkened therefore was not to be frowned upon."

Broadcast all over, via wailing corner shofar, was a study of Iesous into Dru's life- lessons. The herald did announce:
- "For those who are predisposed to meekness," he said, "they shall one day become great persons of property. Many may turn exclusively to the RealEstate trades. Becoming as great Travel Buddy's themselves. Imitating the leadership, command's of thy great Matriarch, – Esther.[18] Who did become a dominatrix in RealEstate affairs. She was to be reckoned on the streets which they tread. Several of them may choose to become moderately decent mucisianists too."

Further reassuring all Unionised labourers,
- "There will be a plentiful supply roundabout of eateries, & pubs, & bars to satisfy thy stomachs & throats after a long day in the fields watching over your sheep paddocks. Or, whatever other laboriousness takes one's fancy." Adding,
- "Humaneness, clemency, mildness will all be offered in measure to those who inadvertently may find them self on the front step of a Law-house. Provided, one's own mildness being fully displayed to the clerk before entering."

With much enthusiasm he did continue,
- "For those with an actual purpose, & backbone. They will become noticed as a rarity. As one with singularity, uniqueness, & oddity. Just like thy presumed celestial."

Pacemaker's were not neglected. The contribution they did make to the life-improvement, & enhancement services offered to their customers were praised.

---
17. Proverbs of Dru.
18. See, Real Esther Tate.

A STANDARD RELIGIOUSLY IRRELEVANT VERSION (S.R.I.V.)

- "Those who do choose this profession will become as thy presumed celestial progeny. Blessed are all thy Pacemakers. They hast offered more life to the needy who did nearly fall off their perches, nearby having to be sent to thy Living Impaired Housing Units. Blessed therefore are the <u>unsoulclogged</u>*. Now they are aligned with pacemakers. More enjoyable are their life choices."

And,
- "Is the latest student of thy "How wokeness is abolished" courses who is of an advantage to any else. Is they who have been given thy good knowledge's & neologies of latest updates."

Concluding this day's lecture series with,
- "To those who would take <u>snuff</u>* at my teachings, lay off! If you don't like what I offer, consider your gratuities with another Itinerant more suited in the latest fashion. Is an individuals write to take up any, or indeed none of what I offer as an itinerant professor. These are but my learnings that I have chosen to offer thee. Not for Prophet, but from my own personal pocket of wisdoms."

Approaching gloaming it not long after became really hazy. Causing snoring of a few who was getting somewhat obnoxious. Iesous did consider it; therefore, a day. Returning to them in the same spot the following week. He did begin another series of lessons. Unfortunately, the very person who'd transcribed the last lessons was back for more. Having made Cu-nei-form copies of the previous lessons which were scattered about the entire hilltop for others to use. These became most helpful as remembrance tools. Interesting pointers, & discussion enders for dinner parties. This day's lecture opened with a doozy; the focus was what in the first hearing did sound quite ridiculous. Seeing that several listeners had begun snoring the previous lesson. Iesous did maybe attempt to lighten the moods, & shock all present out of pride with:
- "Who doest have a real high Cholesterol count? It is that you doest consume too much Sodom Chloride of the Earth."[19]

---
19. The Activation. A reference to (Matt 5:13).

What? This knowledge did astound many physicians in the crowds. For none had yet heard of such a thing. Was then many did grasp onto the idea. It is for this a cause that many otherwise fit clientele do take possession of an eternity box early. He continued,
- "If thou does cut back a bit. Esp., on the fish n' chip night. Healthiness might prevail bit longer." Particularly, while reading & studying that strangely title scriptures: "The Vinegar Bible."[20]

Many of those present did then begin to wonder. Was this fellow just another mountebank?* Loving the prestige of his peripatetic position & the soapboxes from which he banged on with his stories, to win their appeal. Had he finally lost the plot? Was he a health guru. Maybe, a health Rep? Several people began to protest, being the gatherers, packagers, & producers of saliferous products; sodium chloride. Those who worked in that odd 'pillar' looking factory on the shore of the Dead Sea. Disgusted at the insinuations thrown around, they left & did ne'er return. After this, the wholesale, & retail price of sodium chloride was preserved for a lengthy period. Morning tea came & went.

After the break, Iesous did call the ushers over seeking a lamp. His lecture notes had become mysteriously darkened all the sudden. With a new luminari at the ready, Iesous did further lecture the people. Strangely, he began mockingly in the common vernacular:
- "Ye are always to have in ready proximity quality batties for a torchie. If bad batties used in your torchie, any problem is not any contact with me. If your torchie is not ready at hand, you should in the least have a torchiere close by. Never does one really know when it is to be slightly overcast as much that you cannot read easily any longer. After the clouds do shade out the Heat Lamp above a little. Is not a recommendation; however, that when this doest takes place during an eclipse, that you should peer into the Lamp Corona. This will cause much degradation of the eyes, & cause one to stumble about as if on uneven ground. Best practice to get accustomed with. Have a spare lamp source readily available to use 'til the cloud disperses & you can safely replace your reading glare shields."

---

20. See, Bristow.

A STANDARD RELIGIOUSLY IRRELEVANT VERSION (S.R.I.V.)

Lunch time! So, the crowds dispersed for about an hour… returning just in time to catch a volley of wisdoms rarely witnessed in the open. Most were spoken softly in the safety of one's own backyard. Iesous didn't seem to be flustered at the classes tardiness. Beginning to admonishing those who'd begun to spread rumours. He flat out stated in no uncertain wordiness:
- "I have come to abolish law for prophet… (cough), retract that. I Have Not come to do these things. However, be warned that those who do leave out a fly-speck, or period, & generally, write their assignments using their really bad Grammy, instead of using properly a <u>Granmarian</u>*. To use <u>dog- or cat-Latin</u>* during these courses shows you are uneducated. You're a former <u>abcedarian</u>* so, your grades will be docked a decent mark. If it came to my attention that any be teaching this very badness, or, you are prone to <u>uglyography</u>* you too will ne'er receive a passing grade to any of your "How wokeness is demolished" coursework. Would've been in complete vain you attend any lesson."
- "You should have read it somewhere in maybe the 'Olden Bits' that sometimes it is ok to show a bit of 'choleric' temperament. Better, if it be only slight gall, & wormwood. Beware however, allow not this to escalate, that your keep release your vesuvian side; causing someone to be stuck with a case of severe clinomania. It is your fault they decided to join the choirs. This is not a very ok situation. What if they did have other things to do, & were looking forward to them? You have ruined that chance. Did you consider their families? Unless they were born of Parthenogenesis each of them does have a family. How selfish of you to strip that from them. Same goes for name calling; esp., of those of a different education. Dru, also did point this out. Besides, no amount of 'penny pinching', or penny giving will make up for anything, unless you who have many penny's do put his hand in the pocket, & pay full price of their psychologist's fees."

And,
- "In the 'Olden Bit's'. In Mo-she's time some people were spending some of their relations at a <u>Mauritania</u>* camp of bliss? Turns out, this might not be an unusual practice. Look around at the animals.

Esp., if you go to the zoo & sees the monkey's & other primates. They all do it… yet, society does frown upon such activities for us 'evolved' primates. So, just to keep the peace, best to probably keep the Phallus to thyself & she who you did find a sweetheart first. Take heed of the wisdoms of ol' Dru again, regards thy potential states of boredom. You can do it, find a way to really like your first sweetheart again. Boredom, you know it's not worth the trouble. Do your best to reconsider the ramifications, – castration!"

Further stating in the hearing of a few, he continued with,
- "You must have read it, or in the least be warned already: Beware of the lothario, & the coquettish. They shall only "cut the purse." Making all wealth to be spilled upon the floor. Coins will be lost behind the couch, down the drain, or in cracks in the pavements. Making them difficult to retrieve. Surely, resulting in a crestfallen disposition."
- "And, I do tell thee: Is a right of every citizen, to choose whether to find a spouse & begin a progeny. Is, also ok if thou does choose otherwise, – you are quite within your rights to look kindly at apanthropy. Honestly, it'll save a few bucks in the long term. Some may dislike this choice. Calling you all manners of weird names. You will though get over it. Divorce, for the attached at the breaking of material stuff amid an acquirement is ok too. Just be civil 'bout it."
- "You have a saying: "Rip his eye out," or "<u>lex talionis</u>*", "knock their heads together that teeth fall out." But, I say this is insaneness. It will only cause more consternation with the Government. The welfare dental bill will skyrocket, & that is frankly not all fair on those of us who have both eyes, & a full set of teeth still. Get over yourselves, & stop trying to better another. If you like someone else's <u>steam-packet</u>*, might be high time you got a damn job. Then you can afford one yourself. Smooching off another is frankly, so last year!"
- "If someone takes you somewhere you would really rather not be, know it's probably a couple of miles back. So, try securing a camel ride-share back as your legs will surely become querulous; you might end up requiring an odd looking Paddy Quick as a companion when you get home if you don't. When hiring, or hailing one

down do your best to ensure it's one of the deflatable models. You don't want it getting stuck in the eye-of-the-needle gateway."[21]

- "This one's for all the grammar-folk*. Those smart mathematicians. Those drawn to a vocation using all manners of figures (not the lady type figures calm down). I'm talking about all those Accountant types, & numbers people. You have heard of the 'Golden Rule' that was surely used by our people the first time with Mo-she Eudoxus way back when he (she) did take a Census of those that did leave the Kamit. Frankly, this dated 'Golden Rule' which thou hast learnt is kind to rubbish. It has since become knowledge that fractions are not at all that loopy, just misunderstood. Do consider that massive tome of Euclid, – "The Elements" he did call it, as a still most worthy textbook set. But, remember to revise your thoughts when it comes to the using of fractions. Understand it also that "When The Elements were written, math consisted only of counting, arithmetic, and geometry." Algebra was invented much after."[22]

There was much to be learnt this day by the crowds. Some however did listen to boredom who did entice them to leave & go do something more interesting. They did get on with life. Having had enough of being lectured to on things of little relevance to their chosen careers. Others, did suffer it out. Many of these people were thankful that by the end of the day, no transcript & lesson outline was offered as they did depart. Many months, & days past that Iesous did lecture, & ramble about some stuff all day. Some of it was interesting, but, like the proverb does say: "Some people did feel they would be better off as part of the deaf community, or that Iesous himself is part of the muted."

Sundays passed once more, & Iesous did take a short fishing trip for the weekend. Having gnashed the air with much bending the ears of the crowds. He was rightly buggered of mouth. So all he did wish to do was have a bit of time out & did relax with his buddies. Not long after did he & his mates embark on a leisurely boating voyage. In the middle of the trip; however, while somewhere on a lake, a rather fierce Euroclydon* did come from nowhere. It did lash the boat with much

---

21. See, Matthew 19:24; Mark 10:25; Luke 18:25.
22. Hauser, F. See also, 'Algebra' entry, Dictionary of Word Origins.

wind. Making the waters to get as they were read in the Olden Books, when No-ah did a little traveling. All men on board did not much get to finish any of their snoozing times. The rocking of the boat caused much Sturm und Drang*, making it near impossible to rest easy. The swell reminding them to begin singing a sea shanty. Was during the second chorus that Drew did notice that Iesous was happily snoozing. Incensed, he woke him & rebuked him. He did whine & pule how could he just lay there as if nothing were happening. At this, Iesous did look around & smugly stated in a loud voice so to be heard over the windiness, "Bah, what the hell are you worried 'bout? Is only a little roughness. Fishermen you are… you should have expected that something like this might happen. Esp., on this lake. I thought you understood that squall's often did just appear for the amusement & testing of fishermen skills. Besides, look over there, a sand bank!" The pilot of the vessel began citing a proverb: "All freights lighten, just as Peat did begin to throw his companions into the seas."[23] At that point the boat did moor itself on the sand bank. Just as quickly as it arrived, the squall did go east to another part in search of more fun of frightening people.

Days, & months drifted into another. It was on one of these ambling days that Iesous suddenly remembered he needed to file his latest Taxation form. So he rushed off to the nearest Remittance-man*. Walking into his offices, he was met with an odd looking fellow who introduced himself as Matt-Hue. He did oblige to file Iesous's backdated Taxations. But; much to the surprise of Iesous, there was no refund offered. Which kind of upset him, as he'd received one every year since beginning his Itinerant job. Unexpectedly, Matt-Hue was, as payment for services, invited to a surprise party by Iesous. It was a spur of the moment thing. Having just then also decoded the cypher* handed to him earlier. It was a request to have a secret nosh-up for a collective of Tax evaders.

About the time of all this kind of thing, & much else was locally, regionally, internationally happening about the places. A parallel other likeable Iesous was trying his hand at his version also, of an Itinerant job. When he was not reclining on a corner mouthing to every passerby: "Give me coins, & I will enjoy you," as he was strolling the beat.

---

23. Based on a similar German proverb.

A STANDARD RELIGIOUSLY IRRELEVANT VERSION (S.R.I.V.)

Spruiking wears, goblets, & all manners of household goods, & services. Even becoming a moderately famed wailing & spel* MC, & newscaster. Having several follower's pen his broadcasts soon after dictation. This other Iesous was causing quite a stir. Claiming to be the epitome of a thaumaturge*, & other strangenesses. Persistently showing off his acts of prestidigitation. Claiming to being able to wake up some people who had become real tired, had real bad suffering of clinomania & so had to become a clay* resident. He was also quite famed at water-boarding, & barefoot skiing, & other circus type amusements. He did with all his antics cause quite a ruckus with authorities, & demimonde alike.

Then there were actors:

A little parody of the alleged exploits of a troop of a <u>messianic</u>* actors, & colleagues. We see here a bunch of scared little illiterates become intrigued with an explosion of sorts. Which gave some frabjous abilities read about in their bed time stories (Old Testament). A blustering, hot-headed bloke had an epiphany, & suddenly changed his mind about stuff, which lead to even more fame visited upon him. A parody to the Bible book of Acts.

SOME OTHER ACTORS:
Acknowledged by Theo, & Philus, are several things which have already been authored about one itinerant teacher. He did begin to set his operation at the same time, in the same region as several other Iesous. As another regional itinerant he did choose, for the sake of keeping the woke happy. His trufans did insist on the personal pronoun moniker, I Am. Feeling it gave him a sense of importance above another. Often spruiking that his qualifications were of a higher learning than another.

I Am did cause much consternation about the places. But, all tales told of this I Am fellow are controversial. Not being easily seen in verification to veracity. I Am, it is said was a teacher of all unknowables, & magics. He was according to some, a qualified hypnotist, & did spread rumours about how wonderful it is to promote a Welfarism. He did announce to many, his much higher status. Often, retorting to questioning by an opponent <u>D-Y-K-W-I-A</u>?* Then, referring to himself as holding a real high position in the place. Just a bit lower though than the Grand Chancellor to the college from where his qualifications were earned.

In those days, of I Am's career everything he did teach, do, think, or act upon. That all this was likened to being unkosher. Therefore, I Am did annoy, & vex lots of whoever did spy his whereabouts & be in his vicinity of hearing. So much vexing was there, that some very authoritarian's & parochial stewards of the establishment did eventually

A STANDARD RELIGIOUSLY IRRELEVANT VERSION (S.R.I.V.)

be able to cancel, & revoke his itinerant license. They were, so it seemed able also to disbar the organisation he had helped to become reality.

One moment, it did happen a little bit like this from memory. Many of I Am's first followers became fearful one afternoon at witnessing the 'cancelling' in their Head. The punishments too were most frightening. Near all his closest students, & mates then, did contradict having knowledge of I Am. Not willing to disclose what ego ramp I Am did stand on, & teach from. Despite lots of them being known as research itinerants. They did not wish to go through the same humiliations of becoming 'cancelled' like I Am. So, they did lie to authorities at every opportunity when cornered. Not long after did some of the best of I Am's research itinerant's did choose to make sure they did dodge the probable same cursing with Bell, Book & Candle*. They did then seek a clancularious* hideout. Finding a perfect dilapidated, State-owned building earmarked for demolition. The thought was that their usual haunts would be havens for spying. They did need therefore, somewhere totally neutral. Believing this would allay probable targeting, & prosecution. They were unprepared to 'throw a seven' & face prosecution if spied attending their usual conventicles. So, they did hang about hoping the fanaticism of the last couple days would subside. Never quite knowing their fate, or the day when the building would go to rack & ruin. Tension was high, as were their hypertension, & cholesterol levels. All these 'scared little guy's,' as with the comedy troop was just vocating* about while fumbling a poker to pass the time. When suddenly a huge roar of hugger-muggers was heard. Followed by an explosion that was so unexpected a building shuddered a little, swayed a lot, & collapsed into a frightened mass of rubble. Immediately, the castaways did flee to a nearby corner. Reappearing sometime later as part of a crowd of rubberneckers, nosing what had occurred. Finding that an 'oil feeder' wick to an oil street light had lighted up the street ahead of time, & so sent a flaming ball of hot air about the place, lighting one near all passersby.

Nearest that moment a troop of actors, & actresses did erupt into a volley of extreme agitophasia*; electro plasmic* type twaddle. Hardly anyone took any real notice, except the sidekicks of I Am. To them, this tommyrot utterance did remind them of a long past bed time tale. Sounding much as taal. Maybe, this was the reemergence of some proto-afroasiatic, proto-semitic tongue? There was, one of their number recall, a similar happening in one old time fantasy tales of the Olden Bits. The Olden Bits Mo-she is legend to have encountered electro plasmic orations. Anywhen later some of their ancestors are recorded to have also had a similar experience. Seeing the most likeable explanation was closer to Mo-she's encounter recorded in Eudoxus, all did suppose, & secretively yearn that a similar orating experience would become present maybe-then. Witnesses about began to nosing this spectacle. Among the rubberneckers were a vast variety of ethnicities.

There were many politically, & conscientious reformers as diverse as any other commerce center. Several fukubukuro*, & market stall holders were owned & run by a mish mash of phratries, tribes, & ethnic groupings of industry leaders representing the Part-thins, the Medes Gaud laboratories of Gaul (modern France), several cheese representatives from Edam, there were cousins of an Elam-mite farmer. Also, here on a festive trip was numbers of native residence from as wide reaching as the olden expanses of the Mesopotamian districts, hundreds of Everton toffee* lovers from a gang of Southern Palestinians, - the Cappuccino's, members of the Pontahontas clans of Asia, the Phrygian's (cold storage specialists). There were specialist pamphlet designers from Pamphylia, numbers from Kamit, & those owned by Cyrene, & many tourists from Romania. The explosion had caused the marketplace to become a morass of confused activity. TikTok, & other social media platforms crashed. They could no longer upload posts of their latest reviews. Previous tics/likes of approval, for good bartering skills greatly, could not be relied upon. When it was suddenly noticed, - the wine stall/merchant had done a Harold Holt*. During the commotion, somebody began calling out for Joel Cassandra. A minor who was renowned for correctly predicting disasters. He had gotten lost or been misplaced by parent's or, other guardian after making a substantial purchase of grog. Local DFS (Department of Family Services) authorities were unimpressed. But, a kindly stranger did find the child, & directed him to the nearest DFS office. Being questioned about all manners of unrelated things about his wondering, the DFS did engage in much small talk with him.

During these conversations, the young fellow did relay an interesting tale he had been read from his favourite tales of oddities before bedtime.

A STANDARD RELIGIOUSLY IRRELEVANT VERSION (S.R.I.V.)

He did conjure the tale in clear detail, which did concern some of the DFS audience. Recalling, there was at one favourite moment in the tale where a character did become dowsed in Spirits. So, stumbled about acting out the manners of a madman, talking to himself, confusing, & scaring passerby's, & generally being a ripe ol' downer in the entire community. Joel then did announce that the tale told of various celestial oddities, which were promised to be visited upon the spirited ones. In the heaven would be witnessed the moon becoming as a blood red apple. There would be the inhalation of much smokiness, which then did cause those it smothered to blank out, & become unconscious for a time.[24] This was to be reckoned as occurring in a yet future time, or, possibly just around the corner. All in the office did gasp in horror at the hearing of such a tale. They did consider visiting the home community of Joel, that they did find out was at Petra, for they did wish to do a searching through this community.[25]

The DFS officers did decide they must find, & declare the substances the community did use to concoct such tales, as contraband. Soon after, Hades did enter DFS & returned Joel to his parents at Petra. DFS inspectors did visit Petra. Yet, despite all efforts, they did find nothing out of order. The explanation offered them was all residents suffered NHO, Neurotic Homogenous Obedience, which cause them to be shunted as kind of leprous. They had to make good at Petra. The bemusement of this community, was not that for much of the time they chose to live as an anchorite, but doing so lent themselves to a fanatical Welfarism/ Socialism. Where so it had done seem, everyone did commit to a social ideology of sharing near 'bout all things, & owning very little. Some even dreamed this ideology would be known as a Great Resetting of Society. As the DFS officers had done find out. Near every effort was made to sustain the needs of the community whole. Every psychological, physical, residential, ethereal*, authorial indulgence was catered. However, below the surface of this serenity, & bliss, some community members were brazenly advantaging themselves more than others. There was a Balaamite* in a community nearby who did subscribe to the NHO. His name was Han-Annoyance.

---

24. Bible: book of Joel 2.
25. Present day Jordan.

Han-Annoyance did love his wealth, & things of brightly coloured sapphire. He did also assume the religious rights of the NHO. That many of them would be of great financial gain. It was one <u>otiose</u>* afternoon that Han-Annoyance did promise & intend to donate the entire collection he had hoarded over a lifetime. Promising to contribute it all to the NHO., welfare pool, to be distributed among the other community members. That their own <u>hedonism</u>* in kind would blossom. Turned out however, his indulgence of hedonism was very great with him; for he could not help camouflage a little of his most prized pieces for gratification. When one of the community overseers had done sniff wind of his deception, he did rage a little against him with a charge. With much wisdom did he bluster at Han: "He who does not purloin promised donations, choosing to again hoard them has learned to live. When oh Han, will you learn to live?" In remembrance of the maxim of stinginess, he continued, "The edacious, & drunkard will surely come to ruin; his purse will empty more quickly than the cheapskate, or, sensible. It is better to be one of the sensible than waste your energies, & earnings on making wider your belt…" A serious charge of '<u>intemperance</u>*,' & many parchment leaflets explaining the charge were distributed against Han-Annoyance for his evident recusance. He was not long "Cancelled" as a <u>snollygoster</u>*. He faced charges of being an errorist; as someone who inveigles others to error. The community leaders exiled him from all community fundraisers. Word of the successes, & brightly coloured gift packs offered to new comers, did the NHO. community begin to expand throughout the regions. Many plebs, & other internationals did sign up. They did all make commitments to adhere to NHO. publications. To the NHO. ideology; for in their brochure was a promise to compare itself to the political, & reverent scene in power. Even promising to exceed these, the organisation did toot about themselves being much different, & helpful to a wider societal base.

There was 'bout that time a 'stoner', called Pete. But, only at falling out of a trance-like state. 'Stoner' was one afternoon famished. Having spent much time <u>vocating</u>*, & faffling about. In a <u>pantophagic</u>* state, spying a tablecloth covering an unattended outdoor picnic setting nearby. He could barely resist taking a peak

A STANDARD RELIGIOUSLY IRRELEVANT VERSION (S.R.I.V.)

at what deliciousness might await from view. Lifting the corner of the cloth his oculars near fell from his head in delectation & delight. There were varieties of unusual things packaged to be very titillating.

"Go ahead, - wrap your taste buds about these!" "Nobody will mind. In fact, these things should become the 'new' sources of foods." Bellowed a voice through a peephole in the fence. With much honeyfuggling* did the voice continue. "Look. It's that packaging pleasing to the eye. It cannot therefore be all that bad. Take a cook's tour; there's new varieties of 'chips', - cricket, mealworm, & other bug products. I promise you; these are much beneficial for your ailing health. Forget the age old domestic meats, & other standard foods stuffs. They're outdated, & quite puzzomful* for the planet. Go on, I guarantee you'll become a much better person, spiritually, mentally, & physically. If people like you would only transition to eating my chosen foods." Unconsciously, Pete did formally protest under his breath. His mind seeing through this as complete humbuggery*. Not once had he tried new stuff. Not once had he consumed. Let alone touched things considered tref*. Besides, he weren't a bird. He was raised in the 'old fashioned' ways of carnivorousness.' This was most satisfactory. Thank-you very much! The consumption of bugs, leaves, twigs, & bark sounded too icky. Was crazy & real unnatural for any of the Humankind species. Reasoning that such an urge to consume these products, could well be unhealthy, for its abnormality to Human-beings. Concluding, such a push was an excuse for allotriophagy*. Knowing well that in those Olden Parchments, the Olden deity did make provision for a diet that included both plants based, & animals varieties. But, never were bugs, & synthetic types considered. So, Pete did frankly decline. Specially, arguing that if all these 'new' things were of the 'new, better food' variety, why is it that the marginalised only are encouraged to consume them?' The 'Elites will consume, & do whatever they choose. It is one 'rule' for them. Another for the rest. Besides, Pete did again emphasise in protest that he had trained his palate with a workable bias already, & wasn't enthused to push the boundary any more.

"Ah, stop your whining. The rest of you poor plebs hasn't caught on yet. But, rest assured, we're working really hard on it. If you won't take this seriously, well, we'll have to manipulate the immature, &

irresponsible. They'll eat these things without question. Damn it, they will like it!"²⁶ 'Stoner' was much discouraged at this tone. So, he did not scoff or gormandise whatever was available. But, did <u>discreetly</u>* hop it to the nearest <u>metabolic clinic</u>* for a toastie. He did then also visit a library & educated himself about the 'Great Reset'. Seeking further information about the control of the entire world that the unelected upper class; those who believed themselves above others wished to enforce on the world. After much research & observation of world affairs, Pete did became much enlightened. Recognising that accepting these 'new' proposals, or different things as proper foodstuffs, it really is a bad thing. He was of the Humankind. Not a bird, or an animal to be corralled at the whim of some elite class. He did reason, rather, his new knowledge has the great potential to reinvigorate the unlearned, opening one to this insane, deceitful ideology.²⁷

About this time, there was also a rival clique 'heavyweight', - Paul, who according to various accounts did have the following countenance about him: He was "short in stature, head shaved, legs bowed though athletically formed, deep-set eyes, broken nose, and full of charisma, for sometimes he appears like a man, at other times with the face of an angel."²⁸ Paul's activism did often cause much factionalism among his own ideology. He was so dogmatic regards his own; he could not however resist butting heads with the new rival Cabal in town. He did not much agree with anything the NHO & their own babbled on about. Often, resorting to persistent slander, & maligning of their policies, & ideologies. Viewing them as plain dotty, & out right bonkers. He did attempt at every opportunity to ensure the entire organisation was permanently "Cancelled." Most of the time did Paul prefer to show the community his 'angelic styling', opposed to his 'irateness'. For, this did seem to gain much more likeable attention. As Paul went about raging as a typical irate 'man' about NHO operations, & their policies he did happen a minor victory to his cause. He did during one of his irateness interludes happen

---

26. Such proposals as in his hearing did only remind Pete of an ancient archetypal personality considered in the ancient texts to be of a 'tyrannical' nature, Nimrod. The one of whom it is said enticed rebellion.
27. See Postscript for 'Reevaluations' of 'Stoner.' Also, Paul who did become sem priest later for the NHO community. See footnote below for 'sem' priest explanation.
28. Price, Robert M. The Pre-Nicene New Testament. Section VIII. Location 30034.

A STANDARD RELIGIOUSLY IRRELEVANT VERSION (S.R.I.V.)

to stumble upon a lecture series by one of NHO's main lecturers, Stephen. A much educated, & versed NHO community member. Stephen, a Historian, was a senior lecturer. He was one afternoon ranting about his ego ramp. Reminding the audience of 'accepted' histories. Nudging all in attendance to ne'er forsake lessons from a bygone era. Much of the audience was riveted to their ticketed spot of the venue, & applauded much at the conclusion of his lecturing ego ramp act. But, others, Paul among them did rage, & wrath against him with much vexing. They did believe that such a history lesson had been manipulated, & likely after doctored to give great purpose to Stephen's cause. Stephen was soon after arrested, charged with spreading rumours, & fabrications for gain-of-function research to further the operations of NHO, & was permanently 'Cancelled' soon after. After the sentencing & punishment metered to Stephen, Paul did be felt much vindicated. Which moved only him to persist in his goal? Yet, more lecture series was organised by NHO membership. Which did confuse Paul & others for he did know of the 'successful' cancelling of the 'nominated head' that took place publicly several years before. It was enraging to activists such as Paul that the organisation remained valid, & even growing in strength & subscription.

In due time, & much to the surprise to Paul, did he encounter an epiphany. His tune choices, & song selections did get much better, & appreciable to all who had no choice but to listen. He did eventually come to side with the Welfarist's. He too became one of them. Rising to prominence quickly. Instead of persistently banging on about how backward the NHO Communities were. Paul now did shock, & awe his former proponents (which happens to radicals. Seems radicals cannot help switching 'sides.') Radicals often flip n' flop as a wet fish on land. It is amusing that anyone does put up with such inconsistencies. Maybe, these folk are undisclosed ancestors of No-ah?[29] An extraordinary transformation of Paul occurred. Happening after an encounter with a very strange multicoloured vested entity who did quite severely flagellate all his actions to date. The entity was unimpressed at the consistent heckling of the NHO. Paul now admits, he was confronted by blinding light, & effectively, interrogated by a someone, or thing

---

29. See, The Activation.

unknown. The entity was assumed to be from another realm, or, possibly dimension. Who knows, yet those who have lived through such an ordeal became known as 'contacts.' Such contactees rarely are comfortable in brightly lighted spaces. Not long after his encounter, did Paul switch sides. An upshot of the change in attitude soon became real evident. He held the conch over all manners of fatidic exsufflation. He was soon marked as a thaumaturge of influence. If he did sneeze into a fichu, kerchief or swab a nose or wipe a greasy hand, finger, or his brow of sweat. The recipient seemed to become the panacea for all manners of ailments; real, faux, & everything between. Food poisoning, headache, leprosy, burns victims did all present to Paul, & no sooner had they voiced their issue, the malady, whatever it was, mysteriously disappeared. People allegedly became whole. Paul became quite the celebrity among those who were inflicted with 'exorcist' experiences. Suddenly, those 'hanger's on' were forced to lose their grip, & remove the unwanted pounds. Eventually, these episodes became bad news for every legitimate medical practitioner. They found themselves losing many clients; so many, that there were few options than to burn their medical journals, & return to Talmud* schooling to re-skill.

    Life motored on. Countless speaking tours were booked all over. Attended to by hundreds. Paul's celebrity grew dramatically. So much that it was now his celebrity that became as sand in the eye to his former faction. After one speaking tour event, Paul was allegedly attacked by a rival cohort, & was lapidated. Much passive smoke did arise from the stooshie* & battering of words, & various body parts, & ash throwing contests. The 'stoning' however was but a clever ruse he'd orchestrated whenever he did fall asleep from boredom. In such a state, he had organised to set motionless, as if in trance as his old ancestor, Mo-she. Who, if it is known did sit in Lotus as Buddha for many lengthy periods. Paul had organised a ruse with a colleague, Barney. He was instructed around an hour after the beginning of any meeting, if Paul did present as boredom, to wave a shekel about in protest to something. Showing such a semaphore, Paul removed himself quietly from his Lotus position, & both men did slink away in the direction of the local Livestock Derby*. There they watched in delight, the camel, & goat herding trials. Derby was thereat famous for the running of sporting events.

A STANDARD RELIGIOUSLY IRRELEVANT VERSION (S.R.I.V.)

The carnivalesque atmosphere was electro plasmic! Both Paul, & Barney did get into the swing of it. Joining the roping of herds, & several rapping activities. In their spare time between events, neither did forsake their duties to NHO. Never ceasing to spruik the benefits as much as could be accommodated, & accepted. Their efforts did impress certain festive goers from regional areas, like Lystra, home of mouthwash Gourd swills. Also drawing attention from icon manufacturer's from, Iconium, as with Antioch, satellite refrigeration city to Head Office, Phrygia. Paul & colleagues did keep this ruse going for many days, months, hours without cessation.

Overworked, irritable, traveltainted* & downright sick to the back teeth of each other. Paul & colleagues took a break from the other. Each dispersing to a disconnect corner of the map they separated to begin to repair the escalating mischief that was beginning to brew. Threatening to become as a poorly poured beer, - too much froth, & bubbles. Athens was clearly marked as a wonderfully relaxing touristy destination. Paul did head off in that direction.

Leisurely strolling through Athens one afternoon, visiting the touristy sites, & treating his taste buds to a smorgasbord of new delights. He did know in his gut, that Athens were where he did need to be this present. The parchment brochure of touristy things to do while in Greece was accurate. One of the most extensive cosmopolitan of cities, Athens was a Mecca of Western cultural hipsters. One of his favourite treats was the array of flavoured after-dinner ice-creams available. The city he did also find out on a guided tour, was the birthplace of Cosmo. This was a bi-yearly parchment glam rag. Here, one could read of the gossips of the last years, the trends of yesterday, & what was the latest in democratic, & philosophic importance. As with a listing of up & coming Philosophers, & orators. Athens did also house some of the most renowned Philosophical Academy's in the region, like Mars Hill, Areios Pagos.

As was his custom, Paul did strike many conversations at local pubs, sporting venues, & the like. But, mostly at the Cynic-Gogues where he was often an uninvited guest. His proudest moment took place conversing with an Athenian Council atop the Areios Pagos. Where a sometimes heated conversation about some dietary minutia took place. It was also here Paul did converse with several Stoics, & other academics. Each found conversations between them a slow, &

often confusing experience. For, Paul as a sem priest, did often forget he was quite fluent in a little ancient Greek, & their history. But, for smart-arsey purposes he did choose that ancient Kamit (Egyptian) tongue of Coptic/Demotic. While, the Stoic remained speaking Ancient Greek, or a dialect of it. The point each of them was attempting to make to the other was slow going. As, nobody had thought to fetch a terp, or the <u>triglot</u>* 'Rosetta Stone' to assist with intelligibility.

The conclusion of Paul's vacation, he dove straight back into the familiar surrounds of his local swimming hole. Beginning another round of speech therapy sessions while on tour. On one occasion, Paul did use his 'sem' priestly authority. Punishing one audience member who had fallen asleep during one of his lectures. Was Eutychus who insolently did begin snoring loudly. He was a sufferer of either <u>dysania</u>*, or, a form of acute <u>oscitancy</u>*. Not realising the seriousness of his condition, a dyspeptic fellow, showing as much compassion as a starving shark decided to <u>defenestrate</u>* him so the rest could hear the closing remarks. Incensed with this, Paul did immediately remind the young man: (1) to ensure enough sleep before a lecture, & (2) if he was found to have ignored this directive the next time, he'd bare the fullest brunt possible of the power, & authority of knocking heads with a 'sem' priest like Paul. Explaining, with <u>incertitude</u>* that as a 'sem' priest Paul was ordained, & authorised to show off full powers of <u>anabiosis</u>*. Being well versed in the anabiotic trade described as the qualified who "…preside… over the Opening of the Mouth ritual.., in which he touched the face of the [body] with tools to revive the senses… He performed the same ritual on statues, imbuing them with the spirit of the person they depicted and enabling them to act as surrogates for the one who commissioned the image."[30] Paul's warning to Eutychus therefore was the opposite could be performed also to any who did act inappropriately during a lecture series. With that understood by Eutychus, he did immediately cease being sleepy for the remainder of the lecture. After this episode, Paul did venture roundabout a lot & as the hours, days, months, years fell into another & became indecipherable from the other, the more weary Paul did become.

---

30. Teeter, Emily. (A 'sem' was considered the First Priest (hem Netcher-tepy) overseer of the religious order)

A tired Pastoral Paul

Paul, claimed leadership status of the emerging religious faction, but was becoming real tired, & upset at the lack of care some subordinate were showing. Rebukingly, he penned a notekin. Reproduced here are his thoughts. Parody of the Bible book Titus.

TIGHT-AS:
Paul, did soon after all this travelling & acting like a Pope, had become quite a figure; a stalwart for the causes of the NHO community. He was being worked to the bone, having to spread himself extremely thinly in all duties expected of him. He had therefore become completely anorexic, & exhausted in mind, & physique. He did then feel it necessary to scribble on a napkin parchment in a <u>bukateria</u>*, a note to one of his subordinates. Instructing the dream of having his load lightened. The fellow he had in mind, & was scratching out instructions to was prone to continually <u>Hooverise</u>* possessions, & other commodities. So, he was known to be a <u>quaresimal</u>* operator. Paul did hope that his work partner would be encouraged to reform his choices somewhat, loosen his skullcap, & perform, or, in the least take to mind the instructions. The note was directed to Tight As, & fellow workers.

Dear Tight-As, & crew,

Just a short note of instruction to you from Paul, 'sem' priest of the NHO communities. I am exhausted. Why the hell am I burdened to carry the bulk of the load for everything this organisation claims to achieve? I wish through this reminder, that you see it fit to consider taking more of the administrations which would greatly relieve me, & several of your colleagues, allowing us to become slacker in our duties. I'd like little else than to be able to rest for a few more hours a week, maybe take a full week off every now & then? Does your stinginess really have to be at the expense of your fellows? I am one of your elites, & so deserve a little respect for the position. In more time off at the expense of you plebs becoming wearier. So it is our health, alertness that are increased to flourish, not yours. Just seems a little unfair mate. That's all I'm saying.

To Anne, & A-man, please use the following instructions to encourage Tight-As to loosen, & maybe prod him to reconsider his role. First, please remind him of the Proverb: "It's probably not all bad to be quaresimal. With the consuming of goods, & drink, yes. For, if you do not choose to be quaresimal with these, the worst case scenario is. You become fubsey*. Bloated, to eventually fall off the perch earlier than might otherwise have happened." The antithesis, "Stinginess could be construed as giving the people the 'evil eye'." To remind thee, Proverbs of Dru categorically stated: "Evil eyes are a complete suspicion. You shall ne'er be attentive to such for it is a waste of time to chase after irrationalities, & nonsense. Might be, you did happen to catch the glance of someone with an amblyopic eye. It is dissatisfying to be pettifogged & accuse someone with such an issue, labelling them auspicious without proper cause."[31] Stop it. Refrain from all suspicious activities. I am also hoping that I left several 'Crates of Elder-berries' among you all. These need to be returned asap. My stores of wine are running low, & I need to make a new batch in readiness for the coming 'Passover' season. If the process is not begun soon, the chances of fulfilling orders for the next season will be zero. I need the fast maturing seedlings to plant. Many of you may be aware. I supply the Cynic-Gogues of the region, & I'm likely to have that agreement rescinded if their supplies are not replenished. Like yourselves, I cannot afford in the current economic, & political climate to be reproached, neither by a Cynic-Gogue husband, nor his wife. It will not end pleasantly if because of some mishap, I am labelled debaucher, or a headstrong steward, & overseer. If this happens, I'll let fly, because I'll know then the scheme about my personality. The one I've been cultivating, & nurturing for years now, being honourable, kind, hospitable, self-contained, & self-controlled in all dealings with each Cynic-Gogue will be uncovered for the trickery, & ruse it was planned to be. Do you really want me to be known as untrustworthy, quick-tempered, & arrogant? This, will be reflected directly back on you all. Ask yourselves, can the NHO really afford to be sullied like this now?

---

31. See, Proverbs of Dru.

A STANDARD RELIGIOUSLY IRRELEVANT VERSION (S.R.I.V.)

Further, it has also come to my attention, there are among several of your Cretan; those who seek to catch for their own Prophets, as all types of liars, evil beasts? & gluttons. What are those 'evil beasts'? What have they been consuming? Obviously, some kind of soup, causing delirium. Regards those Cretan, I ask that a rebuking sharp eyes be kept on their movements. We cannot afford to let these wacky people out of sight. It might be a real good idea to use petty denarius, & go purchase a kind of tracking device. Like a small gem hidden in a <u>Phylactery</u>*. Offer them as a gift, or incentive for good work; as a thank you gift for their diligence to their Prophets. Further, many of you are aware numbers of our dottery, decrepit companions. That they portray themselves as sober minded. They are also quite controlling; not only of themselves, but many of us younger folk. This is ok, unless they happen to entice you to breakage of another of Dru's Proverbs: "Thou shall always, & within reason, respect & admire superiors in the workplace. You should ne'er go out of your way to cause any consternation between workmates." Knowing from experience, several of these aged buggers will push n' prod for amusement, some of you to puncture your resolve. That you must remove yourself from such a Proverb. Thus, be on the hook for retribution. Don't!

I plead however, that each of you does your utmost to repel the urge. Remind them, though they present as obedient, & submissive in the workplace. It is widely known that they are often there for a tipple only. So, they can desist from the "Holier than thou attitude." Such posturing is an indictment on them. Finally, Please have Arte-Mas, & Ty-Chicus do their utmost also in aiding Nico-Polis this coming wintery season. <u>Deve</u>* & <u>goonda taxes</u>* are still required to aid the lawyer stipend. Just the contracts of our venal <u>grimgribbers</u>*, Apollos, & Zenas. The NHO cannot sustain them without donations. These past years, has been of great benefit. They have done a stupendous job yet in hoodwinking litigants, which have ensured our keeping afloat to carry on with business as usual.

Paul. P.s. In an expectant future for peace & profit. May Grace stay with you. Sorry for the inconvenience, yet, I cannot deal with her incessant whining at this juncture of my life.

One-se please!

A much frail Paul implores a colleague to send him his One-se. One-se, a pun on the word for reconciliation which is the name of a slave - Onesimus - meaning 'useful'. A parody of the Bible book Philemon.

PHILLY:
To Philly, Paul, the sem.
    I just wanted to confer again, regards earlier conversations. I am not getting any younger these days, but am slowly, as expected, becoming one of the dottery, decrepit, skranky* companions to you all. So much as my bones are near showing, & my skins are become leathery, & saggy in places I'd rather like to keep hidden. So, as you can imagine, the nights are becoming unbearably chilly. As it is, the rags I am subjected to don now. Frankly, make me look as a tatterdemalion*. They're all dowdy & flabergudgion* for their constant wear. Could you then in your benevolence, see to it the Ashen Sackcloth 'One-se*' I had left behind last trip, be forwarded by next scouting runner headed in this direction?
    I know I'm only over the fence from your neighbour, but, I'm frankly just too effete. Some are now labelling me execrably limp-wristed, so why bother coming round. It would be of great warmth, & comfort to these olden bones if you'd send that One-se. I only have a few tattered, outdated, unfashionable scraps of electro plasmic loin cloths in the alcove. Cheers for the considering my welfare & warmth. Regards.
    P.s. Might need a wash. Last time I did wear it, I did notice an obtrude grinnow. A belligerent spot of soup that had not been dissolved by my attempts at scrubbing it out. It did look to have dissolved when I last did wear it. But, as you know well. My peepers are not all that well at the intricate stuff nowadays.

'Cleanliness - is Godliness'

A fellow believer of the community implores, in a soft rebuking manner that others take care of what they're doing. Remember their purpose. A parody to the epistle of New Testament book - Jude.

JUDAS:
Shalom, Judas, savant of NHO Communities.

Unfortunate circumstances have forced this parchment poster on all walls round about. Despite being most keen to write you all at the wonderment, & experiences of becoming a presumed valued member of the NHO community. Three years has past since my acceptance into this clan. Alas, I am grieved to announce I am most surely dissatisfied. I am seriously considering hiring turkey bacon*.

For instance, security is way lapsing. Being mostly rubbish in effectiveness, as I have noticed on more than a single occasion that someone, or somebody's are creeping around the but & ben* sometime after my retirement for the night, & are persistently fixing themselves a ripe ol' mess. Nothing is put away. No dishes, utensils are cleaned & returned to their proper placing within the almery behind the curtain. Don't even get me started on the benches, & table.

Guy's & dolls, it cannot be stressed enough. I am not a scuddler*. Read the damn notice - "MICE! DO NOT LEAVE CRUMBS." I am not this organisation's scullion! All should know that it is extremely significant that proper hygiene is practiced whenever one of you considers prepping a 'me-meal.' Even if that is only a snack of parev/parve*. Maybe you did choose dates, olives, & crackers smothered in oil. Or, as some of you have fallen for. Snacks of pet bird type foods, & condiments. I only remind you. You can eat whatever. I don't really care. Just be mindful of correct procedure in preparation. Cease from pushing your ideology surrounding these (inedible foods) on others. They most surely are not fit for human consumption. The NHO, although inclusive, & guided by equity. We cannot be bullied by woke health inspectors, nor other official Roman armed personnel. Its just insane! The earlier occasion cost me no less than a month to make ready the place once more. Frankly, I am sick to my ashen codpiece at persistently being expected to make good on the mess some of you continue to make.

Those who do suffer with the dream state walkabout disease. See a damn physician! Maybe, you could have it prescribed that you are shackled, or locked in your estates during After-Light. A curfew, if you will! Or, just as After-Light does descend, you are knocked out. So you are confined to your bed mats.

By the way. Whoever keeps swiping those imitation E-nock knock party cards. Return them! To scoffers in speech, food, & other things. Stop it. I know your whereabouts. Parading about as if untouchable. Pull your heads in. Do what is correct, & what aids the advancing of the community whole, or, I'll have little choice than to have you all publicly named, & shamed. We all know that such will likely, end with complete Cancelling. I do only point these things out as a warning. I'm not a snitch. Cheers for your future consideration. For the best in Community atmosphere.

To be forewarned

A parody of the epistle of first of the letters of Apostle John. Imploring sound beliefs to become staple to a believer's life. As those who'd prefer them to be subjugated are lurking in the wings, awaiting to pounce. Epistles of John. 1,2,3.

A JOAN CITIZEN:
Since the Activation, we are surely counted among those who are not shown any hinderance to sound locationally, aurally, verbally, visually, tactilely. We have understood, & been taught to witness & possess the animateness of the rationally unchallenged; ours are the expressions of being all these things. We are the fortunate ones to demonstrate these with perfection. So, have been instructed by Logos (Divine Conviction) to proclaim all these things that you too, might become like-minded. That others abide by instruction in the dogma & characteristic of animateness.

In the ancient identity papers still available in all libraries, it is read the olden o'l El did use Logos, & scalped in twain Light, & After-Light. Light, he deemed was most assuredly the better for things. Much rejoicing is borne of Light. After-Light, is frankly, much inconvenient when it is desired that movement persists; as with endless After-Light, all know assists in ensuring all stumble, & knock into the unseen. Causing much hurting, & miserableness to follow for a time. I remind you that the great mystical El you know, doesn't want anyone to stumble about in After-Light. But, there are some we know of who 'claim' to not be tripping all the time. Yet, they do quite often. It is with much disobedience that claims of walking in light are found out to be untrue. Those who are caught to be untrue will be frowned upon, & severely scorned, & maligned. They will forever be known as Apples of Sodom. Those who dissolve into ash, & dust for their persistent captious provocation. The charge therefore is. Remain in light. We do understand, that to do so you are instructed to dismiss an admiration, & galagog* of your place in the entire Cosmos. In comparison to the rest of what is in the cosmos. All must dismiss as irrelevant all that is marvellous, & wondrous, & awe inspiring in the cosmos. Esp., the known histories still available. So, it is stated by wokeness, these were but a blip, a spark; soon to be dismantled as irrelevant, hurtful, & ignoble. Barely suitable for survival in the 'Brave New World Order'. After the 'Resetting.' Seems, those 'enlightened' ones, according to the woke, are those set firm in the 'new' Light of the 'elite'. Despite, the cosmos, all in esse, the heartaches, & joys of generations past were a favourite of Mo-she Eudoxus, & former peoples to admire, & document. Apparently all these former things shall be dismissed, for the satiation of the cabal of 'elite' & their insatiable power grabbing desires. All these folk want, is that they receive all admiration, & obedience. Most assuredly, they are your average snollygoster*. Determined to cheat you out of your best life. The life you have desired to live.

 Have you heard, ye little plebs? There are many rumours about that there is not much time before the elites do succeed in their endeavours. Many are saying that they now roam about all places. Enforcing, & making reckless, irrational policies, & promises. Rebel little ones. Silence the rubbish they do speak from both sides to their mouths; their whining about a looming climacteric doom state. They are boasted to have even infiltrated the halls, & Staterooms of power. This is said to prove that our final hours for play time are about us. It is urgent then, that we completely understand. The emerging 'elites' of many places are those espousing a 'singularity'. That a singularity is spread abroad, & across the techno, & human divide. But, you dear ones are the true elite. Holding power over those claiming providential powers. Have you heard the calls that humanity merge (willingly) with emerging technology. That essentially, humanity does not exist as it has for millennia. Rather, like chattel. Some no doubt prefers to become like a Terminator type entity. Soulless, & pre-programmable. Transhumanism*, & other forms of xenotransplantation* are but one of their goals. Just so most, if not most world phratries are ruled with impunity, by those claiming godlike status. They surely are descendants of those who once sat listening many days ago to words

A STANDARD RELIGIOUSLY IRRELEVANT VERSION (S.R.I.V.)

of instruction upon the hill but, boredom did overwhelm them.[32] Making them to scuttle off and do more interesting things. Like become tech savvy, rich, & politically malcontented. They did then, fabricate all manners of weirdness to their own benefit. So they can live their lives as they individually choose. While demanding the many transforms, & comply in obedience to the desires of the few.

 I know it's a crazy notion, but I recommend that many of you not continue in their fantasy. Dreaming of an indestructible continuance. Vanishing-day*, either post, or pre being dispatched to the halls of quiddity, is but a nice muse. I ask, is it not psychosis you necrotize that you never necrotize? But, their ultimate goal is - an 'overlord-ship' of the many. This is the goal but, will surely ensure you remain idol & cause an upsetting of worldly equilibrium.

---

32. See, Eudoxus.

Reminder

A reminding letter by John to believers, in the same vain as letter one.

CITIZEN JOAN II:
To the crone, that were somehow elected along with her children, Grace, Mercy, & Peace. May you one day be reunited with your fathers, & son in truth! We have all heard it from the beginning, yet I implore you again to be mindful of all those stoical meditations of old. Yes, those that literally were past down to us for centuries. Although those parchments, & other trinkets upon which these are scrolled, have greatly faded, & have been smudged, & become degraded, & so being barely legible now I imagine. Try though to remember their lessons.

On the grape vine is much banter 'bout how unfortunate, are the facts; that there seems to be many now who suffer aprosexia*, - a wandering mind. Paying little or no attention any longer to old meditations, or the benefits of an egalitarian social order. Rather, as usual they do just wander about, shouting the virtues of wokeness. Demanding their ways are the truely honourable. While completely ignoring their own hypocrisy. They do, & say, & live as they want. Never ceasing lecturing a fantastical virtue that everyone must adhere. I do implore you, never be happy to be receiving, or believing of such people. Don't even waste your breath on greeting them. Rather, always be suspect that their forgetfulness, their false virtue, & wokeness. Their inattentiveness to authentic dignity, & the humanness of Human Relations will likely show themselves to be most substandard. They might even attempt to cause you to act in like fashion. Indeed, many

A STANDARD RELIGIOUSLY IRRELEVANT VERSION (S.R.I.V.)

people now behave in like substandard humanness. Being the poorly educated, or brainwashed. Refrain from the honey-trap of civility, equity, inclusiveness. These are but a pretence, & sham.

Last, I remind you of that ancient Sophocles, who shared much to gain: "All a man's affairs become diseased when he wishes to cure evils with evils."[33]

---

33. Kirov, Blago. (His Words - p4 of 42.)

Hospitality

Third epistle of John punned.

CITIZEN JOAN III:
To Gaius,
    In truth, I do trust it goes well now with your sole. That it has healed & in good working order. I hear great things that you are walking again. Great job! Though I surely have much to yack about with you, I don't want to waste anymore of my pen n' ink. My supplies are low, so my intent is to come over in the near future for a coffee. In the meantime, I'm sending our friends over. They have all requested that, along with others, you do at least attempt to greet all by a specific, preference Personal Pronoun designate.
    Warning! You do risk 'cancelling' otherwise. Nonetheless, do be confident that, if you do 'become cancelled', it is their loss. Not yours.

Reexamining the tales of the Revelation to John

The often thought of frightening for its mysteries, the 'revelation'. Final New Testament book of the Christian cannon. The exact John who allegedly penned this is unknown. It was considered, in good measure by various early believers to be bumpkin. Not worthy to be called scripture. A Parody of the Book of Revelation.

A REEVALUATION OF JOAN:
The Reevaluation now in your hands were likely authored by any number of Joan's called Sibyllistai* who did make an impression & living from paparazzi royalties. There are several Joan's who claim high paparazzi status who were followers of the I Am. They did aspire to reinvent, manipulate, doctor several of the Sibylline Books that are in circulation. So, any guess whereto this belongs, is likely a decent guesstimate. Several Joan's had not truely come forward to claim this piece. A reason could be the Joan in question was on another job. Or, was currently incarcerated on an Ephesian fishing retreat, on the famed Island of Patios.[34] If this be the truth, 'a' Joan of some script did begin to scribble thoughts while waiting a bite, about a fellow going by name, I Am. The below narrative; therefore, must be recognised for what it is. The ramblings of 'a' Joan who did scribble thoughts of what is believed memory. Being revealed here first. Such will likely never be repeated, or admired as factual, historical, or sound.

    A Joan did follow the I Am around for the prior three years before retreating for some R n'R to a Patio on Ephesus. Becoming most tired that the I Am did not, or could not leave the 'establishment' alone. Constantly badgering all authorities, to the point of real annoyance. Becoming known about the places as a 'know-it-all.' Thus, the bulk of this rendering sounds, & reads as much as a someone on a psychedelic

---

34. The Isle of Patmos.

trip from the consumption of too many mushrooms, & swilling of Spirits. It is compiled from sources, & articles of influence that are unknown. Thenadays, I Am did seem to have much to unburden from his chest. Whether he had been simply suffering a reflux, or was just really annoyed at the 'establishment,' or in realism was just simple mad, & possessing an angry disposition is the inspector of this material to make for themselves. A Joan is but the messenger. Unsurprisingly much, or in entirety, is the following article Taurus Excretory. Likely not holding to any realism, or authenticity.

Joan,

To the seven fishing mates of Asia, Great fishing spots, & plenty potato cakes, & squid pieces to you. I will not blabber on 'bout our fishing exploits here. This article is not commissioned or contracted for that nonsense. My contractual obligations stand with only pronouncing my thoughts of the I Am fellow. I Am could not resist, but did whoop much during his activities, that he were, is, & will come after having seven 'Spirits' lounging about the throne. Grace being a companion, was also a firstborn, & not one of the Living Impaired. It is said then I Am does come with much mystery in cloud coverings, or probable smokiness; &, all bloodshot eyes shall be upon him. He did also often announce he's not only Alpha α, but likely also Apollo, also, Pi π, Sigma ς, & others just a tic lower, even to Ω Omega. Claiming Xanadu was not too far off.

I Joan, was under the influence of many Spirits lazing on the Patio when someone did begin to startle me. Breaking my meditative posture, I did wail, "Look mate, don't come the raw prawn at me." But, it did ignore my protest & begin in a grandiloquent tone,

- "You should consider writing an opus buddy. I can just tell you are really articulate. I'm enthusiastic others would really enjoy it. Especially, in those educated minor, & major regions of Asia. Places like the maritime fishery of 'Ephesus,' where fishing is unrestrained. What 'bout Smyrna, where you get good Incense resins to cover all 'shady' smells? Once composed, you could send the manuscript parchment to that parchment manufacturing, & publishers of scrolls at, Pergamum. Oh, & please don't forget to mention the 'odour inflicted' of Thyatia. They too deserve some light entertainment to ward off their

A STANDARD RELIGIOUSLY IRRELEVANT VERSION (S.R.I.V.)

afflictions & repugnant odour as much as possible. Also, those at Sardis, - those 'Red Skins.' I'm aware of the controversy surrounding their name, that it is considered now to be 'politically incorrect.' Yet, really, they too deserve proper identification. Ah, neither should you forget to mention as contributors, your 'affectionate brothers', at Philadelphia. Though, questionably, would be the addition in the manuscript of those 'claiming Justice of the People' status; Laodicea. But, it's all up to you."

Spinning about, there was only seven lamp stands. So I asked him in attendance to them. He did reveal himself, & happened to mention he was searching for his son. Said to be fitted out in a full length robe, & having head hairs resembling an old hag. Spying his wandering about, we sided closer. Was then I did notice a peculiarity; flickering flames darting hither, & thither about the eyes, which surely must have become a constant annoyance. The revealed son did also sport Bare Feet that did glimmer bit like tarnished brass, or bronze. But, the most vexing was the voice. The accent was unrecognised. I did wonder if he was a Southerner. Maybe, an Aussie? Nothing articulated made any sense to me, but sounded like a rushing waterfall. So, I did return to my former posturing, & again drop in a line. Besides, I did briefly glance in the 'right hand' of this son. There were several Star-droppers, & from the 'mouthing region' protruded a sword. Knowing it was not the time or region for 'weequashing*,' I Joan suffered naturally, aichmopobia*. Thinking, was this fellow tormenting me before skewering me multiple times? A few moments did pass, & curiosity did get the better of me, for I did eventually face this individual again. For my own safety, when I had done turn round, I did duck, just if there were a Star-dropper headed my way. Then, the robed one did gurgle a bit, cleared its throat, & stopped babbling like a brook, just long enough for me to make out in plain enough words:
- "Don't be daft. Get up, you most dumb-ass of mortals. I do only introduce myself such to get attention. I have yours. Quick, grab your journal. Be a lad, begin to scribble the following thoughts for me. I see you are a keen type fisher. Ephesus? No matter, I require you to author a parchment for me. Write it to those mentioned. See, I am right handed & these Star-droppers are not real good for

writing. They do make too many little holes that the parchment does disintegrate quickly. Write to them at Ephesus, explaining their own sake, they should ne'er consider unrestrained fishing a chore."

His dictation began:
- "To those of Incense manufacturing in Smyrna. Offer approvingly, honorificabilitudinity* to them. They are offering the communities a great service. Despite many up's, & down's, seeing the political, & economic woes 'bout to explode, so it seems. Nonetheless, encourage them to not despair too much. For ol' El's sake, do not consider sticking joss sticks in the ears, as a 'cerumen' removing tool. Refrain much also from using your skills as a comfort blanket. Your skills, & esp., the joss sticks made make a much better pleasant smelling, & odour neutraliser. Stick with that!"
- "To all parchment sellers, & manufacturers at Pergamum, offer this expression. You have indeed these past years published many wonderful, & ornate pieces. Some have passed into the 'classic' category for sure. Yet, I do have a gripe. Your latest publications allow some of its verse to be ignored. Another, is often bought to becoming a doorstop, or a bookend. This is a very grievous treatment of the written prose. It is as the Kamitian do say, "medjet netcher" (word of the God). Such, they must be revered, read, understood to hold some value, & placed away correctly. Otherwise, many of those 'words' could end as some of those scratched, dulled, & barely legible writings on the walls in Kamit. Besides, I warn you all now, if no change is significant I will have no choice than to come over & clip you all about the ears. If you'd prefer, Lapidation stones are another good medium. I can bring a sample if desired."
- "For the odorous, Thyatia. Inform them I am aware. You have been dealt a 'shite' hand. Your unemployment offices have neither been to an advantage, or relief of your plight. Know this, it does greatly vex me to the point of migraine that you all just seem to roll over & accept that Jessy tart on the front desk. How she does sit there in smugness knowing her employment is secure. That as she doest demands that you set there quietly in her room. I know the struggle this causes. I know this test is near an intolerably painful metaphysical experience highlighting your finiteness.

A STANDARD RELIGIOUSLY IRRELEVANT VERSION (S.R.I.V.)

Mark my words. She will soon enough entice boredom to stay for a play-date. Then that very same Boredom, will lead her to doing rash, & sometimes tearaway, or even harmful stuff. She, & the boss will be caught out soon enough. They'll be spied positioning themselves to a high repute in <u>Mauritania</u>*. Spending a year of bliss as masters of the bedroom community there. Much as was spoken of in the Olden Books of Mo-she Eudoxus."
- "For the 'Red Skin' I have little to announce. But, I am much saddened to be told that despite being a confectionery treat, & your title has given you from innocence without malice, or bigotry of another division, or against any other confection company. Despite your title, Sardis having meaning of Red Skins, this does not warrant Cancelling by those who are but 'snowflakes.' Unknowing of your histories, these 'snowflakes' have demanded a form of recompense. Saying, it is an abuse of those of Oxidised- (Rust-like) pigmented tribes, & so must change. What rubbish! Be aware; however, Sardis will be known & loved as Red Skins for a long time coming. If anyone does have ears not blocked by Joss sticks, or natural waxiness, hear the madness about you."
- "To the loveable brothers of Philadelphia write; I gave you <u>Monkeys</u>* that will only open doors on that day. Sorry 'bout that! The master-key to the <u>vomitory</u>* is still being crafted by the locksmiths. Besides, at Mardi Gras I don't see any reason that you can't still wear your crowns with pride. In this day, & age bro's, what does it matter how you identify? What does it matter what day it is? People should be able to let the other live, & wear whatever headgear whenever it suits. Without having to explain, & justify yourselves to anyone. Esp., if your choices do not have a massive personal effect on any other, or their lives. What is not tolerated however, is persistent 'wokeness' that demands the majority bow the knee in homage, promising to never to act in word or deed that hints at the slightest possible causing of grievance of the minority. We should all just get over ourselves really. Grow up the lot of you. Deal with it. Just as Mo-she Eudoxsus did say, rationally, everyone knows there are no questions that there are major differences betwixt populations; some are of the Humankind, others distinctly of The Eve. Some then of each gender type do get along, & like a lot more their own type,

than another. Numbers nowadays are beginning to come forth as undecided or confused also. That's ok. Human Relations do demand that support be shown without partiality. Where's the real issue."
- "For the 'Justice Party' of Laodicea write I Am disappointed much by you. Your 'social justice' system is frankly, crap! Sometimes you get it right, yet, much of the time it is simply wrong. It's fickle as you too often make one decision regards a thing, but that ruling is not widespread. For instance, rulings you approve to do not apply to your opponents. How is this egalitarian? Nay, it is a very partisan position you do hold. C'mon, reform your ways; those stupid statutes, that they are not so biased. Otherwise, there will forever be a quite large divide between those who are favoured, & the complainer of every possible thing. Sensible impartiality that is what is required. Is anyone listening? Or, is this just burbling like a waterfall?"

After this dictation exercise, I was very much still under the influence of a spicy luncheon of psychedelic mushroom soup. Suddenly, the welkin* did ring. I did notice it was really bright, for there were no clouds. Just at that moment I would shield my eyes a little, a great boom box did erupt playing a selection of musical tunes never before heard. Not recognizing any of them, I was informed one of them was called, 'C'mon Eileen.' Strange as it was, for my name was clearly not Eileen. Nonetheless, a few words sounded as if, "Come up here, I've got something to show you." So, what else to do? Grabbing hold of my resume on a rope, I headed for the barnman, as I did feel it necessary to first scull copious glasses of Spirits. After this, I did need my back-stage pass to get to the throne room of the park. Whoopee, wowee! Did I think as I did reach the 'Throne Room'; there being many coverings of Jasper, Carnelian, on an Emerald backdrop. There were many, many rumblings, & peels of thunderousness.

Much relieved, many ocular appendages were upon me as I concluded the Throne visit. I was then handed a rather tightly rolled scroll, with a floret knotted looping. Someone then did bellow, "Hey, why has he been handed that scroll? He has not even washed hands. Dirty bugger. He can't use that as a towel. It's reading material ya

A STANDARD RELIGIOUSLY IRRELEVANT VERSION (S.R.I.V.)

know." At that, I did begin to weep a little, but did make sure to hide my vision. Pondering, did they know I was a little illiterate?

Looking menacing I did notice guarding the scroll, were Seven seals. I did then quickly hand the scroll back! Then, the strangest of things did occur. A little Trojan-type lamb on a cart did roll on into the room, & did snatch the scroll. As the little fellow did this, one 'seal' did slide off the bank, & back into a nearby crystal pool. To my shock, just after this first seal did depart, there was seen a White Horse. It was really just a show pony. Piaffering* about, displaying all manners of conquering, with magnificence all round. His rider wore cute golden booties, & a matching tiara upon his head. Just as he had done finish his Prancing display, the second seal became fatigued & did also depart the scene. Signalling the entrance of a bright red horse. Much in colouring to the Sardinian clans. His rider was offered a sod of the Earth, & with a broad sword did put on a masterful exhibition of swordsmanship with the crowds that became real congested. Unfortunately, all spectators did enter the homesteads suffering a bad case of Hum Durgeon after this masterful display. This shocking presentation did cause the third seal to slink away too. At which, another horse did rear up & did appear on center stage. He was likened to a Black beauty. Interestingly, or not pending how one views it, the rider of this beast did display scales for hands. He did herald in a much loudened tone, about the price of barley, wheat, oil, flax, wine, & other consumable commodities. Warning the dangers of the stock-market fluctuations. Calling all who'd notice, that it is best to keep an eye on that, & only show panic if Denarius can purchase the Lot. If he did, you would surely lose everything. A fourth seal did then bugger off. Frightened by the sight of an extreme pale horse being harassed by Hades. Hades was shouting at him, "I was only joking. Death, wasn't really good as a name, but you have to admit; it is fitting. Considering his home of a dungeon." The issue I did find out was this horse did escape, & had claimed authority over terra firma. Hades, was attempting to explain though that authority was only granted for the fourth orb. Not this one. "Better get thee back to there before real trouble." Did shout Hades. Strangely, when the fifth seal had done depart, the entire atmosphere, & the sets of the play did change. The scenery was painted to look authentically as an altar.

Moments later a chorus of white robed chanters did begin to erupt in rapture. But, were soon told to be silent & wait for the proper cue.

Following the sixth seal did withdraw. Because its sheer size, & bulk, an earth quaking shuddered the place. So terribly frightening was his movements, did they cause the sun to hide behind the moon, which did so get a bloodied nose. The sky backdrop did then fall to the floor, causing a fig tree to shiver as if in the wintery months. Was here, I did lose my place in the scripted scroll I was reading, & it did retract in haste. The little lamb then who was still beside me did get a punctured wheel, & did topple over onto his side. Becoming much animated, thrashing 'bout, he did require help to be uprighted again. At the thrashing about & animateness of the trojan lamb, all present were caused to hide behind the rock, & mountain paintings. Confused about proceedings, the seventh, & final seal did extract itself too. Nothing happened! He had forgotten it was lunchtime.

There was deafening Silence on the entire Stage for a brief half-hour. Then, mayhem again. Much peels of thunderousness, & many other rumblings from earthquake, & many lightning mishaps. Yes, the crew had returned. Much 'under the weather.' Much joyousness, & music, & much merriment with brass bands, & things did the production carry on through the night, into the following week. Was sometime during the celebrations, a burly fellow did finally 'come out', wearing a luridly kaleidoscopic vestment. In his right hand was note-taking on a clipboard. Then, I did hear once more the burbling brook, who did begin announcing, "Excuse me young fella. But, what the heck do you presume to do? You shouldn't presume to be authoring everything. Despite me asking you to do a bit of authoring. Not everything was to be made to be published. Lot's of this was supposed to be a secret." Turning about, it did articulate more to the others something like, "thanks for blowing it guys… can nobody keep anything confidential anymore? - Geez! Why is it so damn difficult to find good reliable help nowadays?" Geez, bewildered shrugged. He'd only recently returned from a dental, so was yet in much unsoberliness for the pain. Turning to me, Geez did motion I needed to take a coffee scroll break. Was about this time I did depart & did block the rest of the afternoon out of remembrance.

A STANDARD RELIGIOUSLY IRRELEVANT VERSION (S.R.I.V.)

Yes, I have witnesses that will oblige, & give testimony that the above is a fabrication; a likely trip induced by soup, & Spirits. Further, there were guys playing the fig trees, & another bloke made out to resemble sackcloth, & also the lamp stand operators. All expressed fear if caught for fraud, said they would use their testimonies, swearing. They would not change one detail of what has been authored here, - not for 1,260days minimum after the fact. Afterward, much chopping & changing of the script, & action sequences did be acted out for a long time afterward. Causing much wrath with the producer, & other staffs.

So great was their wrath, they could not resist thievery when sleepiness did overwhelm the production crew. As determined, this thievery was never addressed. Some later time did pass uneventfully till war broke out between a Baby-lion, & a poor little child. But, the child did beat it at play wrestling. There was much jubilation with all crews. For, they knew they would have felt like a real bummer if the child hadn't triumphed; having had set in motion the confrontation in the first place, just to see what might happen. Then, I did spy during my scroll break another white horse. Ridden by our ol' mate with the flickering about the eyes. He was holding a placard, & protesting there needed to be more 'sincerity', & 'allegiance' in this, his production. Upon his head was a multi-tiered turban with a blue band about it, to keep it affixed. His robe however was this time dripping. Being soiled with much blood. So steeped in <u>Stockholm Syndrome</u>* were his followers they did not seem to mind that he'd declared to rule with iron fisted & jack-boot actions. Then, for the first time, it was I did notice a branding. There was a tribal tattoo scrawled on his thigh. Soon after, & shockingly, I did also witness a multitude of predatory <u>avifauna</u>* feasting. They were gorging themselves on much flesh. The flesh of those slain of some recent hostility. It was unclear whether the slain belonged to a conflict fought in a future, or whether it depicted the destructive mess left behind from a past <u>malaise</u>*. Nonetheless, it was quite surreal, & disturbing to witness.

Not too soon after did a manticore, & several handlers be roasted with sulphur. Much strangeness, & ugliness followed this episode. But, this author is too disturbed to make an essay of it. Having sensed there is quite enough bibliomancy; the assumption of divining a future through these words, already. I Joan, will have none of it! Such will likely send future readers crazy with thoughts of much dystopia arising before a coup de grăce. That will eventually usher in Xanadu ad infinitum. An idea that upon much reflection these past years is still neoteric.

According to my estimates, one thousands or so times might pass before known dragons & other mythic sensations, & superstitions would cease to be believable. A people will rise in rational, logical sentiency*, & come to knowledge that these tales are but vast mythologies. Being no more than a symbolic fabulosity*. Expressions of catastrophonical metaphor dressed in boundless sensationalism. Meant to teach things that earlier generations could not fathom. About those events, places, & visions were a phenomenon that some tricky ophidian did use wily to confuse generations. But, ne'er was it conceived that soon after, another type crowd might arise. Their goal to abolish, denigrate, malign, & 'cancel' all who dare show allegiance to any of this stuff. A crowd labelled, 'progressives.' I was then informed, such 'progressives', are only so in irreverence, ignorance, & regression of life.

In closing, From the "Olden Bits' Activation, through, the "Newer Bits' Reevaluation. They would forever seek to manipulate for gain what they would choose from these commentaries. Whether these things do cause a thriving egalitarianism* to flourish as was hoped, is yet witnessed. Finally: one truth does remain for all who doest read, listen to these tales; "You will be forever known by the fruits, meats, other consumables, & educations you engorge. As well as all your secreted desires, & actions these give to birth." Above all therefore, remember everyone, without exception is a stakeholder in Human Relations. Regardless of all other laboriousness conducted quoditianly. It is not a radical ideology Human Relations. It is therefore impolitic to consult with, & subscribe to alternate positions only. Nor shalt thee grant tenure to much radicalised left, or right methods of cancelling the Human Relations middle ground that is of benefit to all.

Amen*.

A REVERSED INBETWIXT THE NEWEST &
OLDEN BITS. NOBODY HAS A CLUE WHAT MAY
HAVE TAKEN PLACE.

THE TIME AHEAD OF THE TIME BEFORE.
THE ANTE-DILUVIAN EPOCH.

THE OLDEN BITS:
A BIG BANG!

Where it all began. A Parody of the book of firsts - Genesis. The creating of Universal, & earthly things. The 'Adam, & 'Eve', an exploitation of Genesis 3 (human sin), birth of Cane/Able; a Flood episode, Tower of Babel, extraordinary lifespans. A comedian called Enoch. The parents to the Jewish people, Abraham/ Sarah. To imitate the Hebrew text, all Olden Bit commentaries by design are aligned Right.

THE ACTIVATION:
Ab aeterno*; the very genesis of mankind they believed there was assloads, masses, scores, scads, oodles, millions, bi-millions, gazillions, bazillions, & thousands of designations, expressions, & other personal possessions, personal pronouns about. Nobody is quite sure what all that meant. Nobody has a ripe 'ol clue of any of those things yet! We just guesstimate that at a certain but distant & unknowable past. According to a collective of activist persons, it was kind to a special, & specifically inscrutably suprarational period. Where a non-specific, non-descriptor yet deft legerdemain supported oneself into awareness, consciousness, & presence. There was an El Neberdjer inventor, developer, mastermind of all things. Who was as Promethean* as any other ninja*. This El Neberdjer could not help his cacoëthes loquendi*. How reliable this is subjective for its unknowableness happening auld lang syne*[35]. So begins the tale of the celebrated omniscient, omnipotent, omnipresent Argus of some fame. Claiming all provenience over all the inventiveness of unknowableness.

The asseveration* of ere for the activist is El Neberdjer caused an entire range of specific afflatus*. From which somethings were caused

---

35. Neberdjer means "all-encompassing divinity". The all-inclusive, all-embracing Spirit which pervades all & who is the ultimate essence of all. Neberdjer is a truth of Ancient Kamitian (Egyptian) religion.

to materialise ex nihilo. At best guesstimates, the process began in a femtosecond* just over a titch 13billions years ago. El Neberdjer did asplode*. Emitting a great wind. Bloating of ylem* had become too bothersome for its containment any longer. An explosion occurred. With plumes of gasses, & lightnings filling the nullity. All manners of rumblings & reverberating occurred throughout this blankness. The non-present soon began to swirl. Expanding as it moved about the free, uninhabited, unoccupied, desolate that began a series of laps of all spaces. Distending unrestrained as it went as there was no barrier of containment. The potency of the eruption became rich with form. At this rather violent exhalation, extramundane was birthed. Which did give actuality to countless tiny molecules. Electrons, protons, & neutrons. Here & everywhere began to vibe. In this atmosphere, & the excesses of swirling gasses, those innumerable explosive molecules began to coalesce & form larger compounds & stuff. Atoms, along with a strong cousin, gravity, did canoodle together to form a hot dustiness, forming galaxies & the like. Once more, nobody did hear or was witness to such a violent release, or subsequent canoodling. Thankfully. Bien pensant* & compos mentis* epexegesis* knowledge of sound requires a witness, & a medium for the traveling of 'sound-waves'. As with a knowable audience. There were none to be known yet. Phew! Sighed El Neberdjer from embarrassment. Much relieved an anodyne was no longer required. El Neberdjer emerged from the celestial, primordial fog much elated. There was a scintillescent catholicity & spectral spark in the visual perception of El Neberdjer. Called Illumination. There was Illumination, & Anti-Illumination. Illumination was not at all amused at being the twin of Anti-Illumination. The siblings did fight for control of proceedings. So, El Neberdjer did begin with much psychological therapy to celestially diagnose their issue. Under a much powerful anaesthetic, he did scalp the two in twain. El Neberdjer after the operation took a step back from illumination. He did then for the sake of his senility, decide to make handle changes to ease his mind for remembrance purposes when confronting these brothers. Calling Illumination now, Light, & Anti-Illumination, he did call After-Light. Both parties were happy & accommodating to this minor change. Excited at finally beginning a new venture. El Neberdjer was most pleased with the segregation between Light, & After-Light. Insisting that

A STANDARD RELIGIOUSLY IRRELEVANT VERSION (S.R.I.V.)

from now on, each of the brothers would rule over only one segment of continuance for a maximum of twelve long minute's each. After-which, they were required to forfeit, by order of the Legislative Assembly control to the other. Light, & After-Light is living much peaceably now, & for much longer than was expected. However, unknown to After-Light to this very instant. Light would gain the upper hand over its sibling if ever a stoush did erupt between them. Next, El Neberdjer did know himself on a roll. Amusing himself with all manners of exploits in craft work, & artistic skill. Calling for the separation too of a Wet upper, & lower Spaces that were baptised, mayim to reify. Required documentation & compliance legislature was immediately filed with the Firmamental mayim Department, which did favourably offer expedient assistance.[36] All articles being in order. The one above was renamed Heaven, after having its own baptism. El Neberdjer did stumble upon the invention of Below mayim. Winning an award for the Inventing of mayim at a Universal scientific competition. Formulating Below mayim, El Neberdjer did beat several colleagues at an off-site facility. The rival, University of Illinois discovered a new way to make water. Overjoyed at making water from several unlikely starting substances, & materials, such as alcohol.[37] El Neberdjer; was pleased he did beat them. Thinking their operations, & experiments as unnecessary mataeotechny*. Therefore disadvantageous. He viewed their work as nothing but useless & frankly, pretentious science. He was in the knowing that all these Below mayim were a necessary ingredient of alcohol which after that, was known as the traditional pleasant, & inebriating drinking substance consumed at parties, & after much toiling.
Making a successful Below Hydrous, El Neberdjer did give the largest of waters a special name: yám*, with a moniker - 'Davey Jones'. He then did suppose it was good that there should also be a separating from the muck of Below Materials that formed under the surface of all yám, & all lakes, rivers, & streams. He did then try a little prestidigitation.
Proceeding El Neberdjer did call into question the lack of social distancing between the newly formed mayim. Esp., the mayim that were below the Heaven. El Neberdjer did cogitate a suitable solution. Settling

---

36. See, yám 'Glossary' entry.
37. https://www.sciencedaily.com/releases/2007/10/071031125457.htm Accessed, 20/6/22.

on a rule that all 'Lower mayim' shall be established too. Below mayim said El Neberdjer to the mind, should be divorced from many different materials. Especially, the above Heaven. Reasoning, this would be much preferable for the running smoothly of any social event. El Neberdjer had a <u>fatidical</u>* understanding that plates of meat, ungulates, & all lower body appendages would fair much better, & be more comfortable. Having a happier disposition when used at parties. When dancing about any potential Different Materials. Not being hampered by, or suffering persistent water-logness. So El Neberdjer at the earliest waking of Lights made legislation that ensured a separating between all mayim not of the kin to those in Heavens, & different appurtenances. Success brought about acknowledgement that the transparent, & fluidly-cloudy like substance preferring the designate mist; afterwards becoming all lakes, rivers, & streams. As a precaution, El Neberdjer did suppose also that it would be advantageous to salinize specifically the newly formed yám. With neural tremulousness jactitation of near 50thousand 75kilogram jute gunny's of sodium chloride (NaCl) was dumped into yám. Some commentators have become accustomed to reference of this substance as Sodom Chloride, being now the most prized commodity of that hamlet, Sodom.[38] This element, Sodom Chloride El Neberdjer came to understand was a great alkaline agent, & therefore should become mixed with the newly formed yám. Primarily, to stop it getting drunk, & to aid much in the sanitation of everything after using it as a waste receptacle.

In contradistinction to a martini, the yám did become spumescent when stirred & shaken, making it terrible to quaff. Other waterways were set aside as the prime drinking substance. Being prelapsarian; clear, <u>caller</u>*, & sweet to the taste. El Neberdjer was pleased with his thought processes, for their sobriety, sanitation, & cleanliness. Thinking to hisself, "Can't beat it. Cleanliness, is next to Godliness." Proceeding still El Neberdjer did set himself a challenge to beautify & give sparkle to the surrounding caliginous environ atmosphere. So, he made provision for a much powerful Heat Lamp that was much illuminated than the vitiate gelded one he generated originally. Designing a very much powerful lamp to be directed to begin a burning sensation. This burning sensation would cause the still waterlogged Different Materials (that now

---

38. Sodom, synonymous with wickedness. Where Lot's wife was preserved as a pillar of salt.

A STANDARD RELIGIOUSLY IRRELEVANT VERSION (S.R.I.V.)

had begun to rise from subjacent to waterways), to undergo a process that would be much speeded; that invented process called Dry. At the completion of Dry, the moisture-less muck El Neberdjer did rename Terra firma: Earth, for the congregation of the street. Near exhaustion, El Neberdjer tried his artistic skills at all manners of foliage baring things, & vegetations; zillions of trees, pretty bushes & flowers, several thousand grasses; moulds, lichens, fungi, & other much fun stuff such as herbs, & those odd tasting berries he did like to call olive. Some of these were green. Other a shade of black... just for amusement, did El Neberdjer play around with a colour palette he'd recently found in his <u>atelier</u>* during the annual clean out. El Neberdjer was most pleased with his growing artistic skill set. But, he did feel that he was not quite done. On the eve of dinner time, El Neberdjer did use his artistry in different ways, inventing a melange of creature also; the beasts of all terrains, & all the <u>belue</u>* of the yám, other waterways, & masters of the heaven. Arduously inventing all manners of fancy flighted creatures. Small & large. Allowing these to traverse skilfully, all loams, waterways & the Heaven; but, not so high in said Heaven so as to violate the thin blue marker-pen line of the marble he was playing with. This thin blue line did act as a barrier. Keeping all his former creations safely Earthbound which did help greatly them to not begin to drift off into the extramundane; the realm of After-Light. Extramundane had, since birth become very unneighbourly, being sent to Coventry & so, couldn't play with the rest of creation. El Neberdjer did show great enthusiasm for all the marvels & progress he had made. Being overworked He did doze off. Happily dreaming El Neberdjer was rudely confronted by a <u>Walpurgis Night</u>* that produced a disturbing vision; a <u>sanguisugent</u>* <u>bug</u>*. Cursing he was not <u>abmosquious</u>*, when the blighter irritatingly caused a superficial wound when it bit him. El Neberdjer did promptly squish it as retribution. Wide awake after this episode, He did then keep refining his artistic skills. Not long after, he had accidentally invented all manners of <u>nosopoetic</u>* <u>fomes</u>*; stuff that was highly <u>smittlish</u>* & had a habit of inflicting diseases, & viruses, & other unhelpful concoctions & things that could hurt, maim, or other unimaginable at its own discretion. Studying them, he did notice they would turn things pale, itchy red, or oozing black with pustules. Causing a general sense of soreness, & annoyance to whomever they did decide to attack. El Neberdjer now did not fully comprehend till much later, he had just now violated the punk band Pandoras, by opening their gift box.[39] Realising his position soon after. He became most weary of having to begin again all over his handiwork. Deciding it would be most vexing to start the process all over. Before there was a threat of litigation. El Neberdjer did swiftly move to lock all tiny viruses, his invented diseases, & others. As well as all unhelpful concoctions, & stuff that emitted from the box of Pandoras, away in a special vault, called Ark. At this frightfully startling & unimaginable inventiveness, El Neberdjer sat down for a short time. Taking a quick gander at all that gambolled before his self. He was contented with his efforts; yet… but, a niggling soon arose in his mind. Who would take care of all this marvellous artistry?

One of the final artistic endeavours of El Neberdjer, the inventor, developer, & mastermind of all things was his ability at candid*, & bring into being a similar entity. Comparable in temperament & artistic skill to saunter terra firma. Humankind's he did name it. Most pleased was El Neberdjer. Seeing this creation as his greatest of achievements yet. Humankind's was most theanthropic*, receiving a similar cachet to El Neberdjer. Also pleasing was the colour palette, & the skill-sets of Humankind's that El Neberdjer did choose to use with great animateness. Traditionally, some believe the originating form of Humankind's to have been ambosexan*. Others believe Humankind's to have been more an androgynous* creation. There is even a theory that dendranthropology* was the cause to Humankind's existence. That El Neberdjer fashioned Humankind's from trees. Either-still*, Humankind's surely had a gorgonized beginning. Not exactly acerebral*, rather unshirted*: being more like an inert lobotomised being. Plain, naked, & barely chipper. Spending much time just lazing about. Stupefied, & unsure of what to do. El Neberdjer did then break out other skills; that of an abcedarian*. Teaching Humankind's all manners of stuff. The A B, C's, sentence structure, speech. Independent thought, & critical thinking. Somewhen*, Humankind's began to imagine fire*. After, much carefulness, & experimentation, & much training exercises

---

39. Pandoras, an 80's Punk Band. Pun on Pandora of the Grecian Tale where she did have a mishap with a box gifted to her.

A STANDARD RELIGIOUSLY IRRELEVANT VERSION (S.R.I.V.)

fire eventually consented to domestication. Using 'fire' for several 'new' purposes, vis providing warmth, & a sense of illumination during After-Light. In a third eye moment of Humankind's began calving a figure he named, 'Lion Man'.[40] A figure that morphed through the ages to in a much later period, did become Anubis (The) 'Egyptian jackal-headed God representing the evolution from lower to higher levels of consciousness.'[41] Pleasure & delight & amusement to the celestial congregation was Humankind's. Humankind's all the Lights, & After-Lights did joyfully swan, & dance, & stumble about in Adamitism*. Singing far future hit ditties, - like: "Welcome to the World." The Earth realms reverberated with many rebellious moshin' tunes. Such as, "Welcome to the Jungle." An expected winner began: "Can ya feel it. See it. Hear it t'day. If ya can't, then it doesn't matter anyway. You will never understand it, 'cause it happens too fast; 'an it feels so good. It's like walkin' tha grass. It's so good, so hip it's so right. Its so groovy, it's out of sight. You can touch it. Smell it, Taste it so sweet... But it makes no difference, 'cause it knocks ya off ya feet - You want it all, but you can't have it. Yeah. It's in your face, but you can't grab it. What is it. Ya say! What is it? Yeah, yeah. You want it all, but can't grab it." For days on end his head reverberated with other tunes. Which greatly amused El Neberdjer & other Celestial. Then, one morning a faved companion went walkabout with Harold*. So, could not be found again. A complete portrait of woebegoneness, Humankind's over many a vibrant energy undertook much brownstudy*, beginning to pen notekins* to himself. Which were turned eventually into famous ding dongs*: "Died last night in my dreams, walking the streets, or some ol' ghost town. I tried to believe. Saw all of the saints, lock up the gates. I could not enter. Walked into the flames, called out your name. But, there was no answer. 'An now I know my heart is a ghost town." For the rest of the evening, his head muddled about: "Here I lay, in a lost 'an lonely part of town. Held in time, in a world of tears I slowly drown. I should really be holdin' you, holdin' you. Lovin' you. Tragedy, when the feelin's gone, with no one to love you, you're goin' nowhere...Tragedy... when you lose control, 'an you've got no soul, its Tragedy, with no-one beside you,

---
40. See 'Ivory Lion Man Sculpture' images, at www.alamy.com Viewed (19/7/22).
41. Tangas, Sunny. Metaphysical Dictionary 2nd Edition (Kindle Locations 415-417). Kensho Thinimi Society. Kindle Edition.

you're going nowhere."⁴² Absolutely <u>comfoozled</u>*, the Humankind's was haunted by <u>ozurie</u>* feelings. A <u>solysium</u>* that cascaded through his head until he did fall into an unquiet sleep.

Ol' El ad interim was showing signs of his age. It had been near on several chiliad. According to his own reckoning of fact since his last coffee break. He therefore did again <u>ensconce</u>* in his favourite Throne, & sat down & snapped open a coldie. Breaking out a fresh pack of Cube-an' Cigars, & filling a tumbler from the decanter of his dearest 1265hundreds year old Tomintoul Single Malt Whisky. Following with a <u>bishop</u>* chaser. He put his feet up & did read till falling asleep, the latest copy of "Celestial Magazine." As a pioneer, he thought himself did most deserve considerable encomia. He was after all an originator of <u>abracadabrant</u>* things. So satisfied was he with his own accomplishments that he believed they would from now become <u>sempiternal</u>*. So wonderful were all his artistic skills. His <u>auripotence</u>* did radiate with ever bright authenticity. He could hardly cease praising all his accomplishment. With much adulation &, <u>blurbing</u>* did he know these were incorrigible.

Somewhere to one Light-time El Neberdjer was strolling about in eminence, admiring all that had been achieved in a mere six, or seven chiliad. According to the reckoning of many later journalists. When all the sudden there was a faint, but audible <u>gollohix</u>*. An annoying grumbling of Humankind's mid-section which did cause much insomnia. Upon which El Neberdjer did feel obliged to convene his assembly of advisors to inquire of their opinion. Knowing well other Celestial did make snipe remarks; that he were too <u>gormid</u>* for the position he held. After all, his favourite motivational poster in his offices contained the acronym: "You are TMPDITU - The Most Powerful Deity In The Universe. Strive for Immortality!" His own trumpet being repaired he could not blow it for attention sake. The reckoning conclusion was that to skite ones own opinion, & achievements too often really did just set others' teeth on edge; to the point they want to sock you a Shinar.⁴³ Begrudgingly knowing he'd much <u>R.B.S.</u>*, or prefer

---

42. 'Welcome to the World' - Noiseworks; 'Epic'- Faith No More; 'Tragedy' - BeeGee's; 'Ghost town' - Adam Lambert; 'Welcome to the Jungle' - Guns' & Roses.
43. Pun on the word 'Shiner', 'black-eye'. Shinar is the designated region of southern Mesopotamia. In Gen 10:10, the tyrant Nimrod, built 'Babel' in the land of Shinar.

A STANDARD RELIGIOUSLY IRRELEVANT VERSION (S.R.I.V.)

other things being done, El Neberdjer however acquiesced, & consulted the Conscript fathers out of the power of Appeasement. He did scribe a Celestial-gram, & sent it instantaneous Angelic-post to all other Celestial. To quell this constant grumbling; an obvious cause of the now persistent <u>famelicose</u>* of Humankind's mid-section. It was Prolocutor El (of the Mesopotamian districts. The most learned one versed in sleeplessness & grumbling Humankind's.)⁴⁴ He did <u>indagate</u>*, & while <u>justing</u>* assorted possible resolutions decided the finest solution. Declaring two feasible outcomes: First, wipe all Humankind's out. Or, there could be made a provision of sustenance. The most agreed upon (that incidentally, both Prolocutor El, & El Neberdjer disagreed) was that the advantage of everyone would be to offer Humankind's <u>ovolactarianism</u>* as part of the predominant regimen. Provision for this chow was soon after sanctioned. It became so. A much restful sleep was again had by all.

One particularly <u>uhtceare</u>* After-Light El Neberdjer did remain in a wakeful dream-state for all the <u>nighthawks</u>* circling about. Staring at all the glistening lights upon the ceilings, which were enhanced by his gaudy multicoloured vestment that he'd forgotten to replace to its hanger. He did come to understand Humankind's were real <u>unky</u>*. No wonder. El Neberdjer had not offered Humankind's anything significant by which he could occupy his self. Rather, did just assume Humankind's would be overjoyed living as an <u>anchorite</u>*. El Neberdjer was in a state of <u>betweenity</u>*; of concern for Humankind's emotional state, & letting this pass. Surely not he did think, just as the Humankind's songs began plaguing his constitution… Was then that El Neberdjer became real fed-up that his head would not quieten down all this After-Light. He did then rise & begin to scheme much.

Was at the <u>aubadoir</u>* peek of a new Light when El Neberdjer did conclude that it was not suitable to a fulfilling reality that Humankind's are subjected to an anchorite reclusiveness all their alone times. Thus, at next After-Light time El Neberdjer, after consulting several thousand medical scrolls, so as to not completely balls it up. He did begin to winnow his creative notes of Humankind's. Searching for obsolete aspects of Humankind's person, & character. Those that could be either

---

44. El, a Babylonian deity. See transcript of the Babylonian tale, When the God's were Human.

remodelled, or that which he could safely extirpate. He did then cause all Humankind's to fall into a deep persistent vegetative state, & begin to make a separation carefully of half the comatose Humankind's. He did perform the delicate surgery of adrantomy*. Breaking off an 'extra' rib, called Phallus*. Which was then disposed of in the furnace. This part, it was reasoned, would not be required by his 'new' invention; a palingenesis*, so some would say of Humankind's. Was during this inventive process that El Neberdjer did also develop newish different surgery practices; a particular kind of 'plastic' treatment that allowed the puffing up of the new Humankind's' mammaries; sometimes just a little. Chancing the poker* other times, some were quite pendulous. He did whisper to himself, these new mammaries might be labelled Tarta's, or, an Apple dumplin' shop*, or waps* by Humankind's. With these results, El Neberdjer did cachinnate* wildly as a hyena which did draw too much attention that he'd meddled with Humankind's without consultation. Council consultation was assented after much pressure to kick-drop* the renaming ideas of these newly formed mammaries. Whereto, the 'official' naming brand of the tumefied glands of new Humankind's became breasts. A much less triumphing term. So it was believed. Cackling cheats* became outraged in protest; court proceedings still prevail. With the new medical skills gained, & a 'newer' kind of Humankind's coming into being. El Neberdjer could not help himself. He ran about the place mumbling that everything was 'Oh so copasetic, Jes' copasetic.' Turning on his music box he began singing his favourite tune, Evie, parts one, two, & three. Coming to naming this new Humankind's, The Eve ever-after. The Eve did possess the finest qualities of muliebrity*. All was very pleasing, & entertaining. Humankind's not much longer continued to be "Pat Malone," or under confinement as an anchorite. For The Eve was soon after seen as a total hottie; being proved most desirous for her womynness*. A most compatible & sought after companion for all Humankind's. A very pleasing restfulness the next After-Light was had by dream states of El Neberdjer.

Other Millennia past, yet nobody really took any notice. There was then much frolicking & gambolling about as the norm of day-to-day practice. Both Humankind's & The Eve did befriend plenty of the other life existences. Drudgery, & dullness being from their

A STANDARD RELIGIOUSLY IRRELEVANT VERSION (S.R.I.V.)

consciousness. El Neberdjer was accustomed to joining with the frolicking now & again. Betwixt his other duties as Grand Chancellor; which he found rather taxing. All was very serene in all the places where El Neberdjer's fingers did happen to bring into being of things. In all places where multitudes of beasts, fishes, birds, vegetation, seeds, & nuts & much other stuff had been spontaneously erupted into being. All was very frabjous & copasetic indeed. These are the interpretations, as several journalists can recall of all those unknowableness' which did cause several specific something's to materialise. Before retiring on an <u>idlewild</u>* <u>vacomacation</u>* a while El Neberdjer did also plant adjacent a much prized section of his fashioning of stuff, a not well sneakily, or hidden grove one Sunlight. This was a beautiful <u>coxa commissure</u>* allotment supporting a wonderful array of superb fragrances, fruits, & foliages that were most attractive to behold. The centrepiece was a budding copse of woody perennials & shrubbery, & other bushy plants. Which did deceptively look uncannily like the 'heritage' tomato plant. It was christened at the opening ceremony, The Joint. Everyone rejoiced with much idolising. In honesty El Neberdjer did aspire that this grove & its content is secreted. Wishing it to be his personal sanctuary. For retirement & recreation purposes, (of course!) El Neberdjer gave charge of The Joint, to experienced & trusted <u>Ophidia</u>*. As a matter of courtesy to the Humankind's he felt obliged to whisper his express wishes that Humankind's not trespass this region. Despite Humankind's & The Eve's perceptions that certain trees, plants, & celestial bodies were beginning to be twigged as endowed with 'animation'. The Humankind's were warned emphatically they were to especially not mess with any of the foliage. Being cautioned that to consider even touching one part of The Joint, would be extremely <u>nocent</u>*. Causing unappealing harmfulness. Leading, one to find oneself up a gum tree, & other kinds of distressing tormenting. It may even cause the user to become <u>noceur</u>*; a famished reveller. Convening a <u>tête-à-tête</u>* soon after with Humankind's. Both Humankind's & El Neberdjer did reach an amicable understanding at this <u>latrocinium</u>*. An accord was signed. This was the first ever gentleman's contractual pact; whereto Humankind's also received the first 'rule of engagement' carving. Which Humankind's did keep secretly hidden in his library. The carving was kept as a special tablet called Cu-nei-form. It contains strange cuttings, & wedge shaped markings, & grooves upon it & quite a bit moss. The Eve, having sent an <u>essoinment</u>* earlier. She was not present at this meeting. So, it fell upon Humankind's to be the special envoy & inform The Eve. To this, Humankind's proved trustworthy, & dutiful.[45]

It then came about one sprightly midsummer Tueslight afternoon, irrelevant to 4:30. That The Eve was mucking about with a pit of ophidians, & other similar genus types. Chasing the little slithery buggers through a game of "Hierarchy & Ophidians," when The Eve unwittingly trespassed into the 'special' Joint/grove. The game board did protrude a little into it, as El Neberdjer had forgotten to cordon it off. The Eve had tripped while chasing one reptile. Landing in the midst of The Joint. She was assisted in becoming upright again by a very kindly spoken Ophidian. Of what turns to be a very special kind & high order. His being a special 'Grandmaster', called Druid. Druid also had several intriguing surnames. Having the official title, - Druid Wise-craft. Wizey, being one of his beloved nicknames. Bemused at Druid Wise-craft, he & The Eve got to chatting. During their conversations, Druid Wise-craft thought to put to task the knowing aptitude of The Eve. Much banter followed where The Eve did impressively hold her own. The Eve however did become perplexed, for Druid Wise-craft did occasionally begin to throw all manners of stuff into the aether. What's the aether anyway? Which, the answer offered her did only seem to perplex her further. Registering this via his wise-craftiness, Druid did side up to The Eve to explain it. Attempting harmony & balance to the conversing Druid did begin much philosophising like several other of his companions seeking to proselytise The Eve. Announcing, that it is only fitting that all become as a Phoenix.[46] The conversation then soon after turned to him seeking knowledge's about a particular tree of his guarding. The very tree The Eve was leaning against to catch breath again. Immediately, The Eve did leap from the unmindful encroaching onto the copse, & specific evergreen that was verboten. She was warned

---

45. Cuneiform. The earliest known form of writing. Written on clay tablets using wedge form pits, & markings throughout Mesopotamia.
46. To ancients, the Phoenix (bird) represented the power of resurrection, creation, & long life. In Egyptian theology, the Phoenix is a corollary of the meaning of the presence, & word of the deity which was the destiny of the world, & humankind. Parallels with the Judaeo-Christian concept of death/resurrection are regarded obviously present.

A STANDARD RELIGIOUSLY IRRELEVANT VERSION (S.R.I.V.)

she'd end up a gum tree, & become distressed over other kinds of distressing tormenting. Whatever, up a gum tree, & other kinds of distressing tormenting meant. For she knew it not whatever that was to be having never experienced such before. Druid Wise-craft did spring over an <u>electro-plasmic</u>* windbreak. He did begin reassuring in a kindly voice The Eve that the particular tree she was leaning against, & the miserableness a gum tree was meant to cause was just tosh; was nothing but the highest order of 'Taurus Excretio' knowable. The Eve, now standing amid a <u>kettle of fish</u>* confessed she knew not what either word meant. For she had not learnt whatever tongue that was. Druid Wise-craft then began to explain both the understanding of 'tosh', & 'Taurus Excretio'. Much appreciative, The Eve did feel reassured, registering the understanding & so coming to realising that Druid Wise-craft was not at all unscrupulous. Rather, should be regarded <u>licksome</u>*. The very opposite to what was told to her by Humankind's. The Eve did recall soon after, Humankind's had warned against a particular tree. The Manchineel that was the kind to steer clear. This tree, yes, is a most dangerous tree. It is much like 'Apples of Sodom', being pleasantly delightful to behold. Yet has very <u>puzzomful</u>* qualities, & properties. Such 'fruit' of this tree comes with a warning label: "Please don't handle Fruit, - ask for Dru. Handling fruit, does cause you to remain up a gum tree, & other kinds of distressing tormenting."⁴⁷ Querying this warning, Druid confirmed, The Manchineel tree, cannot possibly be the tree out-of-bounds. Simply, it is not a gum tree. Neither is it native to The Joint. Rather, is native to only several other world regions that are seriously beyond the black stump. Places way beyond this immediate <u>rabbit-proof fence</u>*. Those regions with strange names, like in the America's districts. The Car-rib-bean (steakhouse). Both situated further from eyeshot than the horizon. Relieved in mind The Eve did manifest great thankfulness to Druid Wise-craft. Appreciating his candour, while also having learnt a stack of new things of real value, & had a new mate to converse with. While departing his company The

---

47. The Manchineel tree has very toxic qualities. It bares apple-like fruits that cause burn-like blisters that is potentially lethal. Rain, & its sap falling off its outer foliage likely contains an irritant. Touching the tree could prove irritating. Causing much miserableness, & distressing tormenting. The term, 'Apples of Sodom' is delightfully tempting fruit. Yet, such delight turns to be an illusion.

Eve did mention her intent to open the kimono* for Humankind's. That both she & he had been duped by El Neberdjer for living millennial memory regards this copse. She smartly hopped it home to tell Humankind's about her new found knowledge & understanding. Hoping to convince Humankind's of his silliness, & his gullibility. Why had Humankind's remained such a snool*, & not questioned the motives El Neberdjer had for banning Humankind's & The Eve from The Joint? What was with the disallowing haptic contact with any part of it? Surely, this was to only ensure a pretentious & false narrative was adhered. Clearly, such instruction had caused much conspiracy & possible dragon's teeth* to sprout. Giving nascency to justifiable disobedience. Causing untold unhappiness, & other kinds of distressing purgatory. The Eve had begun to philosophise clearly. Concluding this was a massive 'porky' that El Neberdjer had told. Swine in earshot soon began complaining of some undefined hurting sensation. Undaunted by the squeals in complaint of anti-animalism of her three closest hamlet* friends The Eve regarded their sufferings not. But, carried on with her desire to expose The Joint, & esp., the tree in its midst. Improbably, The Eve did possess the abilities of an autodidact; to discern, divine, or philosophise like this. But, she did sneak about the Library one evening when Humankind's were mulling about something else. She did set about studying the unattended Cu-nei-form that had been left out of the stone ossuary that usually housed it for safekeeping. To her delight, she did one Light time intuit the wedge-type marks, deciding they meant: "Confidential", in BIG RED MARKER-PEN, & "Not For Public Awareness, nor use (Private by Order of El Neberdjer.)" Cosigned by finger identification, Humankind's. Hotfooting it in remembrance of this The Eve did finally approach the entrance to her humpie* Pope o' Rome just on owl-light*. Entering, she suddenly became slightly vertiginous*, & light-headed, remembering that she had not eaten anything of substance since about the time that the Great HeatLamp was high in the Heaven. She was famished. So The Eve did dash quietly through to the kitchenette to fix herself a course of opsony*. A Hummus, & veggie dip sanga of garbanzo* bread. The milling of wheat for bread had not yet been thought worth the effort for it was not refined where sticks & little pebbles were removed from the doughy substance. That, when baked

A STANDARD RELIGIOUSLY IRRELEVANT VERSION (S.R.I.V.)

with a boulder, it was found that the boulder was more edible. Well watered, & fed, The Eve had to scamper past the library on her way back to the lounging rock to catch the bioluminescent* display before bunking down for the After-Light. This pass, she noticed via another most intriguing intuitive sensation. That something was non-identical this time. Compared tother similar times she'd snuck past the library door. There was a faint kind of whindling* coming from the dimly lit frond-light entrance to the library. Recalling that every Tueslight just before retiring for the After-Light himself, Humankind's did spend several long minutes, he called hours here. Unsure of what exactly went on every Tueslight. What the Humankind's were doing is all a mystery! Reading books, authorship, & studies & similar other stuff had not been thought of, or invented yet. As The Eve, as far as she did know after a Captain Cook* one evening the only rock piece in there was the before mentioned Cu-nei-form tablet. But, The Eve was too excited to again watch her favourite bioluminescent firefly display to worry 'bout that just now. So she did just believe Humankind's were feigning an issue. Mayhap, Humankind's was in a state of half-delusional consciousness. Terrorised in a hypnopompic* dream state. No further thought entered her mind about what was taking place in the library. Ramfeezled* from all her play time, she snuggled up to her rock comforter not long after, & enjoyed an admiral's watch*. Next Light The Eve did wake refreshed. It was not until about 9 o'clock when The Eve took strode busting for a pea, the few steps to the kitchenette, & fixed a salad of twigs & leaves & a little golden gooey stuff for hers & Humankind's ariston*. While jenticulating*, this bass* but unflavoured brekkie at the entrance of the antre*. The Eve did peer out just in time to spy Humankind's about to leave via the rock garden. Bailing Humankind's up just in time, she did press Humankind's for a conversation regard a few things she said were really, really important. Sheepishly, & Humankind's did slink back inside & stood about. While The Eve did begin to then divinely devise a form of proto-Volapük*. Humankind's, not truely understanding, did nonetheless stand motionless, & taciturn so as to not be off-putting. Much boredom did come that Humankind's could not wait or listen much longer. Explaining to The Eve that he must depart. During the night, he'd been awoken several times by a series of strange noises.

Besides, it was his charge to go inspect the grounds every Light-time & catch up with the flocks of his favourite Macaws. He promptly departed. Sheepishly, just maintained upright motionlessness, being dumbfounded. Having not a clue about what just happened. The Eve for the remainder of that Light-time was joyous at having the burden of knowledge of the scheming of El Neberdjer lifted from her consciousness. It was a great relief that she believed Humankind's too did get the picture. Seeing the potential effect of the disruption to life the secret of El Neberdjer could cause in later seasons. Having it handed down for eons she could only guess would be the case. But, she had only completed half of her mission. She still thought it best to confront El Neberdjer. So, that's what she began planning. Several Light-times later. After much carefulness, rehearsal & refinement The Eve did feel confident & comfortable in confronting El Neberdjer. Besides, she reasoned that "Ministry of All Things" confrontation desk was situated only a short walk away. Sensing that because of whom she had been, she felt it not egregious to not make an appointment. She was wrong! Either the eve 'womyning*' the desk that day was new to the position; (Jób having resigned over the treatment received).[48] Or, the other eve was ignorant to whom. The Eve represented in the scheme of things. Maybe, it was a case of jealousy? The Eve was flat refused admission into the offices of El Neberdjer. So, she had to make alternate arrangements. The Eve then went home.

The following day-raw* was a bright Thurslight. The Eve did not much appreciate or understand a Thurslight. Esp., this Thurslight as it was rather a gelid aurora. Unenthused, she did hastily make a Lucifungous* retreat out of the streaming light. Snug under the cover of darkness, she could not find solace from the surrounding chilth*, so she just laid there in a zwodder*, grumbling that Humankind's had not attended the vibrant energy since the beginning of After-Light. Only having to arise some moments later with an intense desire to micturate*. Resolving to not fall into cunctation* this time regards the stabilising of the worsening breastsummer*. She no longer thought a hypaethral dwelling would be a fine alternative during the swolten* months. Deciding to

---

48. In the Bible book of Jób, he was sorely inflicted by the deity; having loosing his wife, & being inflicted with many other hurting's, & maladies. There was an 'evil' entity in the tale also. Who did attempt bargaining for Jób's loyalty with the principal deity.

A STANDARD RELIGIOUSLY IRRELEVANT VERSION (S.R.I.V.)

attempt, despite the tempestuous weather approaching, the Augean task this Thurslight. She did begin to faffle* about tidying the entrance of their antre in preparation for repairs. While doing this, a new thought began to coalesce & take shape in her mind all during this Thurslight. She pondered: what if there was not sufficient Light this Thurslight to make things up as the Light past? Would that hinder her Light-time moments? Over time, would she lose much Light-time & have to go to bed early again? What if there was not sufficient Light to watch the new Firefly show? Could there be a way to extend a Light-time. To make it seem, there is more room to fit in everything one did wish to do on any given Light? What if an extension of a Light-time were achieved? Could that also drift into expansion of actuality? If so, might succeeding Mankind's, & Eve's stay wide awake without tiring easily? It was musings like these that occupied the energy reserves of The Eve's head the entire Thurslight. Except for the interval period. When she packed 'Snaks' her sleepover pal into her marsupium Sacreligious*, after emptying it completely in readiness for an outing. More Lights had come & disappeared without much fuss, when from frustration The Eve did appeal for much courage. Deciding this was the Light that she'd confront El Neberdjer. Not forgetting to grab her Sacreligious, which she did remember already contained Snaks, & a banana she did leap off the side rockery, & disappeared to 'Ministry of All Things' local offices. The Eve had gone long before Humankind's had even roused, which was quite strange. She was often logy every morning from her rockery bedding. Ensuring the position of knocker up* being one of Humankind's duties. He now refused this task after she had one Light, insensitively smashed her new expergefactor*. A rooster that Humankind's had found wandering alone, & decided to offer it to The Eve as a proxy tocsin. The Eve very appreciatively the following fateful early day-peep, misused it by snogging it on the beak too hard. It never worked well afterward, but had to be put away in the darkened alcove. It just now collects dust, & mites, & other tiny things. The Eve was much abstracted* while in the waiting room of "Ministry of All Things." She was woolgathering, which soon turned to jouska* about how those fluffy white misty things in the cerulean spaces above her head. How these often gave the impression of some of the cuddly things she liked playing with. She also thought about the 'hanging out times'. Or, as Druid referred to them, the 'lapidation*' times. When both Wizey & her had spent some long minutes tossing rocks, pebbles, & little stones into the nearby channel. Until, the locals began complaining that is…& had a rather inauspicious sign erected: "Anyone found throwing stones at this sign will be prosecuted." Fed up with the wait, The Eve did rise & walk to the front desk. Gave her detail, & promptly returned to navel gaze some more. Not sure why The Eve gave her details to the desk, it was empty. She waited, & waited… some little moments* did go by. Then, she felt a tap on the shoulder. It was an usher who did shepherd The Eve into the most colourful, & sprightly appointed appartments ever witnessed. The two began a conversation about the decor & several other items of interest that decorated the room. There was the most glamorous murals & ceiling artwork. Even better than those painted & sculptured by that famous Arch-being - Michael Angel-o. In one corner was a gaudy multicoloured vestment. The Eve was informed this was rarer than hens teeth. She did notice that this article did shine like the great HeatLamp, & the lights of the spaces above her head that did nictate frequently at her every After-Light. The opia* these caused her was mesmerising. Seeming to wink at her every time they were in eye-shot she did feel their glittering was equally intrusive while causing an intense vulnerability of her soul. The warmth of the drying sensation of the heat-lamp gave her a huggable feeling. The garment; however, she was told, was to always be placed on these specific hangers. As it did too often put to shame the heat-lamp of the Heaven. Which, disorientated all inhabitance of terra firma too often. Much like the planet, now known as Saturn. Which by several ancient cultures & their remaining texts is recorded to have been cognisable as inter alia, - that is, "Lord of the Law of the Universe."[49]

The Eve did also seek the whereabouts of El Neberdjer. Answer: ol' El, as he's affectionately called in these parts, well she had missed the opportunity to catch the ol' El. Feeling dejected, a pooling of salty fluids began; "Oh no, no, no. My dear he's not … well, not yet. He's on sabbatical in the Car-rib-bean & would not be returning till well into next millennium." On the way out The Eve just happened to spy from her periphery vision, a stunningly decorated box vault thingy

---

49. Cardona, Ch 3. Page 121.

A STANDARD RELIGIOUSLY IRRELEVANT VERSION (S.R.I.V.)

thing. Seeing this object, she thought that it awakened a dream state memory she'd had once. She'd seen something like this before. The colours, & decorations were astounding, even mesmerising. There were what the educated called paragon types. It was covered in celestials. Most interesting, there seemed to be a very cool looking Lock-Tight attachment sealing the hinged cover. Yes, the same Lock-Tight type used to ensure nuts n' berries & things remained in the bowl next to the Firefly remote that Humankind's used to stop house inspectors nicking them. Standing near the top of the Ark thingy The Eve did also notice it had very similar scribblings she had remembered in The Joint. About the Ark's surface among the celestial decor. She wondered while peering at it. If like before she might be able to decipher the markings? The same red marker pen had been used. After a few more little moments shuffled past, - heureka! The Eve did begin to divine as before that these scratches, wedge markings, & other pits did seem to explain: "Under No circumstances, by threat of very bad hurting sensations is this Ark/vault thingy thing to be opened. Yes, even by you. Now, bugger off. There's nothing to see here. Let it be!" Well that to The Eve was just plain simple rude. She murmured to herself, "what is ol' El now being so secretive over? What is being concealed from us this time? For what purpose? Not on my watch… Crash, bang, whoop, vroom, smack, biff, poof; were some of the expressions that blared from the soapedy* broadcasting device that showed a moving panorama viewing of distant events. The Eve promptly departed at the conclusion to the cartooning display.

Arriving back at the apartments of ol' El again the following Light. Not wishing to awaken the cherub bacon stationed in the heavenly basement. The Eve did cautiously jimmy the Lock-Tight covering the security pad on the main door. Fortunately, right beside the coded pad on the wall was a text of "Cracking Codes, & Cryptograms for Dummies." Cyphering while thumbing it, she pored over the several highlighted texts. Noticing that when strung together, the security code was revealed. In the exact symbolic sequence, pressing the keys of the Pad, she entered the code. Entering, she did reenter the appartments of ol' El; lo' an' behold. Nothing had changed. The room was exactly as she had remembered it. The Eve did head directly for the Ark vault thingy thing that happily sat idle in its favoured corner. She opened the

Ark, again picking carefully at the Lock-Tight to loosen the seal. Peering inside, the Ark was stacked completely with numerous little clear dishes. Several odd scroll parchment type things rolled up. One very odd looking Paddy Quick that she could tell, had earlier budded, & several other shiny luminous objects. Viewing all these objects with intrigue. The Eve did decide then to 'condiddle*' several items. Placing within her Sacrilegious so to keep Snaks occupied with quietness, an assortment of the little dishes. As with a curious Paddy Quick. Despite its unappealing knobbiness. She thought Paddy would be a great walking aid when her legs tired & complained. Later The Eve did come to cherish Paddy. Having it in her presence did give the impression, & authority to others of shrewdness, which she did appreciate. When home again The Eve did unpack all the little dishes that did immediately sparkle & made impressive & pretty shimmering & shapes about the antre walls. Snaks also greatly appreciated the ability again to stretch out the limbs, & not long made snuggery* out of its favourite corner, & slept. Cogitate; in similar fashion to the cluelessness of After-Light, The Eve did have no indication that those sparkly dishes did contain an ominousness that to this Light-time is an often great, & terrible menace. Their having no discernible detection without the assistance of extremely efficient optic attachments. The content being very difficult to perceive for their Lilliputian* qualities. At this time, an occhiolino would have been very useful, & enlightening. Which, of course, had not been invented. Let alone conceptualised here in such a tale & era.[50] A handful of Lights had passed since her venturing into the suite of ol' El, did both Humankind's & The Eve begins to notice the atmosphere of their surroundings did perceptively be non-identical to before. Attitudes, & personalities of all their playfellows, both animals & of other eve's, & Humankind's began displaying pre-sick. Soon, to acquire the unseasonal taste of bush oysters*. Snuggled up watching their bush tellies* they presented lively protein spillage. Several other folk did begin to resemble a pin cushion, having a showing of many spilus*. Some of these festering ireful marks began to discolour, weep, & blister. Beginning to ooze a fouled, noxious substance. Many inflicted were enveloped soon after in a cloud of fogo*. Others presented with ague;

---

50. An 'occhiolino' (Ital. for "little eye"). The name given to a microscope by Galileo, 1609.

A STANDARD RELIGIOUSLY IRRELEVANT VERSION (S.R.I.V.)

an unknown febrile condition. Resulting in acute body aches, often scratching, & sneezing. Several suffered with a Churchyard cough* at some unknown irritation, only to be visited by Mr Grim, soon after having their own homegoing*. Many became increasingly etiolated after finding relief in darkness. Those unaffected in the neighbourhood, then mostly cleared out. Often, crossing to another path at the sight of the other, or, they did run away entirely. Rank distrusting of another soon became an every moment occurrence. Much disappointment was felt by all The Eve's & Humankind's. Yet, what to do? The shifting of attitudes, & personalities, as if by magic? Had spread tentacles throughout all post codes. Several Humankind's did attempt to palliate the situation. But had no recognition of where to attain the appropriate styptic agent.

Upon returning from his vacomacation* to the Car-rib-bean, &, noticing this non-identicalness of the atmosphere of things as before he'd departed was very vexatious to ol' El. He did commission an investigation. Ol' El did begin his investigations by doing the rounds of all the cognisable communal spots where The Eve, Humankind's, & associates were likely to be. Becoming pretty narked at the realising that everyone was not as cooperative as before his break. In hopes of a better reception, he did depart those places & decided to head directly to the antre-stead of The Eve, & Humankind's. Reaching that rock face, to his disappointment neither The Eve, nor Humankind's was home. It was a balmy late Light-afternoon. Too good to waste so he headed next to The Joint for some R an' R to calm down. Arriving at The Joint soon after, near everyone it seemed, had not only trespassed the place, but, had made the Joint to seem de-Koshered. Throngs had taken to playing "Ophidians & Hierarchy" just as The Eve did often enjoy, & had subsequently messed with The Joint's serenity. Defiling it with all manners of unthinkable's. Several crowds had violated the instruction banning tactileness & were acting strangely. There were groups mingling, & smoking it up* having invented a new round-robin escort game. Others, proved to be famished, & had become sleepy in the midst of The Joint. All the while, Wizey, Druid Wise-craft was content to just fudgel* the day away. Chilling in the shade of The Joint. Enjoying the concert of the newly formed contraband*. He was totally disinterested in all orderliness, or actually doing his job. His demeanour being fedifragous* on all accounts. Having broken the established concordat* between Dru & ol' El that was initially signed in confidence. The present gaiety displayed by Humankind's & The eve's caused a stirring of an emotion within ol' El. Unable to withstand it any longer ol' El did crack the shits. Asploding* with an almighty caterwaul* as if he'd just stubbed a toe, he wailed: "Aargh! Fie* upon you all." Such an outburst soon pricked his conscious as one of his most vexatious emotions rarely called upon. For it did embarrass him that he'd let his keep* free for all to see. This scared the begeebers out of ol' El. In his wisdoms of ages, he did know better than to quicken unchecked such emotional outbursts.

But, irateness now seemed a good descriptor for his inner bursting leakage. Luckily, nobody was seriously injured at this accidental escape. Many of the Humankind's & Eve's in nearness suffered minor burns & bruising. Apologetically, ol' El continued the investigation, attempting to get to the bottom of the cause for the now abundantly evidence of vagueness's of change that had recently made known its sensitivities. Some moments & several Lights did come & vanish as was obligated by treaty to happen with Light & After-Light. Before ol' El did saunter into his office at "Ministry of All Things." Entering his rooms (infinity ∞) did flash through his unoccupied mind… as his jaw near did hit the roof. An early Light routine of his was to do a few limbering headstands to impress the worker eve's, & celestial Heads. In the midst of the routine, he did notice several unordered things. His beloved overdramatised multi-coloured vestment had been removed from its tethering hanger & safekeeping perch. Being left in a rumpled mess. Some mongrel had also swiped his favourite piece of artwork; of the sauntering platypodes around a coffee bar, playing ping pong. Then, as if under the direction of forces that often mysteriously shook a wobble board, his feet turned to face that other corner, - yes, the one where the Ark was joyful to be placed in, as there was a lovely view from that recess. The best one of all the Lot, being the perfect panopticon, allowing the viewing of the entire Spaces of the universal objects simultaneously in all possible directions. Fainting in shock his eyes rolled around the room following his feet, & not long after, did his mind. Ol' El did have to scramble to recover & call them back to his person. Gathering all his self together, & resting for a nanosecond.

Ol' El did realise the Lock-Tight thingy had been tampered with, & loosened from the hinged covering of the Ark. Peering within the bowels of the Ark, ol' El did begin to shudder a little. Noticing several petri's, as

A STANDARD RELIGIOUSLY IRRELEVANT VERSION (S.R.I.V.)

he called them, had been swiped. Several shiny objects had been shifted from their originating positions. Assorted scroll parchments had received a floret knotted looping bow. The only evidence remaining of his knobby Paddy Quick was dried buds on the floor of the Ark. Fervour for a new investigation was stirred. Just at that moment, the music of a mystery film played an ominous score. Signalling his roomy 'Luch' had arrived for lunch. Ol' El decided to turn his music box off, & headed for lunch. Next Light, Ol' El arrived at "Ministry of All Things," even before Light had arrived as he did want a surprise a beginning to the investigating he'd thought about yestreen*. Down to business, he first summoned all animals, questioned them, & promptly released them without charges laid. They're proving useless spectator's. For all of them did no longer comprehend speech, & questioning or the concept of answers. Rather, suffering severe aphasia their efforts at answers were phatic*. As a mafflard*, sounding more as stammering, or a blundering fool. They did also just stand around playing cards, chewing the cud, or something else that suited them. Somewhat perplexed, ol' El did leisurely take a gander ponder* the Ark's window to figure the next move. He did at that moment spy on a sonrock* in a parkland, a 'brain-shaped' container. Ocularly, focussing he did notice the side label, 'Intelligence'. Hurrying downstairs, as all lifts were marked 'Out of order,' ol' El did reach said sonrock just in time to read a dymo label-writer sticker attached. It read, 'property of The Eve'. Just then, a raven did speeded off with the container in tow. He gave to chase & soon found he had put 'on a few'. Probably, during his last break at the Car-rib-bean. Following the raven, ol' El did reach the rock face residence of The Eve, & Humankind's just before his great friend, ol' Nick of time, Inviting himself into the antre, ol' El did begin asking a series of questions of The Eve. None of which were relevant, or originally intended as part of his investigations. He received no good answers. The Eve, out of compassion for ol' El & his cat Cenile, offered them a pitcher of Thistle milk & a slice of her famed mixed berry sonker, & refused to answer any sillier, & irrelevant questions until Humankind's did arrive home. They waited passing the moments beating their gum's.[51] Humankind's arrived home several long moments later. Ol' El did by that stage have prepared a few questions

---

51. 'Idol chatter'.

for him. Which, he did give nothing but green answers to the blue questions* asked of him by ol' El. In a manner of speaking, 'twas only slight articulation, but quite viscerally punchy.

Soon after, The Eve was again pressed with the same questions as Humankind's. But, not too hard for fear of harassment charges from the #Metoo auxiliary. With these many irrelevant questions to the investigation, The Eve did oblige. Answering as Humankind's had done. But, her words showed much cunning, & shrewdness. Slightly amused at the burble of obfuscating answers ol' El did seek to know whether a piper's bidding* was by The Eve, or Humankind's offered to Wizey for tea? Short answer, No! But, as The Eve did have Wizey's formal contact details, she obliged again & hollered out the nearest hole in the antre. The nearest to The Joint, in the direction of his silhouette that was in the place where it always was. Belting out that ol' El desired to have his camping gear back, but was too tired to fetch it just now. Could he bring it at his earliest convenience? Within more unspecified moments, while anticipating Wizey's reply The Eve, ol' El, & Humankind's did make merry moments. They did box with much badinage each-other's ears over scandal broth*. Truly, it would have been more advantageous to enter The Joint & retrieve the desired objects. Yet, ol' El realised he'd already upgraded its security. Having recently installed an alarm that by the brochure, would surely disintegrate every trespasser. The newly invented "Quaquaversal* Obstructive", as it was labelled. With signage reading: "BEWARE OF PEOPLE - "Caution: Do not lean on fence. It occurs you much pain, & troubling. To touch, or look at this fence causes instand death. Anyone found disobeying will be prosecuted.""[52] The safety code to disarm it had been left beside his thunder-box.[53] Wizey finally arrived, but had forgotten the gear. Ol' El did then alternatively reach into the pocket of his robe, & retrieved several question cards & did press him more harshly than he had done to The Eve, & Humankind's. All pressing did not help much. Other than grant the impression that ol' El had a more powerful constitution. Wizey also answered perfectly with correct answers to the question cards. The reflection being seen by Wizey; shown to have been scribbled by ol' El's answer-jobber* on his backside.

---

52. The 'flaming' sword. Gen 3:24.
53. Outhouse, privy, toilet, earth closet…

A STANDARD RELIGIOUSLY IRRELEVANT VERSION (S.R.I.V.)

Announcing that he would collate some answers to several questions not yet asked of them, & return momentarily. As to the immediate investigative answers & questions ol' El decided it would be sufficient to offer his verdict the following Light. Moments passed in silence & ol' El did break it. Apologising, he did say his adieus. It was late in the After-Light, so everyone did retire. Next Light came & disappeared. It was a leap-Light that moment. So, Light went out. When Light had returned ol' El did apologetically shout, Crikey! Universally apologising for his absent-mindedness. Returning to the local rock Eisteddfod. The four of them; ol' El, Humankind's, The Eve, & Wizey did hold a lengthy gabfest.[54] After which it was agreed they should all go out for dinner. Some further pressing concerns required discussion involving each The Eve, Dru & Humankind's. They did wait flapping the gum's again. Dru had departed momentarily to cover his feet.[55] The three of them, ol' El, Dru, & Humankind's stood around a while making hero chatter. The Eve, bored with waiting again for Dru, & tired of all the raw-gabbit*. She had gone home to relieve herself of their pedestrian, nonsensical conversations. Knowing well that both Wizey, & Humankind's were but siolists* of the topics. Returning elated that she had, in those absent moments for some reason, made their antre into a comfortable hibernaculum*. The four went to The Joint for an interview without coffee*, settling on biking* afterward. Relaxing at Moe's bar enjoying a homerkin* while watching a hilarious episode of The Simpsons, ol' El did decide that now was the perfect moment to inform The Eve, Dru, & Humankind's. Some major changes were soon to be made to the districts. In unison Dru, The Eve, & Humankind's queried what was going on? Ol' El had again lapsed in mind. Taking stock of their facial rictus expressions, He did then pose the age old question, What? Was it something I said? Not realising he had offered the conclusion & had forsaken the beginning, & middle bits. Having to take leave to gather his mind again. Returning moments later, he began the entire verdict announcement. Not leaving out either the beginning, or middle, or ending bit. Which did leave Dru, The Eve, & Humankind's not so confused. The Verdict: Dru, The Eve,

---

54. Eisteddfod: (Welsh) festival. Eistedd = 'sit', fod = 'be'. Sitting together. See Wikipedia.
55. Hebrew euphemistic expression of bodily excretion. Saul entered the very antre that David was hiding in to 'Go to the toilet!'. See, 1 Samuel 24:3.

& Humankind's must pay reparation for some personal undisclosed infringements. The Eve, & Humankind's were initially despondent. Having to declare their rock antre as offering ineffective living standards. Soon after, being forced to perambulate* as a flâneur* after a new cross-country course & arena was demolished. As compensation, The Eve, & Humankind's had received marching orders that gave precedence for others to egress & relocate tother freedom lawns* in other regions. However, the most vexatious contention was that after being removed from familiar grounds, The Eve & Humankind's were forced to become a ne'er-be-gone*. Involuntarily wandering through life as a here & thereian*. So much so, it was a weary prospect to familiarise oneself with all the new requirements. Humankind's for instance, was coerced to compromise often just to scrounge out enough suitable dead horse, & beverages; that complimented perfectly counter lunch, & tucker bag. It was for Humankind's quite an aleatory experience. Having to often invent new meal plans with much reciplay* from ingredient scrounged from their eco-roofing*. Dru ad interim did not fair any better. He suffers debilitations after insistence of accepting an amputation surgery of all external limbs. Being confined to endure the snake-bit effects of choking dustiness by passerby's & persistence of threats to paste & squish, & pulverise his crown. The Eve, she was sentenced to labour much in the instructing, & delivery of a new venture. Much unsavouriness between Dru, his latter spawn, & the progeny of The Eve, & Humankind's became commonplace. Which continues to this moment. Decades & chiliad past. Humankind's & The Eve would have sent an illegible hand-printing of condolence had their whereabouts been known. Sentient essence was difficult to fathom for both Humankind's & The Eve. Despite them forced to inquilinate*, they each did scratch it out. Caves, & rocky homesteads were eventually replaced by a newer inventiveness. Dwellings became refurbished to suit the chiliad. From Rock, to Rock plastered with mud; to combinations of tuff*, mud, & wooden. Other harder more durable products. Boondocking* soon became a thing of the ancient Neanderthal types. Thus, The Eve, & Humankind's have often with much silliness. On many occasions, several found a way up a gum tree, & other kinds of distressing tormenting. All endured, evolved, & invented greatly to this moment.

A STANDARD RELIGIOUSLY IRRELEVANT VERSION (S.R.I.V.)

Was on one After-Light there was Much chill-axing beside a vibrant energy. Leading to much firkytoodling*. Humankind's, concupiscence for The Eve did grow to a point he did soon begin to breakdance. Gyrating rhythmically while snapping his fingers to the beating of the thunderous dog soup outside.⁵⁶ Humankind's did break into song: "Mmm yeah, t'nite; I wanna give it all t'you. In the darkness, there's so much I wanna do... I wanna lay it at your feet. For girl you were made for me, I was made for you, an' I was made for lovin' you baby. You were made for lovin' me, an' I can't get enough of you. Can you get enough of me?"⁵⁷ Hitting the highest note of C, impressed The Eve so much. It sealed the deal. Unable to contain her excitement, The Eve did shout 'Gladiola!*' They celebrated with lavish bowls of Supernatural* falsetto* & other gedunk* tastes. More firkytoodling soon followed. Either-still they began experimenting with interconnectedness*. She & Humankind's soon after did decide they should officially call their relationship. Having first had it framed above the niche set aside to keep all present in safety of vibrant energy. De facto, was all too obliging. He promptly drew up the officiating stonework, & soon after presented it. This was prior to Humankind's realisation that The Eve would soon prefer the cute acronym moniker, "SWMDO" - She Who Must Be Obeyed. After much practice with interconnectedness The Eve's person particularly did change. She did begin to some lights not feel like any ariston in the forenoon. Rather, was wamble-cropped*, suffering unprecedented stomachichus*. Assuring Humankind's she was not at all suffering Hum Durgeon*, or other nonsense. For, many months The Eve did remove herself from Humankind's presence; often to the growlery* thinking in confusion on those desanté* moments that she did experience acute illness. Especially, when her matutolypea* became frightening. On better lights, strange cravings were coming. In an increasingly gravid condition, she was found very teemful* thenadays* that could not be blamed on the quotidian prandicle*. What seemed to them, the best part of a full-cycle did The Eve remain so. Until the moment of parturition; a progeny arrived. Which The Eve, & Humankind's did begin to wonder. Was this event given by Parthenogenesis*? The giving of the wee tyke did surprise all involved.

---

56. Dog's- soup - Rain.
57. 'I was made for lovin' you...' - Song by Kiss.

It likely did not happen near exactly as this. But, does make for good story telling. When it had come time for the aborning of the primogeniture, not The Eve, nor Humankind's did know who, or how it was? Never having met the butter-print* before. Sadly, there was no officiating naming card, or documentation of instruction for proper care or use either. Nonetheless, this first of many offspring did shock The Eve, & Humankind's. Being an unspecified miniature of themselves. Similar in structure, & temperament. Having initially been of a miniature stature, a maquette similar in species this first urchin* was labelled by The Eve, & Humankind's, Cane. The Eve, & Humankind's did come up with a corny type label for Cane, - sugar. Little did it become known till it was too late. Having varmint* teenage years, Cane did not live to his nicknaming of 'sugar'. A more relevant moniker would have been shiesty. The more sizeable his self became, the more did benevolence depart his self, becoming quite the agent provocateur. Always seeking to provoke another into committing wrongful deeds.

More moments past & Cane did become well versed in several occupations. His passion however, was directed at the Construction Industry. Particularly, showing great enthusiasm for all things of natural, environmental materials; sludge, & rare pipestone* material that had to be imported. It was a natural progression that Cane's métier was so. Several moments past again when The Eve, & Humankind's did experiment once more with interconnectedness.

This time, with the assistance of ol' El, did The Eve, & Humankind's weariness & expectations be overcome & tempered. With much labouring, did a second maquette moppet arrive. He was much different from Cane, however. Was therefore known as Differently Able.

Becoming sizeable in similar fashion to his sibling, Differently Able did represent primo waters* in all manners of skill. Becoming a professional crackerjack barman* who established the first-ever barcodes*. That each of the successors of The Eve, & Humankind's were non-identical in temperament, interest, & skill-set to the other meant that the rearing of each were as much experimental, as an exercise of trial & error. Somewhen Cane & Differently Able were

A STANDARD RELIGIOUSLY IRRELEVANT VERSION (S.R.I.V.)

both hobble-de-hoy* they were mucking about in the fields, while rehearsing for a pantomime.⁵⁸ Out of the blue, Cane purposefully gave his brother the 'fuzzy end of a lollipop'. Soon, after Differently Able became 'green about the gills'. Leading to him to "faced the Wall." Was not long hence, that Differently Able did soon accept an invite to 'join the Majority.' Afterward, he did become 'completely lost.'⁵⁹ When The Eve, & Humankind's found this out they each became bitterly vexed at Cane being so damn yemeless*. For as far reaching did they search out Differently Able, he could not be discovered. Genuine de profundis*, was evident on the face of ol' El too, when he did approach The Eve, & Humankind's seeking to hire Differently Able for an important roll of overseer of his 'flocks'. But, was ernfully informed that Cane had 'lost' his brother & he could not be located.⁶⁰ The suspicion was Cane had known his refractory personality had turned the diablerie* corner. Turning sharply toward his brother. That he did forethink the deed as dishonourable. But, cared not for a consequence. Cane suffered much Jobation* & accusations of fracticide by Humankind's & The Eve & others, including ol' El who did threaten him with an assessment of his person as humgruffin*. Unless he divulges the whereabouts of Differently Able. But, Cane did forswear, with incessant pleeping* & did lodge numerous antanagoge's*. Not timid in showing his animadversion to the persistent barrage of questioning. "Am I as you say, Differently Able's keeper," snapped Cane with acerbity. "Who rattled your cage?" "How am I to know every move of Differently Able?" Cane did make much pleeping; that he should not be Differently Able's persistent walking companion. So, where he had gone was all a mystery. All the while being instructed to retrace his steps. Which did prove lame in result. Cane soon after felt victimised at threats of being sent to Borstal. Particularly, seeing for his troubles Cane did receive

---

58. Pantomimes were originally performed as acts only. No speaking role. Acts were presented by gesture, movement, postures. The performers also wore full masks to hide facial expression.
59. 'Fuzzy end of the lollipop' - a bum deal. To 'face the wall' - Not technically necrotize. Rather, to be close to death, (at the end of a life). 'Green about the gills' - to look ill. 'Join the Majority' - Died.
60. See, The Disappearing Dictionary. To be 'ernful' is to be grieved, mourn.

on his forehead a tattoo. A <u>scabulous</u>* Cane took some pleasure in displaying & explaining the meaning to whoever asked.⁶¹ Not long after, it became painfully evident after these unfortunate events, & because of persistent name-calling, did Cane legally have his name changed to 'Coward'. Being forced to 'think with his legs', Coward did <u>absquatulate</u>* with his girlfriend. To whom, he later married. 'Coward knew his wife who had <u>wyrd</u>* ancestry, & like himself was fated. Possessing Destiny who at that stage was an unknown child. Relieved at departing the seas on the shores of a distant crannog after an <u>extraneous</u>* swim. Coward & his missus did eventually make settlement as far from The Eve, & Humankind's as much as possible. Soon after, they too became familiar with the interconnectedness concept. Not long after spawning, did Coward & his wife come to know a special quality possessed by the Humankind child. Naming him E-noch. The tyke did grow in not only sizeable fashion. But, was known to be more Hibernarian than his fellow Milesian. Possessing the mind of a <u>wisenheimer</u>*. Having a stupendous ability to jest, & gab flippantly. One of his friends did coin the term, <u>Jocoserious</u>*. This moniker did appeal much to E-noch; for he loved a damn good <u>wheeze</u>*. He was in the habit of concocting pithy sayings that livened the places up. Like, "If your child, or mate has run out, please take another!" Also, "Ladies please leave your garments here, & spend the afternoon having a good time." As well as, "It's clear, he who laughs last, didn't understand it."

One of his most famous jokes: Question:"Which African animal is most likely to be a crime boss? Answer: Awry-noceros. Or, what about these ribbers? What unsurpassed sold product makes the best headlines? Corduroy Pillows! Is it bad luck to be superstitious? On other occasions E-noch would just let his mind wonder, and… Other occasions called for E-noch to show his serious kind of thinker side. In his later years, he did become the inventor of famous E-nock knock Jokes & many more amusements. To entertain at various venues like pubs, & festive occasions. E-nock knock amusements like the classic: "eh-nock knock. Who's there? Woo. Woo who? Glad you are excited too!" Here on after, interconnectedness, while enjoying E-nock knock tomfoolery,

---

61. In Gen 4:15 Cain received a 'marking', presumed tattoo on his head, given by the deity. The meaning of which is unknown.

A STANDARD RELIGIOUSLY IRRELEVANT VERSION (S.R.I.V.)

did explode in popularity globally. For eons did the family tree of The Eve, & Humankind's expand. Stamping their beetle-crushers about the places. There was plenty of baguette's & the buying, selling, & packaging of all manners of merchandise, & other inventions, which soon followed. E-noch knock wisecracks too have never ceased to prevail as good ice-breakers for drinks, & games nights everywhere. For their harmless silliness will always be an appreciated relief to tension at anserous* parties, & festivals.

On another of his vacations that ol' El did happen to be in the same pub in Ireland. E-noch was principle entertainment at a game nite for the real inebriated. Ol' El did show much enthusiasm during the night. Offering E-noch, at the calling of doch-an-dorris*. He did swipe the remaining E-knock running cards. Along with E-noch himself he did take them all with him, back to Ministry of All Things. Sentience, life, & much animation spread. Many moments occurred when the curiosity & mastery of interconnectedness spread also. Humankind's, & The Eve's population aspiration tentacles did migrate in vast numbers to many regions. They did attempt exploring, & made their presence known to far-flung, earlier un-known & exotic regions. Though all their dwellings spin on an invisible axis, still nobody does get all that dizzy. Except it would seem, those that over many moments do become outdated. These folk naturally become the ceremonious citizens of the Dodo hospice for the living impaired*. Those who, though weren't all that great vocalists. Did shuffle off to the choir invisible. Others become forsaken, & lost. Some of these unfortunate* folk vanish just as their ancestor Differently Able had done. Having an unfortunate moment & encounter with a Cane/Coward type. Suffering the disrespect of Qi, & pneuma that was vital to all anima. Cane/Coward types again causing them to become exanimate. So goes the cycle of things.

Suddenly, there was the invention of Light time extension. We know this for at another instant both Humankind's, & The Eve's seemed to remain awake & sentient, & animated for very long intervals. One life was reputedly animated for 962years. Another is reported to remain animate for 969years before succumbing to tiredness. So inspiring were these feats they nearly made the "Guinness Book of Records" for the most extensive, uninterrupted animations around. Yet, forgotten by many praising these records, is that according to numerous reports given by a collective of certain persons, there is one other who beat these accounts by a factor of infinity. E-noch. As any can tell, he does remain uninterrupted, & is believed to remain animated. Continuing actuality by entertainment in "Ministry of All Things" of employees & other staffs. A fact of existing; it does continue to happen that everywhere Humankind's & The Eve's go; expansion & much interconnectedness follows. Soon after the coming of Light-time extension, it did seem to several in "Ministry of All Things" that they were missing out. There was much protesting that there should be a kind of by-partisanship. They did then, decide to visit, & even date the eve's of outside the Ministry. Many did choose to take up partnership with them & engaged in miscegenation with them. The progenies of which were known throughout the place as Nephi-lim. Nobody is really all that sure about why, or who came up with this moniker, for it is of most unusual etymology* long since forgotten. The Nephi-lim are purported to have been great arriviste's*; becoming Great Celebrity Prevailers. Possessing really powerful minds. Toughness, & real big proportions. They did increase to a significance never witnessed before. They did also possess a wonderfulness that made some look upon them as if an Adonis*.[62] Some say Nephi-Lim did engage in much persecution. Often disempowering & terrorising the progenies of other Humankind's & the eve's. On examination of these, & other reports ol' El became incensed. Calling for a ban on employees of "Ministry of All Things" from interacting with the progeny of Humankind's & the eve's. Under pains of expiration, & certain termination of their employment contracts. Those Humankind's & the eve's that continued to 'shack up', or submit to future exploitation with Nephi-Lim types had their right to enjoy Light time extensions greatly reduced to no more than 120years.

INTERVAL.

During interval, there came into being a particular Humankind. He was a truepenny. Known as a true, & trusting well-natured, & very committed initiate to that most ancient ol' El. He was known about the neighbourhood as No-ah. For despite all his pleasant

---

62. Adonis, derived from Phoenician adon, lord. Related to Heb. Adonai, God/Lord. See, Jospeh T. Shipley. Kobo Ed. Arriviste, an educated term for a 'social climber'. Not a true compliment.

A STANDARD RELIGIOUSLY IRRELEVANT VERSION (S.R.I.V.)

qualities, he was also prone to hold one negative opinion about stuff, & in the next instant seem to volte-face a decision. Hence, his nickname became, No-ah. No-ah did make great friendship with ol' El. They did visit many nite-clubs together & their friendship did grow. On one of those nite-club outings, ol' El did confide in No-ah of his disappointment with many Humankind's, & eve's. That it was very bothersome that many Humankind's, & eve's were still unscrupulous. Likely, they were still hanging about with Nephi-Lim types. Obviously, a hangover of their ancestors. Which, ol' El did have to abjure all the conspiracy theories. Before explaining the reality of history to No-ah. After coming to an arrangement to honour several ancient Law Codes; scribbled by a wise King, Hammurabi*. These were the legislated set of cause, n' effect codes of conduct as offered by Hammurabi. On the same evening of signing both No-ah, & ol' El had each become real bumpsy. They did make several anserous assertions to the compact. A strange compact, as No-ah was certainly not a neptunist* by any stretch of the word. For an unknown reason, No-ah did choose as his primary métier, shipbuilding. No-ah was awarded the contractural rights to build a stunning floating barque-shrine.

(235) If a shipbuilder (yep, me - No-ah) builds a boat for some one (You - ol' El), and do not make it tight-laced*, if during that same year that boat is sent away and suffers a Keak*, (& becomes deformed, buckled in water) the shipbuilder (No-ah) shall take the boat apart and put it together (puritanical) at his own expense. The tight boat he shall give to the boat owner. (236) If a man rent his boat to a sailor, and the sailor is careless, and the boat is wrecked or goes aground, the sailor shall give the owner of the boat another boat as compensation. (237) If a man hire a sailor and his boat, and provide it with corn, clothing, oil and dates, and other things of the kind needed for fitting it: if the sailor is careless, the boat is wrecked, and its contents ruined, then the sailor shall compensate for the boat which was wrecked and all in it that he ruined. (262) If the animal be killed in the stable by God (an accident), or if a lion kill it, the herdsman shall declare his innocence before God, and the owner bears the accident in the stable. (263) If the herdsman overlook something, and an accident happen in the stable, then the herdsman is at fault for the accident which he has caused in

the stable, and he must compensate the owner for the cattle or sheep.[63] These are, but a few of the regulations & amendments made that both party's; ol' El, & No-ah & his crews were obligated to adhere seeing they were to partnership in the offer of ol' El in building a <u>transmarine</u>* <u>zoological</u>* <u>marvel</u>*. No sooner had an entente parchment been signed. No-ah was gifted an open cheque account to fashion & fit-out the 'subjectively' grandest ever floating barque-shrine to be built. This was a very strange arrangement to win. The lands that No-ah did call home, were most <u>xeric</u>*. Never witnessing much by way of 'open' waterways. Like <u>Centralia</u>*. Much of the earth that he called home was rather seas of sand dunes & desolation.

Being the soul contender, & having won the contract did also shock No-ah. As ol' El did let it slip after becoming much <u>cup-shotted</u>* one After-Light. He did intend to deracinate with <u>omnicide</u>*; that a liquidation of all Humankind's, & eve's, & all creations should be visited upon them. They were all 'born on the wrong side of the blanket'. So, were bastards in his eyes. Holding all humankind's, the eve's, & all creations <u>peccable</u>*. He did make many threats at <u>noyades</u>*. Not being able to satisfactorily expunge his disappointment that his, & El of the Mesopotamian's favoured option (1) was voted down & was earlier pooh-poohed by Council. Ol' El had decided to bring about a great elemental maelstrom, an environmental apocalypse. A momentous event so devastating that would engulf, & reverberate around the world. So disastrous was this event, many other cultures scattered about were effected. Survivors made records that are present to this day. <u>Cabobbled</u>*, & totally <u>blutterbunged</u>* by this information, No-ah did set about quietly as foreman for the proposed construction effort. Knowing that if such information leaked to the media. It'd go <u>lick-for-leather</u>* around the globe in seconds. Causing worldwide condemnation & belief that No-ah was again <u>pixilated</u>*. Finalising contractors, & tradies alike. The materials supplier was no other than the famed (Five Star) award winning Gopher-Wood Constructions. No-ah & his fellow contractors were ordered to build the barque-shrine using the following design parameters. It was not bog-standard, but was to be prepared as

---

63. Law Codes 235-236-237; 262, 263 of Hammurabi. See Hammurabi entry in Glossary. (Parentheses & * my addition).

A STANDARD RELIGIOUSLY IRRELEVANT VERSION (S.R.I.V.)

a bespoke construction. Strictly, only being 137.16meters in length, height, 13.7meters, & 23meters breadth. Not at all an astoundingly mammoth barque-shrine in the scheme of things. It was either to have two, or three decks. It was to also be a not very well-camouflaged barque. Having both inside & out, the cosmetics of 'pitch'. That sticky, resinous black, or brownish substance used for 'waterproof' corking. The yacht, as that is what it effectively is, was to house not only No-ah, & his immediate family members. But, also 'every known' species of animal. There was either a single pair, or several pairings of each species to be 'housed' on the barque-shrine. Accordingly, the 'instructions' handed to No-ah meant that up to seven pairs each of creepy-crawly, mammal, & beast was to squeeze onto the yacht. It was a requirement that up to seven compatible pairings of the 1.5million species, including the 400 or so that were violent to Humankind's. All were to become a floating resident. An amazing undertaking if pulled off! It is granted that the 1.5million species found 'room' on this yacht. Including those mentioned 400 that were particularly violent; passively, & aggressively to Humankind's. These, no doubts were often sent to the 'solitary confinement' holding cells until they could prove their benevolence among the general population. Confusion remains to the precise population aboard. Maybe, while scanning the plans, No-ah did spill his Java? No-ah & his crews were successful. Commissioning the near finished barque as The Zoo Marvel. However, several spats did overtake during construction. There was much confusion regard the specific suavities. How these were to function efficiently. Secondly, how all <u>pabulum</u>* were kept from spoiling, & how best to stow them properly for each species. These were the most vexing concerns that drove construction efforts. Agreeable resolutions were eventually decided. There was built a dinghy that dinged loudly behind the Zoo Marvel to let everyone know it was still fastened to the stern. Having 'climate' controlled compartments containing the various dietary needs of species, which included the pilot, No-ah & his immediate household, who for some strange reason chose to be sustained the entire duration of the voyage on hardtack. Solving the provision issue. Incidentally, No-ah's household was all qualified vets, or specialists of animal husbandry. Both Zool Marvel & the dinghy were outfitted with the very latest sanitation apparatus; a series of holes,

& gangways. Most importantly was the placement, & construction of a purpose-built 'seat of ease' for a waste receptacle, hanging precariously near the surface of the seas. It's a miracle that very few became lost when attending, for disability railing had not been thought necessary yet. A retractable sunroof system, & several window shaped openings that did allow fresh air circulation were also constructed.

No-ah was of the Light time extension generation. Being reportedly over 600years aged. After the Commissioning of the barque-shrine, organisation of the residents began to take shape. The processing took about 150hundreds 'cycles' to complete. No-ah's household was required by legislation, to ensure the best settlement & correct allocation of suites to each pair that filed into the departure lounge. Unfortunately, the potential maiden voyage occupants who did saunter to the departure lounge & register for the allocation of a suite; the Sauropods, Apatosaurus, Brontosaurus, T-Rex (as he was later given as identifier). All their flighted cousins did all perish where they stood while awaiting departure. The time for the world to lay down its knife & fork* arrived. But, many residences failed to take the weather channel seriously, & it did take everyone by surprise. It was regrettably, forecast as the most sensationally unseasonal & bleak Light time. It was swale*, & thwankin*. Consisting of torrent winds, mingled with angry gloomy clouds which did let fly much torrential rains. As the Zoo Marvel pushed away from her mooring on her maiden, & sensationally Titanic voyage. The mores of the populations that ignored anything to do with her did not change one fly-speck*. Everybody not involved or interested in the voyage, or contracted builder. They all stayed away. Not only because of the forecasted rapid close to the Ice-Age. Having not invented a bumbershoot* yet, wet weather gear, or life jacket. Nobody thought seriously about a major flooding event occurring. So, nobody prepared a sandbag, dam, or levee bank in time. Subsequently, the torrent winds, & violent rains were persistent. They did also seem to harass the Zoo Marvel, following it about its journey for about six full months. The rains & windiness both did seem to take much pleasure in tossing the barque about, & generally making the voyage as unpleasant for all aboard. The 'sunroof' & open-cut window facilities proved as a bad design flaw. It could not be opened without flooding the galley & other compartments. So, there were limited fresh air circulation; aside the

A STANDARD RELIGIOUSLY IRRELEVANT VERSION (S.R.I.V.)

open-cut windows, which did cause some of the residents to become persistently, miserably saturated. The resident veterinarian household of No-ah all suffered much fatigue. Being each required to diagnose, & then treat all manners of ailments. Those never before encountered. Let alone become qualified to treat with efficiency. Ailments such as pertussis, a touch of the vapours, 'mal de mer' (sea/motion-sickness), Ross-River fever, measles, & Phytoplasmas*. The best the household could do was attempt to ensure all occupants that there were millions of antibodies. Along with other immunisation sensations of the body working real hard to combat their specific issue. They were all pretty positive such existed. Though there was no true proof at that moment.

They also attempted to boost this via a concoction they had recently procured from the Chemist Warehouse. Prior to its great liquidation, they were convinced by the shelf-shouting positive advertisement of the flyers. They had stocked up on some stuff called vita-mines.

Not one animal, insect, plant, or mammal understood what was occurring during a 'consultation'. The vita-mine supplements supplied did seem to cause more issues than they potentially resolved. There was widespread ataxy*. Disturbing loosening of certain bodily movements. Many plants found they lost much condition with painful asteroids*; often turning brownish before withering. There was much generalised sickness still felt by all. Procellous* Lights, & After-lights prevailed for what seemed to the thalassic mariners, 1000years. Before the seas did begin again to become serene, & kind. Undisturbed by an uncontrolled violent force disengaged from sight. The weather did soon after show, & remained in a state of kindness on lown* waters. In all the regions of the seas where the Zoo cruise-liner hanged out bobbing about. Despite an easing, there was much vomiting, & illness, & receptacle fumigation required. Drifting for what was imagined an eternity, the Zoo Marvel did eventually come to Port again. Slotting into the appointed berthing.

She was yet required to undergo further 'lockdown'. Preventing any from departure from the barque-shrine for a month. It was reasoned that there could be no chances of the maladies dealt with during the voyage that they could present an outbreak among the forever terrestrial populous. There was great fear that a touch of the vapours felt by the shrine residence, would spontaneously erupt throughout the lands, causing much other maladjustment's of populations.

The conclusion of lockdown came. All 'passengers were finally unassed from the vessel - they did disembark in an unruly manner. They could not wait to reenter the societies they knew. Several passengers did find it too upsetting, & so joined "Ministry of All Things." Others did suffer long-term effects of the issue they most disagreed with on board the Marvel. Still, more had a complete sea-change (pun intended), - moving to richly fertile regions to begin a new vocation. This, No-ah & his household chose with much delight. He did become a success. Becoming known as a famous elbow-crooker*. Cough (ah, - vintner). Establishing himself as a most ambrosial liquor; wine, & Spirits merchant. Installing several chains of 'juice bars'*, & zythepsaries* about the places. It was after one particular night, following the establishing of another juice bar. That No-ah did promise to not tope*. He failed for he did enjoy a little too much clamberskull*. Becoming so swine-drunk* that there was 'egg on his chin'*. Soon after there was an issue with his twiddle diddles*, & plonker*. Becoming unfortunately exposed after the inventing of several maxims during opening night festivities. One of his most enthusiastic & fondest began: "Oh brother and husband, priest of Ptah, never cease drinking, eating, becoming shickered*, making love, passing the time in merriment, following your heart day and night."[64] Of this, we can tell. No-ah did succeed by his own advice. Was then during that present time that while No-ah & others did get about life with their juice bars. Ol' El convened a newly invented forum. FLAC; the 'Food, Livestock Administrative Council'. During their first deliberations it was decided that the previous 'law' of Sustenance Provision (enacted by El of the Mesopotamian) was greatly outdated, & so must needs be cancelled, or, minimally amended. The new administrative body did from now on enact a fresh legislation. Written to accomodate the perceived, & latest polling desires. Within the new legislature, an amendment was ratified. Stipulating that it is perfectly lawful, & most goodly for "Humankind's, Health, & Happiness," that it become a provision. Carnivorousness was permitted now for Humankind's, & animal varieties, & their progenies from this moment forth. Consuming rights for 'Health, & Happiness' was to become norm. Choosing to revert to the 'olden' provision was also acceptable. Was to be respected if this was deemed tolerable.

---

64. Teeter, Location, 567.

A STANDARD RELIGIOUSLY IRRELEVANT VERSION (S.R.I.V.)

Carnivorousness by raw consumption; however, was only permitted for the sarcophile. For they had all long forsaken any former knowledges of 'cooking.' A knowledge long misplaced by ancestral lineages. Humankind's also, had a proviso attached; that consumptions of the Zoophagous were ne'er sanctioned at being prepared for the dairy products of the consumed. To be so unthoughtful, was to enact great grievousness, & bring a shame on the consumer. Such 'new' regulating action was formerly consented by the consistory. Since, however in ne'er every region whereto do Humankind's, The Eve's & their progenies reside there has always been a faction of revolutionaries, & activists consumed with insisting that the former ancient law of ovolactarianism is the truely better. So, no matter does the new Zoophagous provision apply. Many accede still to the ovolactarian provision, & do badger the concession for all Humankind's. Affirming it must be reinstated as the predominant provision. General icons came, & did often pass through to many other, preferable places. It happened that the early Eve's proto-Volapük did begin to catch on. Becoming widely in use throughout some regions. Numerous users of this tongue were the countless nobody's that did not crack a mere mention, or were authored about in the news articles to be left about in Stone Cu-nei-form histories on any local store table of Café, & eateries across the lands. The cause; few understood the tongue. Having elusive, & linguistic forms, & complex intonations difficult to justify. Attempting to be thus schooled in this tongue was like trying to teach vellum, or a stylus board the alphabet. Expecting these to automatically offer an audience a prose. The histories of Humankind's, & The Eve's is chockers with the silence of these non-events, & non-exploits. Of countless of these & other words, & unimportant persons that they did have spoken, & had achieved throughout their days but were ne'er recorded. There came a certain afternoon; however, when quite a few of those <u>pilulous</u>* person's 'knee high to a mosquito'. That they did decide that they had enough of being insignificant. Always ignored, & forgotten by the victors & elitist class of whom exploits are recorded. For the pushing, & shoving to remain in the spotlight always, the nobody's did see as just selfish, & so did want in on the action. <u>No afternoon farmers</u>* among them, a collective of several tens, & hundreds nobody's of any repute did decide & banded together. They did buy a plot of prominence, & set about organising a

Conference of the Pontifical, - COP as it became known. As a rival to everyone else's recognition the goals of COP were to establish themselves as the authority on matters of atmospheric conditions, & redistribution of all wealth. Plans of construction were drawn, & submitted for ratification, & soon after were received back favourably. Full manufacturing soon began. The nobody's did choose to erect a splendiferous edifice. Assuming they could rival <u>Sybaris</u>*. Who were known for their luxurious & sensual lifestyles? The edifice was to become a very multi-tiered memorial in celebration of themselves, & all prior non-exploits, & stories. They did speak, & act upon. It was to highlight the nobody, & offer inspiration to generations yet arrived. Unexpectantly, halfway through the fabrication of the edifice intended, for an unknown complication of sorts when the fashioning of their enterprise did begin to go awry. Contractors in employ of the nobody's did suddenly begin requiring attendance to a special asylum. Many had become inflicted with dementia, & so, kept misplacing their tools. Several more, began to spontaneously combust into a maddening of hypothetical hysterics. Sprouting grandiose plans to reinvent the reputation of cheap, reliable energy sources. Others did break into earlier unknown foreign, or, Proto-<u>Glóssa</u>*. They did make much protesting in many uncouth tongues about things unknown. That these 'unreliable unknowables' as they became widely known. Others, became inflicted with other maladies too upsetting for description. The place began to resemble a madhouse, for the entire region it did seem, was prone to catching affliction. Family groups broke apart. After extensive investigations, it was concluded that the cause to much of the <u>spike-bozzling</u>* came as a direct result of a planned deviousness. Set in motion from the earliest planning stages. Meticulously orchestrated by the Luddite elites in the planning offices of the 'Head Offices' in a distant place called Davos. All sapient Nobody's were unsurprised, & set about their lives as usual. Lots of other generations past by, were forgotten, & ultimately lost to time. In the mean time, & as a cause to generations walking the <u>Til</u>* about the earth, much progress in inventiveness did remain prominent. Like, the invention of a <u>barometer</u>*, which saves lives & the wallets of the little too <u>disguised</u>* after a night out. Where ever tribes, & <u>phratries</u>* did settle on patches of gravel, near flowing mayim, or scattered in desolate places were there both good, & bad happenings, & things.

A STANDARD RELIGIOUSLY IRRELEVANT VERSION (S.R.I.V.)

There was the organising of society, which did take place all over. All this seemed to be causes of being. Humankind's, & The Eve progenies do alway survive, & adapt accordingly. Just as they had done successfully before. Language, & more expressive ways of communication evolved alongside other inventiveness. There were countless hand & pocket shops*, & other places of leisure springing up about the places. Offering all manners of consumables that delighted a passerby. Humpie's became elaborate, more extensive, & morphed to suit the era.
It was around such moments that much ancient history became forgotten, & replaced with other more exciting accounts. Was among these accounts that there became an elderly geezer who, through no fault but his namesake, did frighten the begeebers of several others. His name being Terah. Terah did sire several Humankind progeny. The most famous for our telling of the following replaced history tale, was A-bram. A most unfortunate name, for in the vulgar tongue A-bram does mean, Naked. There is to be found no conclusive or logical reckoning to why he was labelled this. Except maybe, that this identifier became his label concluding a pranking dare Terah did lose. That A-bram was potentially known to prefer the locomotion of an innovative rundle that rotated when pushed, instead of the spindly Chevroleg* & Toyotoe appendages he was born with. Famously, & undeterred by his fondness for the disk. A-bram did marry a sweetheart. Sar-ai. She was the famed dressmaker of legend. Maker of the wonderful Sari of South Asia. A great portion of the 1.8billion most densely populated geographical regions employed, & praised her skill & mastery of craft. There are numerous tales of A-bram, & Sar-ai already in circulation. These will not be repeated. Except by way of a short statement allowing smooth transitioning & continuing to the current narrative. The A-bram, Sar-ai lineage famously expanded. However, through unfortunate uncontrolled circumstances, some of their progeny did happen to settle in a strange land. A rural suburbia area ruled by a people of the frog, - Kamit, they did call it. Was while spread out, & scratching a subsistence in this land one of A-bram's own progeny, Jacob, & then his son Joseph & their lineages who did make their labels quite famous in Kamit.[65]

---

65. Kamit, ancient title of Egypt.

Exit stage Right, & left if you must!

A Parody of the book of Exodus. Meeting with Moses who encountered the deity after fleeing Egypt. Conference between Pharaoh, & Moses, The Exodus from Egypt. Concluding, some commandments Moses was instructed to give to the people after a lengthy meditation session.

EUDOXUS:
    According to sundry estimates when throngs of A-bram & Sar-ai's descendants did be forced, because of a 'climate & humanitarian crisis' to relocate; Kamit was a much ancient & elderly retirement rural region (30,000 - 50,000b.c.e.). A-bram, & Sar-ai's tribes were forced through elemental issues moving in on their native Canaanite lands into exile* & advance to an adjacent suburbia of the Kamitian Eastern Delta territories. In search of retirement lodgings, & for the ablest still of them, steady employment. Many of their people did choose, & prosper in livestock of both cattle & geep* & other possessions, in the not-too-distant suburb of Go-shan. A semi-desolate, homely expanse that was vast enough to accomodate all political stereotypes. The ancestors of A-bram did view living this region as Arcadian existence. Time passed some moments after their great grand folk Joseph had become a popular celebrity throughout Kamit society, becoming the vicegerent to the Prime Minister of the lands. Many days did pass, & Joseph was shown great honours when he did celebrate his own dodo homegoing*. When, in his later moments Joseph did stumble into an elderly fashion, & soon followed becoming a somnolent resident that could not be awakened. As did his spavined* patriarch, Jacob before him. Undaunted, their latter kin did continue to throve in the land, but ever so less well off than their Great grandpappy had done. There came about an election cycle, & a new Prime Minister swore as he did enter his new power position. He did rule over all lands of

A STANDARD RELIGIOUSLY IRRELEVANT VERSION (S.R.I.V.)

Kamit & the suburbia region of Go-shan. As the new Head-of-State, the new Prime Minister did think he had won a mandate to inflict upon the population an agendum that heightened his personal environment concerns. Regardless, how outlandish, or ineffective. It did seem he, & his patrons, & closely tied political faction members pleaded ignorance to Kamit producing a fraction of the environmental concerns as a whole. Rather, he, & his newly formed administration, was excited about new policies. Desiring a forty-three percent reduction of the slightly larger one-percent changes to the whole environmental concerns. This, or it was a self-indulgent, calophantic attitude that allowed the instalment of unwelcome policies as this. Like the new PM, his administration, his A A sponsor knew less than nothing or was so self absorbed, they cared little about unpopular <u>nomothetic</u>* requirements, or the concerns of governed populations. Following winning the election, the new Prime Minister did therefore ensure that all previous actions, & administration judicature became obsolete; either having them burned, purposefully lost in bureaucratic red, green, blue, or other colourfully tape. Or, buried deep within the vaulted passageways of an ancient building achievement. Such as, under the paws of the Sphinx.
It had been twenty-score moments since Joseph was granted a send off in typical Kamit style, during a State-wide celebration of all things green, & slightly connected to frog welfare, & worship. That the new Prime Minister was clueless to previous administrations, & popular mores, lent itself to him becoming a ruthless, disdainful, & malicious type ruler. Particularly, of resident foreigners like the largely philistine Canaanite kindred & ancestor of Joseph. There was no unionised organisation, or legislature to oversee, or ensure a fair, & proper treatment of any workforce. Native Kamitian, or other. Nor, was there legislature to protect the endurance, & compliance of 'The Ritual Of Opening the Mouth'[66] for a foreigner who does suffer extreme <u>clinomania</u>* at Kamit's hand. Rather, as a Trojan, esp., the kindreds of Joseph had been compelled to constantly file an "automatic stay" order of the many unreasoned often distributed <u>ASBO</u>*. To halt further forfeiture proceedings on their mortgages that may persistently

---

66. A ritual performed during the burial celebrations of the dead in Egypt. See texts in explanation by Jan Assmann; Wallis Budge etc.

continue by Government officials, just to keep building all manners of monuments of public, but, more government interest.[67]

The kindred of Joseph were severely inflicted with inconsistent unfairnesses. Never knowing the reality of any situation they may stumble into. The government did take umbrage, & inflict them with much harshness. With much ethnic intolerance, & bankruptcy, & great soreness of body; bone, & psyche the people did suffer. As the principal corvée labor force of Kamit, they were forced to endure also the most unhygienic labour conditions of the region. Having a curfew in place from the moment of entering a work site; unable, by much pain in the belly, & bowel, to relieve themselves except for the briefest moment when Nebnetcheru the "Chief of All the Works on All Monuments"[68] averted his appearance to evacuate, & cover his feet. Building operations were appalling. Having several questionable tuff* materials; porous volcanic rock, or Sandstone mixed with straw, sand, twigs, Palm fronds, reeds, pebbles, or bone, & ash, & beer. These materials were the only available substances to complete building the numerous Totems, Statues, great public housings, several hundred boutique ecumenical establishments, of the numinous, impious, & bondieuserie variety. The most famed of all, the Sun Triangle structures, & other monuments. All which has to this day become famous, iconic tourist attractions. It is striking that many monuments weren't suffering acute basiphobia like much of the population did at certain seasons of the year.[69]

Esp., after, & during the yearly monsoon, & windy seasons. These events continue to this moment, to wreak havoc in the region. Despite minor inflictions of walls, pavements, & landscaped gardens, all iconic monuments stubbornly remain in an upright posture to date. Thus, any damage required that the corvée* labour force, bound by duty remains to make repairs. This most surely kept the welfare bill high, but unemployment to a minimum. Many citizens, esp., the allochthonous who made up most of the corvée labour force received a visa & other documentation proving legitimisation of their citizenry status, which

---

67. An "automatic stay" goes into immediate effect the instant you file for bankruptcy.
    That means no other person can proceed with forfeiture actions against you.
    https://www.assetforfeituredefender.com/news/235-how-bankruptcy-affects-asset-forfeiture
68. Teeter, Emily. Location, 571, 573.
69. Also, *basophobia* (fear of falling). Related, but different to acrophobia - fear of heights

A STANDARD RELIGIOUSLY IRRELEVANT VERSION (S.R.I.V.)

was required to be authenticated by authorities daily. For any breach, a writ from Nebnetcheru & his overseers was issued. Or, they did face a court-martial. Many of these infringements were issued to not only raise revenue for the building of monuments, but more so as a bribe for controlling, & manipulation of citizens, which gave authorities a sense of amusement, & power trip.

The official branding & sponsors of the corvée labor force, & suppliers of all work wear were the founding couple of the Levi Denim Producers Company (LDPC). Few outsider phratries did qualify for the receiving of such a hard wearing, chaffing uniform. Thus, the official uniform of the workforce, & population at large consisted of denim over all, or summery dress/tunic type attire with matching brimmed skullcap. Unofficially, were the acceptability of cool wicking type bamboo undergarments, & Akubra. Clerics & bureaucrats to a work site, or residence received several pairs of denim budgie smugglers or, bikini codpieces*. Also, novelty sunglasses, & a tattered secondhand four-and-nine trilby. All garments & work attire had the strangest embroidered Instructions for Use scribbled on the backside of each garment in full view of any who stood or walked behind. In giant lettering was; "WARNING! This is not underwear! DO NOT attempt to put in pants…the final instruction reading in bolder lettering - DO NOT WASH!"[70]

Upon receiving work orders, & employment it was required that a 9month period is endured waiting for the official stone tablet work order to be filed & legibly chipped correctly. The stone certificate replaced the required visa of the outlander, & was approved as a heavy but necessary burden to carry. Despite the official line, anyone could falsify them. Banging one up using an off-cut of the stone materials used on any work site. That is until preparations were being made by the LDPC to design & officially issue a government issue tablet. Such tablets were known as Anonymity, & were a requirement of all common folk, being an identifier.

Was on a late Friday afternoon when one couple had decided to try the practice of interconnectedness. Having a yearning to secure a lasting patrimony in Kamit. It did happen one balmy weekend afternoon, an

---

70. From actual instruction for use labels. The instruction to not wash from a label in Egypt.

extraforaneous* concert for all Levi owners. So, several close relative friends, each with their stack of Anonymity identifiers, did be took to a parkland seatery on the banks of the Nile for a picnic luncheon. Being well fed, & watered (to be polite), the Levi crowd began relaxing enjoying the concert. While drying out, each of them did nod off, leaving the stack of Anonymity unattended. The stack did be reclined, as if Commander, & crew of a fleet on the closed lid of their ossuary-type varnished igneous containers patented, -esky. All esky's waxed so much they slid off the bank & into the flowing waters of the Nile. Yet, the Levi's & relative friends stirred not but did stiffen in slumber under the tranquil heat lamp. The current then did bore the esky with passengers, Anonymity aboard. It did be travelling along the river for about 500meters before coming to an abrupt rest in the shallows among a tussock of reeds. So abruptly was this stopping that many esky did up end & did become as sunken. Drowning those Anonymity aboard. All but several copies of Anonymity were lost to the depths of the Nile. The survivors receiving numbers of bumps, scratches, chipped corners before finally settling as clinging to a life raft yet precariously to their esky. At that very moment the half-sunken esky's did become among the reeds, an angler did catch a 'catfish toughing it out with an anguilla*' on one, & immediately called for assistance to come indagate, & retrieve the catfish.

That it might become an attraction at the local aquarium. Clinging precariously to its esky, all surviving Anonymity were rescued, & taken to the local DFS offices (Department of Family Services). The angler being an officer of the DFS enjoying a day off duty. Handing the tablets, & the esky's to the regional Manager they were placed at the back of the room where a child prodigy was under the instruction of the Principal educator in matters concerning Kamitian (DFS), Kamitian Politics, & civil service. Although the identifiers did not officially participate in any of the classes, or had an influence on the curriculum, for a strange reason known only to the student, the several rescued Anonymity identifier did receive an honourable award at the graduation ceremony. For the child did on occasion, outside study periods consult them. If only to study for some gems related to personal issues. As a graduate, the student was recognised as well versed in poetry, songs & ditties, mathematics, philosophy, astronomy, & public health concerns of the Kamitian dialectical elite. But did lack relational skills. The graduates name was released to the

A STANDARD RELIGIOUSLY IRRELEVANT VERSION (S.R.I.V.)

public soon after. It was the orphaned non-native to Kamit, labelled after being adopted secretly from a Levi clan, & schooled in all DFS, & Kamitian mores; Mo-she Eudoxus.[71]
The years spent at DFS schooling, & other Kamitian activities did weigh heavily upon Mo-she. Mo-she did become a confused matured individual. Despite the evident talents, Mo-she suffered what a future generation would come to empathise as a psychological, & emotional dissonance of birth status. Unable to decide which gender was to become most favoured. Mo-she had spent much time studying the ways of the Neoteric's. Leading to a rejection of all current Kamitian literary, & social norms, becoming a proto-imagist, inventing a new fashion sense by beginning to apply masculara*. Which trended well among the well-bred priesthood, & DFS Kamit populous. To simplify life, & please the conscious of Mo-she, a choice was made to use the supplement of personal pronouns, Meander* /him-her. Others chose the nickname Androgyne. Anonymity, to the contrary suffered nothing. Rather, did remain so for several decades after graduation on the shelves of the schooling apartments. All surviving Anonymity were eventually lost thoroughly. Having succumbed to the ravages of time, to eventually become careless to existing. Despite all efforts taken since the time they did enter the 'muted service' of the DFS, neither the rescued esky, or rescued Anonymity tablets did be claimed by any guardian. All personalities contacted declined ever losing their identifier, for Anonymity served their confidential patentees perfectly. Even those of Levi residents of the suburb of deNile; the swanky burb owned & administered by (NBC), the Nile Bankers Consortium declined a claim of ownership of the denim tea-towel that was found inside one of the esky's. Much indefinitely continued progress, & events passed uninterrupted to a future just as they had earlier.
It became one afternoon that Mo-she did require inspection, & investigation of possible breaching of one Levi couple. The charges were of the potentially serious breach of Family Service guidelines, & an indenture for destruction of a tablet. Approaching with caution, the residence of the couple, it was noticed that several items of denim

---

71. From, Eudoxus (of Cnidus) [390 B.C.E.? - 337 B.C.E.?]: A Greek mathematician, astronomer who mapped a star-map of the then known world. He influenced Aristotle.

work wear & undergarments were unceremoniously strewn about the place. Just at the point of note taking, & writ citation Mo-she Eudoxus was clipped about the ears, & chased from the courtyard under threat of legal proceedings for invasion of privacy, & being a suspected gadabout*, Meander did be forced IDP* sufferer.⁷² Charges that the DFS was all too familiar. Unwilling that Meander should be forced inkyo* & become the latest 'victim' of DFS internal affairs, charged with solicitation. If guilty, Meander'd surely be sent to Privacy/ Gossip Reform School or face cancellation by society. Mo-she Eudoxus did cite a commendation of unemployment, & promptly uprooted to the adjacent lands of the Mi-dians.
There was in that place, Mi-dian a collective of seven women activists, called "The Sufferer-Jets." Their CEO, Dianna had jet black hair through sackcloth, & ash, as was the requirement of all participants. Their mission statement did outline they should stage protesting. Particularly, of foot ailments, & other bodily sufferings like chilblain, & scorching. As with other non-specific inequalities, & sufferings common to women, men, & children. Was on one afternoon suffering tongue bearishness because of much protesting the seven Sufferer-Jets by happenstance did ogle Mo-she at the local hairdresser. They had come to read the legal transcript & charges pending accounts, & were curious to know whether Mo-she would join their cause as a protest to the ridiculous & overbearing charges the DFS of Kamit was pursuing. Mo-she did promptly sign up after some further considering, & submitting to having undergo some minor cosmetic augmentation. Including, not least having all heady hairs lengthened with extensions, & the parrot-top* coloured to match the Jet black of the others through the same sackcloth, & ash process as Meander's fellow protesters.
On another afternoon, about late dinner time that Mo-she Eudoxus was busily carrying out the duties of a swivel-chair sinecure, finalising the following calendar of protests applications, & following up on potential graffiti artists that Meander did become a snoop. From the window some distance away, was noticed a strange sight. An ignis fatuus*, & much smokiness did be shone abroad as with a hungerful smell of sizzling bacon. Habitually compelled to indagate such strangeness,

---

72. Used here as a trapesing gossip. Not as a flitting about socialite.

A STANDARD RELIGIOUSLY IRRELEVANT VERSION (S.R.I.V.)

Mo-she did grab a vade-mecum of fire-readiness, & a "Subpoena ad testificandum," & several close-at-hand hosiery*. Meander was reminded of this as around the room were plastered several helpful warning prompts that read: "If of Fire, try to use the ex-ting wisher." The most instructive, "All Fire extinguishers must be examined at least ten days before any fire." Meander therefore waited, using the Ten-day lapse wisely to study all ex-ting wisher instructions. Only grabbing hold of the nearest fully-prepped distinguisher* after reading its Instruction manual completely. In BIG RED lettering was the instruction: "First, - carry to Fire." The strange ignis fatuus noticed in the previous days had not died off. So, in case there were a breach of 'Back Burning Legislation'. Mo-she did head off in the direction of the flames. Nearing the site there was no burning, nor bacon to recognise. What Mo-she did confront was Shadrach*, not euthermic at all. Rather was much likened to a brazier of imitation branches with flickering of a flame type. The kind that Meander had seen advertised as the latest Shadrach products. Those advertised to be fire-retardant/resistant. Instead, the closer Meander sided, the more this strangeness did focus to become similar to likeness of 'electro plasm'*; that other-worldly material that doest seem to spontaneously appear when called for during séances. Mo-she had only ever read about this, but never had experienced it. Coming more intrigued; Meander sided closer. Strangely, every lick of this electro plasm types, did seem to become more as a germination of disembowelled voices. Listening with intent, Meander could be sworn such was attempting comprehension & intelligibility. Noticing that this imitation log display was not aflame, Mo-she did come to thinking that this material might be really good as foot facelift for all exeshoetion* of their sandacle* footwear through the hotness of the sands. Esp., when it was required that at protests standing around in hot sands, just made the trinkets adorning their sandacles often melt. Maybe, this type of stuff could lengthen the life of all zuri & other footwear? It could also be real utile when attempting to bring forth a hotplate from the stove. The thought was such materials could also benefit households in dephlogistication*. Could also be having much advantage for other indiscriminate things. Like when explorers do take to consider the other places about. The advantage seen by Mo-she was that small enough pieces would not require much hard labour security. Mo-she did scrounge around for little pieces to try in Meander's own footwear, when. Plain enough intelligibility did begin to speak saying in some uncertain terms that the crying out for such a material for explorers & the like had indeed reached a really loud pitch. That it were up to Mo-she Eudoxus to embark on a journey to supply all known regions with such warm, & fire-retarding substance. Taking several little moments in comprehension, & calculation of this new summons, Meander did request the courage to inquire. "Who do thous believe thou is. Why hast Meander was just now made to comprehend this charge? Who the heck art thou, oh, electro plasmic voices." In reply, the disembowelled articulate uttered the following statements: "Well, my little Mo-she Eudoxus, the one of multiple personal pronouns that just confuse everyone for silliness. This is I am I, & my personal pronouns are any of those that seem at present to not be over used, as a possessive determiner patented through another's voice. They, Them, Sar, Yoself. For, 'I,' 'It,' 'Me,' 'We,' & 'My' being taken by those who talk of themselves, & theirs incessantly." Following with, "It is the greatest 'They Them', seller of all useless objects, & other stuff. Sar, does command Meander, Mo-she Eudoxus, & do send thee to sell these, thee multi-fire retarding, & warm comforting products. Thou must make these available to thee poor & unbelievably wealthy alike. Thus, forget thee Sufferer Jets. They hast well serviced the purpose, yet, hast now are but whining insufferably. Get thee, Meander from these places, shod feet & fix thee burnt sandacles of all short, wide, narrow, & large, & small feet. The great 'They Them' through thee Mo-she shall provide it to all in need. Get thee back to former places, & sell <u>Shadrach</u>* products, fixing all burnt feet, melted gladiator-style fringes & other trinkets & appendages because of much hotness of sands, & cooking places. Sar, Yoself Out. Look! This rainbow is my guarantee that all these announcements are true & I am IU is inclusive of the peoples who do revere a good rainbow for its prettiness. I am IU do adjust I am IU's personality pending me am's mood & desire for acceptance by all persons!"

Experiencing <u>heartspur</u>*, Mo-she did tuck shirt sleeves into trouser pockets, hitched the robe, wrapped a wimple around the waist as a belt, & darted off to home. Arriving, Meander did read a cu-nei-form message left in the inbox. It did announce that the long sufferable kin had

A STANDARD RELIGIOUSLY IRRELEVANT VERSION (S.R.I.V.)

recently arrived in town. They did have a job offering return to Mo-she to the former position at DFS. Early the following break of day, Mo-she Eudoxus formerly recanted knowing any kin. Making amusement of Ah-Ron, & Mir-I-am who it was stated were Meander's legal siblings. After much giggling over naming rights, Mo-she did offer a benefit of the doubt to Ah-Ron, & Mir-I-am. Further conversing & bantering followed as Mo-she did reject their offer again, having countered that offer with another. Ah-Ron (Egyptian: Harkhuf) was known an expertly versed individual, an overseer of foreigners, & the seal bearer of the Prime Minister (King), as well as holding the station of lector priest. With these qualifications, Ah-Ron was therefore offered the position of ADC (aide de camp), the 'spokesman', & personal consigliere to Mo-she. Mir-I-am (Egyptian: Maaike, rebellious womyn) was a qualified insurrectionist, & prognosticator despite her physical affliction of leprosy, & so was often treated with apartheid.[73] With much deliberation & compromise both Mir-I-am, & Ah-Ron did accept the offer of Mo-she, recognizing the importance, & seriousness of Meander's disposition. The three did form an alliance, vowing to right the wrongness of all burnings & foots, & bodily inflictions that did happen by accident or decree by authorities. They did not long after begin their journey back to Kamit in hopes to be received by the Prime Minister, his marketing fixer, & housing & furniture safety privy counsellors. A perfect Capitol chariot, with an intriguing instruction rear sticker attached was commandeered. Ignoring that the sticker amusingly read: "Be attention to the environment around & abide by the traditions. Do not operate when you are in poor health or bad spirit. WARN: The manufacture not be propitious to under 6 years of children & elder use."[74] The three, arrived back in Kamit a little earlier than expected. So, they took to leave, & visited the Levi factory to inspect their operations. The following day Mo-she, & Ah-Ron, was permitted to brunch with the Prime Minister in his Commerce Chambers. Mir-I-am was absent for it was the custom, because her stature as shorter than the others. From a sensitivity that she would likely have to recline in a highchair. Likely being known as an insurrectionist who could have thrown a

---

73. In the Jewish Bible (Old Testament) Miriam the sister of Moses, is struck down with leprosy by the deity. See Num 12:10-15. In that case Miriam was shunned for a week.
74. Real micro-scooter Instructions for use.

spanner in the works, she was excluded. All the same, Mir-I-am did use her spare time wisely. Showing great interest in several 'pet stores'. She became much excited for their exotic array of insect, & animals that were popular with citizens. She was also amazed that some of the most popular creatures. Chosen as pets were scorpions, gnats, frogs, ants, (Scarab) beetles, locusts, & the many ponderous <u>zoological* antre's*</u>. Later, she did also visit the great library containing all the knowledge of the world, at Alexandria. Here, she did be met with a most intriguing Neoplatonic Philosopher, Hypatia who forthrightly invited Mir-I-am to attend one of her lectures. Afterward, Mir-I-am did brush up on the environmental issues, & theories of the region.

In careful consideration of all that she had learned at the feet of Hypatia's lecture, Mir-I-am did read & study the weather patterns, as well as past documented records of Kamit's BoM (Bureau of Meteorology). Understanding from these records that fascinatingly there were frequently occurring weather oddities. The Nile waters flowed on occasion in a deep shade of red; as if of blood. There are numerous deadly warring bouts on the landscape, between the local locust, lice, ant, fly, gnat & frog populations. Many of these were joined by various dissatisfied 'pet's'. All the creepy-crawly's & animal populations were in a consistent flux; persistent <u>brangling*</u> disputes, & fighting among themselves. More often such fights did spill over to the communities. Many Kamitian families became real annoyed with the intrusion, & desecration of their properties & person that resulted. Not too distant from brunch, did the first conferences commence. But, it was a flop. There was no real organisation, or protocol. Everyone spoke over & above the other with ever increased frustration, & height of pitch. Each participant then departed embittered, & sought counsel from their lawyer, instructing them to collaborate with other Statesman to hatch a plan. Several days later, the lawyers returned & entered the second conference. This also did prove just as shambolic as its predecessor. For, they had failed to reach due consensus. All lawyers involved in discussions were instructed to revisit their objectives again, with the clarity that the 'Law Code' of Hammurabi offered be included.[75] Those that Mo-she, Ah-Ron, & The Kamit Prime Minister

---

75. Hammurabi's Law Code. The oldest known Code of Law still extant. Approx. 4000 year old.

A STANDARD RELIGIOUSLY IRRELEVANT VERSION (S.R.I.V.)

had initially instructed in optimism to reach an amicable solution to all the issues Mo-she, & Ah-Ron had voiced. Several nights passed before the lawyers had been able to reach a consensus. Where, in celebration to their agreement. All connected with the result then did assent to a matinee puppet show. There were numbers of deity statues, & several corvée labour force onogata & <u>soubrette</u>* for authenticity. They did perform for their regent, & his guests, a <u>supermarionation</u>* pantomime of 'The Great Escape'. The night became very silly; Just for kicks an assortment of coagulated cheeses were brought out. Whereupon, they did each try their hand at <u>tyromancy</u>* despite none of them being especially skilled <u>turophile's</u>*. There was much bibbing of wine, spirits, & beer. Consuming of many cheeses, crackers, cricket paste, & many bug, & bird food condiments. All stated to be 'environmentally', & more healthily beneficial than the consumption of natural domesticated livestock meats; like, sheep, cattle, goat. Despite the illusion, much happiness was far from sight. Lactose intolerance, & much other <u>crapulence</u>* soon followed. Persisting in the wake for numbers of days as nobody had thought yet to tempt penmanship of a universally accepted <u>Theolobotonologia</u>*. Which was written by English Herbalist William Westmacott many, future decades after. Many days after everyone was still <u>stale-drunk</u>*. Those days were too bright to handle for a hangover. It was decided that these would be missed by no one if ignored. They were! When the final conference between the Kamitian Prime Minister, Mo-she, & Ah-Ron had been concluded, they each did take seating as near the waste receptacle. As all knew <u>anywhen</u>* Lactose, & other bodily disturbances could show up unannounced & ruin proceedings. Seated patiently, a ruckus did begin as Lawyers did enter the Chambers as partygoers. Each was carrying a newly wedged cu-nei-form tablet expertly scribed & painted on papyrus. The lawyers had taken to labelling their work expertly: the "Coming Forth By Day".[76] Included, were snippets of the Law Code of Hammurabi. Which was expertly & decoratively portrayed about as a purfle decoration throughout the body of the sheets. The Kamitian Prime Minister, Mo-she, & Ah-Ron each received their statute approvingly. With gladness, & a great sense of achievement did

---

76. Commonly known as *The Egyptian Book of the Dead*.

both The Kamitian Prime Minister, & Mo-she sign the back of their parchment. Sealing them with a cerumen seal. The final agreement Mo-she, & Ah-Ron had fought really hard for had been delivered. Arrangements for distribution & service agreements for the wholesale manufacture of spruiked product lines to the population soon followed. The undertaking for the manufacture, distribution of the products fought for by Mo-she, & Ah-Ron, was tendered to by the Levi's. They were the only large-scale operation in the region after all, able to handle the scale of operations necessary. All was going swimmingly, when. There was a great comedian thrown out of Kamit. Being 'All Holiday*' for him as punishment in extreme wokeness. Incensed, townsfolk all over rose up in protestation to little effect. Following, thousands of armed forces were deployed, being charged with enforcing a curfew, ensuring all households remain within the confines of their residences on pains of fines. Meanwhile, across town word had spread that there had been war declared. Frog, lice, & gnat armies had taken to swiftly move in on the territories of ant, fly, locust, & other insect/animal gangs. Unfortunately for the residents, all local convenience stores & pet barns ran short of their stocks of pooter. It was then declared by the Kamitian War Counsel that it would be necessary to seal every attainable crack in monuments, & tourist attractions. Set traps about prominent areas to catch the buggers.

Not long after the announcement did millions of agminate* insect armies show their true force. Marching forward all over the land they did block out the great heat lamp for the next seventy-two hours. After-Light had begun to rejoice. Had it finally victored over his sibling? Thousands of warring insect, & large family Ranidae, consisting of 433 species in twenty-four genera of frog warring, did pillage & cause much mayhem. The entire province of Kamit soon came under a frightening stygian darkness. That the Kamit Humankind population soon began to feel the worst of chilblains, & other frostiness complications like severe colds. Such colds inflicted in great numbers, as if by sentients, the firstborn of all life. Animals, Humankind's, insect, & other warring gangs were sorely compromised, - for, the firstborn of these did soon after-become a new owner of a newly fashioned eternal box*. A decorative wooden, or stone overcoat. The numbers of the living impaired became so great Dodo hospices were overwhelmed, having to

A STANDARD RELIGIOUSLY IRRELEVANT VERSION (S.R.I.V.)

refuse numbers of new applicants for residency. They did then, pile up so much that either end was caused through warring, or cold mattered little as the results of casualties did begin flowing to the Nile. Making its waters smelly, unpleasant to look upon, & unsanitary for consumption. The warring had become a blood bath, of both combatant, & civilian casualty. Mo-she, & the team of volunteers, distributors, & many manufacturing staffs did become as a cloud, & departed the chaos.[77] With them were hundreds of camel loads of unaffected product they hoped would become trade worthy for other regions. Ah-Ron (Harkhuf) did arrange for '300 Asque's* laden with (joss sticks), ebony, precious oil, grain, leopard skins, elephant tusks, throw sticks: all good produce."[78] Taking their chances elsewhere, it was known that to remain in Kamit, the resulting of this warring would be higher insurance premiums. So, they did each feel obliged to uproot, & take a chance in another province. Trekking Eastward, so it was thought, once the throng of Mo-she had been spied as departing, the Prime Minister, his Ministers of Council, & other officials did become real incensed. They did begin to realise that their cheap labour forces were dwindling, & having to be replaced by more useless citizens for them being superannuated. So, incapacity. Particularly, through retirement into a hospice for the somnolent. The Prime Minister, his Ministers of Council, & other officials not long commissioned the sending forth of emissaries. Along with the Chief of the elite military forces to the PM, - Onuris-moses. He was chaperoned by several Serf's Department officials, carrying Subpoena's in the attempt to halt, or better subvert the mass exodus from stage left & right.[79] Charges of neglecting civil duties were filed, but, unsuccessful however. So, all cost incurred fell to the Kamitian Prime Minister & his government. Many of Kamit's finest-trained civil servants who did chaperone Onuris-Moses soon filed for bankruptcy. They were never to enjoy such grand employment again. It was handed down in judgement, that the arguments put forward by government officials required a complete 'passing over' for their ultra

---

77. The Exodus from Egypt.
78. Wilkinson, Toby, (p. 33).
79. *Onuris-moses* (Dynasty 19) held the titles of God's Father, Chief of Seers of Shu, and High Priest of Onuris, as well as those of royal scribe and scribe of the elite troops of the king. Teeter, Emily. Location 574.

vires, partisan, & self-serving interest. Therefore, it was officially granted that Mo-she & the 2million or so who did follow from Kamit, was free to depart the mayhem.

The departure from Kamit proved as not entirely the most pleasant experience. Those that did make a mad rush from Kamit, unfortunately had forgotten their 'national certificates,' their Anonymity. Therefore, there were major delays at the boarder checkpoints. It did seem the right thing to do initially that those who found their way to a checkpoint ahead of the others, they were forced to wait for the (cough) 'laggards'. No wonder it took, according to numbers of authorities anywhere to 40years downtime before Mo-she & others found a plot of gravel, & settled down to make something of themselves, even becoming a State within its own right. Fortunately, while they waited there was plenty supplies of those utile materials that stave the body from scorching, or getting uncomfortably cold. It would have been a ripe ol' bugger if there weren't enough of those materials. As the After-Light dipped to astoundingly frosty temperatures. Each Light time was surely stifling; so much that they could have frozen eyebrows off, & scorched & crisped their soles.

While waiting for the others gifted <u>gyromancers</u>* did begin to <u>circumambulate</u>* wildly at an increasing pace. After sculpting an <u>aureate</u>* bovine from plans pilfered from a temple. Their antics did entertain everyone. Until they had become so <u>dansey-headed</u>*, a cause of their spinning, they had no choice but to fall to the ground. Bets were taken from which direction the stragglers would arrive depending on which direction the gyromancer's limbs did face when they collapsed. Such skylarking was prior to lookouts keeping an eye on two weather phenomena that did soon begin to stalk the people who did flee the misfortune taking place in the Kamit. There was a familiar flame of electro plasm that did light up near all the camp from dusk, to the early light. Then, an angry <u>tourbillion</u>* funnelled down to touch the plain. In a whooshing rumble, & wobbly manner did this dust devil calve a path.

Now, the practice of gyromancy became popular with the people of Mo-she. When the military wished to sack a town or province they did on several occasions employ this tactic. It was especially effective when combined with the ruckus of musical productions. On one occasion, a combination of military, & ordinary folk did wish to raise the township

A STANDARD RELIGIOUSLY IRRELEVANT VERSION (S.R.I.V.)

of Jericho. Mo-she did instruct them to use their gyromancy skills, & the clamour of untrained music players. They began walking around the town in a clockwise fashion. Then, with a change in note of their shofar players, & drummer boys they did cause the township much dizziness, spinning about Jericho in the opposite direction. The town did get so disorientated that the protective walls about the places began to crumble. Thus, the township was 'captured' by the people Mo-she set against it. According to interpretations, the walls did collapse inwardly. Jericho's mayor & other officials were most unimpressed. But, nonetheless, did yield. All this was very entertaining for the people following Mo-she. The sacking of Jericho did take place many years after the followers of Mo-she did leave the Kamit. The use of Gyromancy as a weapon of war was prior to the invention of other, more effective natural means of sacking a province.
During their travels, the throng eventually did follow closely Meander to a water hole. A place evidenced as recently having been exposed to what can only be described as a slaughter of insect battlers. A body of waters that had once been stained as blood. This is why this body of water is today known as 'red', see! Despite the decomposition of the combatants, having long passed, allowing the waters to return to a pleasant shade. How this was to be traversed successfully without spoiling their attire? Mo-she was confounded. Mo-she, & all advisors eventually decided on dividing the people into two equal lines. One side had brooms, mops; they swept the waters aside. The second line did have shovels, & spades & dust pans & did use them as buckets. In expectation of clearing a path. Having laboured like this earlier. The people did begin to take umbrage. It would have been much easier, & much less arduous on all if the decision were made to side step it & walk around to the other side. Stating in no uncertainty, "It would have been much better if we had not decided to follow you, Mo-she. We should have stayed put in Kamit!" Hearing this Mo-she slinked away to another part of the camp until they did become untroubled.
Several Lights, & After-Lights came, past, & shot off in another direction completely. For, where Mo-she had parked the camp, was to the shoulder of a great freeway. Being a busy thoroughfare, it turned out to the surprise of many, to be either the still used road 'called in

Arabic the Darb el-Arba'in, 'the road of forty (days)'.[80] Or the Silk Road. Either way they were far off the 'official' path according to the latest diagrammatic representation in Mo-she's possession. The following morning, Mo-she did have a Damascene <u>moment</u>* & ordered the throng to Chuck a <u>U-ie</u>*, & double back. The issue & concern was; someone the previous night had not tethered twister to the tethering stake properly. The tourbillion, being temperamental had by earlier light then wandered off. The throng was instructed to keep an eye out for the dust devil. While searching for twister, the pilgrims broke into song. Formally punished for 'breaking' the peace, they were soon after commanded to desist. Thus, it was in deafening silence they did proceed. Aimlessly they did conduct searching for twister. Several more lights, & After-Lights went by. Everyone wondered if they had just <u>Ouroboros</u>*; ambled in circles again, & ended where their tail began. When all the sudden, a moment scuttled by when someone swore to smelling the aroma of twister. They, & a few others did scuttle off then. Headed in that general direction. They were never recovered, but, were assumed to have had obviously become extinct. Or, they had buggered off to a distant & much pleasurable, & accommodating futuristic neighbouring cityscape. For lack in moistness, & sustenance the throng did become delirious, & soon after were pictured as becoming fallen apart. Near approaching their dehydration, & practicing <u>memento mori</u>*, they did begin looking as corpses. Rumours did spread among the stragglers, & much dissenting <u>kvetch</u>* was brought against Mo-she for complete lack in Human Relation skills. Aggrieved at their backbiting, & inconceivable intolerance at beginning to become extreme in moisture-less. Voices did raise again against Mo-she, that it might have been a different tale if they had remained vigilant. Vassalage for Kamit meant their lives were uncomfortable, we found <u>querencia</u>* within its confines. Mo-she did after that, cry aloud, "Wherefore art the skills, to slavish amusements one hast before endured?" Hast thee been so un rememberable of the olden ways of toughing it out?" The long & distant electro plasmic utterances did then briefly make a return in reply. In a kind of whimpering, it was overheard that Mo-she was to task & enshrine former skilled operatives.

---

80. Wilkinson, Toby, (p. 36).

A STANDARD RELIGIOUSLY IRRELEVANT VERSION (S.R.I.V.)

Esp., those of water-well drilling, & oil merchants, & suppliers of other hospitality services. All these specialists were sought to begin to use their skills, talents, & diplomas again. They were summoned to supply the requirements of the jaundiced, & near fallen apart of the populations with sustaining properties. Satisfaction did soon after follow. Not all in the population was joyous about their situations; however. Two neighbours specifically did begin to brangle* with much loudening. The houses of Amal-ek, & Reph-I-dim; they did begin to quibble over the soft-headed fencing arrangement between their allotted tents that had become extremely polymicrian*. It was disputed who should appraise & put up a blanket barrier between each, while suitable hard wearing petitioning was erected. It was not until Jo-shua; a skilled "Conflict Revolutionist" did arrive on the scene that a minor settlement was agreed. Twas' a member of a Pygmy people inhabiting sections of Burundi, Rwanda, & The Democratic Republic of Congo (Zaire) did also become involved following Jo-shua's intervention. This encouraged Mo-she to fix an E.B.A. for many people, as a way to make settlements lasting. An E.B.A. was also affixed between the exiled Kamitian, Zaire, Burundi, & Rwanda.

Not long after, did three moons decide for an unknown reason to do a 'flyby' exhibition in one season. This phenomenon greatly excited onlookers, including astronomers like Mo-she Eudoxus, who had skilfully been documenting the probability of such a marvel occurring. It was all laid out in his/her writing of an 'Almanac of After-Light Amusements, & celestial phenomenon to study.' The flyby exhibition occurrence took place when several communities, including Reph-I-dim, & others were busying themselves at Wilder-ness's twilight garage sale. So, for the most part, it was missed. These communities only became aware after they had from curiosity, purchased an earlier edition of the almanac.

It was a couple of moments after these events that Mo-she did happen to sight the probable appearance of twister. It seemed to be waiting on a yonder distant monadnock*. Immediately, Mo-she did leave Ah-Ron as stationmaster of the mini trains, & bumper cars at the Amusement Park the community frequented. Mo-she did then scamper off as a straddle-bug*. Hoping to dekna* whether Meander could entice twister to again lead the way for the community.

It did turn out however, that the hilly yonder outcrop was not just over the nearest ridge. Rather, it did take Mo-she a couple of weeks to finally approach it. It did not help one bit that Mo-she was insistent on scampering as a beetle; especially, when two of your most lengthy limbs, are shorter than the other two. Making much soreness, & cricking of the neck; as humankind eyes only do face front ways, the direction of the future. They are not monocular like a Chameleon. As the proverb is: "A Chameleon is a prophet, viewing both the past, & future instantaneously." Unlike these lizards, Mo-she had a rude awakening that despite all efforts, 360degree vision is unattainable. Mo-she soon after reached the hilly outcrop, & did have to rest a while with a hot-pack on the neck & shoulders to induce relief. Idling to the vertex, Mo-she Eudoxus did be met with the sign: "STOP! You have reached the Summit." Dignitaries, Statesmen, & Earth climate protestors were there. Ignoring them & their illogical doomstering speeches, Mo-she did bugger off to a close by park bench, & did eat his lunch in silence. Atop the hill, Mo-she Eudoxus wondered was Meander created by Benny. For, at the peak of the mound, were much comedic happenings, & virtues of silliness. Engrossed with this provocative idea, Mo-she did begin then to sit down in meditation in Lotus position. Hours, turned to little lights flashing before the eyes, when for sitting like Buddha*, Mo-she Eudoxus did experience an ataraxia*, & soon after an enlightening. Thereat, Meander was offered by apparition a beautifully sculptured slab of basalt. Where-upon 'electro plasm' did make numerous markings, explaining to Mo-she these were the wordings of the Great Hammurabi. The very same Hammurabi that became the decorative boarder to the Cu-nei-form papyrus received back in Kamit which did secure the deal with The Kamit Prime Minister. Mo-she did begin by automatic writing, to make a copy, (Fig. 1.). Having then authored a rough copy, Mo-she was instructed to return, with his copy to the theme park where all the peoples were, & deliver to them the instructions scribed. He-she did again sit in Lotus position for a little time further, to formulate these instructions.

Sclerotic, & sore from so much Lotus sitting for what seemed an eternity, Mo-she did after sit in a new position. Breaking into a stretchier posture. With much pandiculation* did Mo-she begin a salutation of the heat lamp. Feeling much limbered, Mo-she picked up

A STANDARD RELIGIOUSLY IRRELEVANT VERSION (S.R.I.V.)

one edge of his roughened slab, & attempted ungraciously, to hotdog it to the bottom. He'd forgotten how declivitous the elevation was, so had to ride it as a toboggan. Most disappointing, as him-she did begin the ride, the sled did crash often into many obstacles. Making Mo-she to stumble, & be tossed as a salad from it. The slab soon after, became as chipped, cracked pieces barely legible. "Oh Bugger," remarked Mo-she, & did sullenly saunter back to the community. Returning to camp, Mo-she did call a community meeting.
Here, Mo-she did discuss all the benefits, & pitfalls of extended meditation. Explaining to whoever did notice, the meditations Mo-she did conduct while atop the hill, were concluded with democratically attuned niceties. Assumed to be of benefit to all <u>gentes</u>*, gentiles, phratries, & tribes. Those present was not impressed at the academic <u>acumen</u>*, waiting to use the facilities. The crowds did conclude that him-her should continue meditation practicing while they all waited their turn. Which Mo-she obliged to indulge. Months did pass by but little did change about the former Kamitian peoples. Despite formerly acknowledging, showing great enthusiasm for Stoicism, meditation practices, & potential wisdoms gained from these, few took the charge of seriousness to the point of consecration.
Concluding this was seriously deficient Mo-she did attend the hilltop again in meditation to how best to approach the matter. Another eternal series of Lotus positioning followed… Returning, Mo-she again did convene a community meeting & discussed the latest developments pondered upon during Lotus. This time, Meander used more wisdom than was expected. For, Mo-she did have printed parchments in readiness, that were in easy to comprehend point form. An outline to the latest conclusions & thoughts. Mo-she had indeed begun to learn the benefits of being astutely versed in Human Relations. The following is but the bare bones, the first dozen or so of six hundred+ Stoical Meditational Commands. Those that Mo-she Eudoxus had formulated & concluded that were of most likeable, reasonable, & helpful for proper Human Relations.
1. Everyone, without exception is a stakeholder in Human Relations. Without the learning of the instinctive parchments, & those parchments which these assisted in creating later that officiates over stakeholders, drawn up by Kamitian lawyers for Mo-she, under the direction of

him-she, & the Kamitian PM, using the Hammurabi Law Codes, populations would still be acceptably governed by tyrannical Kamit types. Fewer still, would recognise that all are known by the fruits, nuts, & cheeses consumed. As well as the other laboriousness conducted quoditianly*. It is not a radical ideology Human Relations. It is impolitic to consult with, & subscribe to alternate positions only. Nor shalt thee grant tenure to much radicalised left, or right methods of cancelling the Human Relations middle ground.

2. Thou shalt ne'er use selfies, & other images. Specially as a means to gain remarkable wealthiness, fame. Particularly if these are gained at the expense of another.

3. Social media shall always be used sparingly, as these do assist in the preallocation's of very bad feelings of another, & has caused much complaint. An exception to this rule is the statuary making of statues, & the pictorial imaginings in likeness of ancestors, parents, siblings, other kin, & beloved pet. In a catacomb under the residence, or, on a cu-nei-form slab cleverly & discretely placed on wall plaque, bench, or sitting room table is acceptable. Reverence, & homage paid duly to such images assures the departed, by magical inference, do not reside forever in a Dodo house for the living impaired. Why destroy a lucrative, & beloved Kamit tradition?

4. Lookism*, is not a freeing of someone's obligations to Human Relations.

5. The acts of graffito on walls, & parchment with hieroglyphic cartooning is the, medjet netcher (words of the God). Thus, the reading, & scribbling of such characters about ancestor's needs, & all luxuries on walls, & parchments do keep them existing & in happiness. It is the pictorial hieroglyphical depiction, either by statue, or other is but replica's. These are counter images of what once was in animated expression. Do never practice necrolatry*; however. 'Tis an abomination to show excessive reverence for the insentient. Vaucasy*, though could be quite true for some, is a product of society. Sentience is much more than the sum, & product of circumstance, & stimuli. There are choices.

Remember always, the dead are never dead until they are forgotten. Which is reasonable. We are all eventually forgotten. Best get thee over it, & cease whining for eternal remembrance. Was by the great Thoth's hand which did teach all manners of the skills & wisdoms of graffito.

A STANDARD RELIGIOUSLY IRRELEVANT VERSION (S.R.I.V.)

Any that do take umbrage with graffito, & wisdom as though these are a mere abomination, must be sent to writing, & artistic reform schooling.
6. The 'Large in Bone', the fubsey*, & those labelled giants are just as even as the svelte, fashionista, & the disfigured in physical structure. They do only require a slight lengthier, more expansive homely configuration. Will be a more suitably fixture for their well-being, allowing them to also prosper alongside the much daintier classes. If it can be restrained, no one should even consider waiving a subversive finger in the direction of a giant, lest they do wish to have the rest of thy fingers broken, & needs are placed in a place of Welfare. Is not by some imperfections that the large of bone structure, the fubsey & great in height, that they might contain an extra digit, or toe. For personal safety, best not consider without permission, in nicknaming them '24', or Titanic.
7. It is most sensible to be mindful, & honourable to the elder, separately from the statues in the catacombs. Be mindful of the animated, & unmated still elder. Do not subvert their past acknowledging, or achievements without due, & proper causation, & the full hearing of those achievements. Those who do insist on practicing, or championing ageism. They will be caught out, & reprimanded severely, likely to suffer having familiar ties restricted or sent on an expenses paid All holiday*.
8. Cancelling the past efforts, & acts for minor grievances, or irrationalities not aligned to the here n' now, is just plain silly projectioning of modernisms. It is patronising. Stop it.
9. Do everything probable to keep one's foes, & friend in a state of well-being. Thou shall always reconsider the tragic state of affairs it is to change your life*. Eventually, you will come to 'face the wall.' No longer to enjoy the benefits of Human Relations.
10. Do never go out of the way of subversion, to become the agency of grievous bodily disfigurement, mutilation, or minor scratching. It is grievous that it might become open to the elements. Lead into tormenting, & miserableness, from many nocent happenings.
11. Never, upon the same being visited upon thyself, be the provider of another having to relocate to the resting accomodations. No longer requiring a ventilator*. Neither, to one's kinfolk, nor the unrelated by lifeblood. The reaper will surely require of you too, in a good, & proper time.

12. One's word, must needs be the most honourable endorsement to sustain. For the lame, hearing impeded, simple in mind, & lapse of tongue, & all possessors of other commonality to ailment. You shall be managed, & thought of as any other. Just as the other who does not show a hinderance to sound locationally, aurally, verbally, visually, nor the rationally unchallenged state of being.

13. Of all beasts of burden, & domesticated livestock. These shall in reasonableness be happily consumed, as the 'Laws of Carnivorousness' did set in motion after the ancestor No-ah did become reanimated on the dry lands. They shall be consumed in a nonviolent, humane manner. None shall be seen as acceptable if treated severely, or with any harshness. It is of no greatness that one should continue in the consumption of only leaves, twigs, lichen, fungi, nuts, berries, fruits, creepy-crawly's, & the like. A full nutritional value is offered only by the consuming of red meats, chicken, fish, & various other tasty's. Forget not broccoli, or the little cabbages & other vegetables. To abstain from a variety of natural meats in thy diet for all time, & to only consume bird foods; seeds, bugs, 'synthetic type' meats will surely lead one to becoming agrestic*. In likeness to "Nebuchadnezzar: king of the Maddening living as an anthophilous parrot, or other creature."[81]

14. If persistent concern is shown for the emitting of smelly gasses from domesticate food sources, know this. No true affirming consequences, or major effects will be seen in quality, or quantity of the flavoured breathable gasses or consumable.

15. It is of most advantage to consider several sources of energy. Coal, forest wood, winds, & heat lamp above the head. All do provide in their own manners, usable efficiency of energy. It might be worthy to also try thy hand at projecting thoughts to a future yet unknown. It might be thought that there is a source sufficient, & long-lasting. I Mo-she while in Lotus did happen upon a thought for a 'nuclear' type. Whatever that be. The electro plasmic articulations did confirm a reality. But, for a much futuristic people. Open the mind to advancing of yet the possibility for unrecognised ideas. That not all days are their abundant wooden pieces, sufficient winds. Nay does the great heat lamp beat the

---

[81]. Nebuchadnezzar, most famous in the OT book of Daniel. In Dan 4:28-33 Nebuchadnezzar is forced to live as an animal.

A STANDARD RELIGIOUSLY IRRELEVANT VERSION (S.R.I.V.)

brow but for twelve long minutes at a time. Sometimes, less. Become innovative in energy consumption, & not so damn parochial* & anserous with arguments about your favoured energy source only. Not all those things are always here.

16. Without bigotry, but a considerableness, & rationality knows there are no questioning that there are major differences betwixt* populations; some folk today would rather unsex* themselves & deprive the gender & qualities first of belonging. Rife are the Humankind who like to think as a boi*, & become Nail* in appearance, & orientation. Others distinctly of The Eve, want to think to unsex & make themselves Mail*. This is confusing for all involved. Lots are now shunning true muliebrity. Yet, some still insist, despite their wimmynhood, they do wish to change, & indeed abolish basic bio* distinctions. Some, may desire this to satiate their misandry*? Some still further cannot seem to decide if their womanhood is true, & honest. This is ok for them to think. As long as that ideology does not attempt to abolish outright standard knowledge, & wisdom. There is nothing terribly disturbing about such confusions. One always has the right, be it biological ineffective, & deficient to insist on something at the expense of the considered, substantiated other reality. One may ne'er be bigoted that they do badger, malign or call ditzy any who does like to think as the collective propose. Esp., if for the sole purpose of gaining of an upper hand in life. Life is complicated. We are here, we do things, say things, we become things then we disappear. Sometimes as Differently Able, but, more often naturally. Human Relations, & the getting along with another, despite persuasion must be of the highest of conduct.

17. It is of a high standard, & a much valuable commodity that the teaching, & rearing of the younger in mathematics, philosophy, astronomy, Human Relations, the Sciences, histories, & the humanities. All traditional educations shall be lauded above another, less sensible, but more confusing of reality, & goodness. It is considered of great disservice to the younger of our generations to be grievously replacing all these with an encroaching of irrationalism, ideologisms, insensitivities to reality. Those things that only espouse a maintenance of superficiality, & dumbness of attempting to reshape or abolish all prior learnings, as with any greatness in deed. It was these, & many other meditations that Mo-she Eudoxus did make available to the community. As a little booklet or parchments to be

rolled up & placed in a special almery* to be articulated periodically, in the hearing of the townsfolk. Several other formats are now available also. To suit one's own taste; there is a tightly rolled away parchment piece placed in a little wooden container that fits, & protrudes from thy brow. It is to be a reminder to the grey matter that one is to always be a Human Relations advocate, & consultant. Also available, are several periapt* stones, gimcracks & other trinkets. Some might prefer a cheaper wooden formatted decorative ring, a trumpery* earring & necklace set, or as a plaque to be nailed upon the door frame of the housing apartment. As a reminder when leaving, & reentering the home. If this not be conspicuous enough, for those who do wish it, a fashionable article of clothing, doubling as an 'entreaty fabric' will avail itself, & truly satisfy. At the hearing of these things, there was much civilised debating, & questioning.

The popes of the communities all did agree, & did cheer with much fanfare, "Yay team! To thee Mo-she, you have surely outdone thyself this time. A stupendous service ave you completed in our hearing. A grand idea was the parchment pointers. The peoples that did leave, some more permanently than others the regions of the Kamit on that fateful warring of insect, & tenebrous afternoon of chaos. Though we all cannot guarantee fullness, & loyalty to all these meditations, for it is difficult to be remembering of all 600+, we in all moderate agreement acknowledge these words for great consideration throughout our days. They will be of greatness in relieving the mundaneness of our lives. Encouraging some to new paths. Well done to you sir." Concluding all proceedings, & pageantry & after party the crowds did disperse hurriedly. They had forgotten that the boyler had, by now been emptied of all liquids, & likely melted. If so, a new one would be needed to be fashioned from the slag. It was story time in the central camping tent. This night the tale of 'Esther Tate, the famed RealEstate companion' was being read for the first time.

As Instructed

Short parody of Bible book Leviticus. Instructions, rules, regulations. All required by the deity. The deity follows some, so why not them?

LEAVE-IT-TO-GUS:
There was a fellow, an employee of the Levi empire. Was he who was called upon to set up a series of offices, & make properly all factory flaws. In these places were to take place all the constructions of all manners of denim attire; tent, office, & sporting fixtures, & other niceties that give pleasure to the sitter, when reclining leisurely under the Heat Lamp reading the latest crime fiction. It was Gus's work ethic, & charge as janitor of the Levi factories, to make the knowing of all the preconditions, & proper uses of Human Relations that Mo-she Eudoxus did bring to the communities last time him-she did descend the loftiness of the hilltop, & attend again to more Lotus Positioning.
All current employees agreed Gus was the best for the job. Specially, regards janitorial duties, as nobody wished to get their nails broken, only to have them redone after a manicure. After his janitorial duties were completed, Gus set about every afternoon to the awareness, & reminding of all 'bout Mo-she's words, & meditations to be found therein. To a point of persistent knowingness, these might give some reason for denim curtain manufacturers & many other persons, to cease their incessant pettifogging about their in-differences. Gus's arms got really tired everyday at having to point in the direction of the wall hanger; the one containing the framed 'wedged' Cu-nei-form painted expertly on papyrus. That which did contain, & include Hammurabi's Law Code, as a major part of the decorations.
Directly underneath said painted papyrus, was a tattered, dog eared, smudged scribal copy of the point form parchment sent by Mo-she to all the towns people; the exhausting to read, six hundred so Stoical Mediation commandments regarding Human Relations.

STEVE MORGAN

Was to these Gus was charged with reminding the employees all meditations regards Human Relations, whether they are at the workplace station, or the homely tent, or indeed carrying on with their social & sporting activities. Was expected & wished that all persons begin to look favourably upon such meditations as it was felt that to adhere as best as one could to these that a peaceable & joyful existing might become a staple of generations. Unfortunate for Gus, there must needs be several meetings in a several day period. Meetings had needs be repeated to drum into the hearers the requirements as set down in Hammurabi's Codified regulations. It was pointed to directly near lots that if these were sufficient for that olden ancestor, No-ah. Well, they must needs be ok for all else. Quit the complaining, & just get on with it. Remember, those codes of Hammurabi had been once manipulated, pilfered, doctored, discoloured, repainted, re-scribed repeatedly. If only to ensure the people became understanding. Esp., for those who did long days hence, depart the Kamit, went walkabout, did about face & retreat to the former paths, & finally settle on a patch of gravel & made a go of it. It was burdened on all employees of Levi, that they become very familiar with these codes, & meditations of Mo-she. Harsh penalties would be issued to those who willingly, or otherwise, break the slightest, most insignificant regulation, or meditation. Becomes known nowadays, all meditations, & other six hundred authorisations were given by a true autocrat. Nobody in the community was even able or offered permission to sort a complaint, without the express consent of either Mo-she, Ah-Ron, or other appointee. None were permitted by much painfulness, likely leading to end to forget, or lapse in cognisance, or astuteness. Not to dismiss even a singular fly-speck*, brass buckle, tac, thong, or tiniest gem of jewellery. Rules, regulations, permissions, diktats, legal threats. Many other punishments became the order of much business of all those who did escape the warring in the Kamit, as also those to who were charged to work in the Levi factories. Surely, the truest form, & beginnings of Stockholm Syndrome*.

More than a lot of people

A parody of the book of Numbers. Of those who left Egypt, their encounters after settling on a patch of gravel after leaving Egypt.

CENSUS:
It took place in a deserted backyard, & cattle station holding paddock of Wilder-ness that Mo-she Eudoxus was compelled to take a Census of those still left that originally came 'fourth' in the race to leave Kamit. He/she did not consider those of the right, for they were not of his/her own faction & did not comply to a certain favoured point of view. Rather did too often for liking argue another point of view. A point that also showed the silliness of the other view. This was an upsetting standard as it was not so recently pointed out that factionalism, & favouritism was not the best way to ensure the happiness & well-being of at least one half the population. Nonetheless, seeing Mo-she Eudoxus was left-leaning (having the left leg a smidgen shorter than the right leg), Meander did be got on with the job. Thus, Meander's counting of only the leftist's stands as:
Of the houses of Reu+Ben, their numbers were, 46,500. Of the house of Simon, their number was 59,300. Gad, the emphatic ones were numbered at 45,650. Ju+ wife Dah, had a clan of 74,600 (Their lives were extremely busy as you might have guessed). Issa's car most surprisingly fitted 54,400 miniature Ceramic clowns. The houses of Zeb-U-Lan; those of the 'orchids' & fruit tree groves of Vietnam & Chinese provinces numbered 57,400 who all worked seasonally roundabout. Eph-Raim's able bodied warriors were counted later as they had to wait for stragglers to finish their military training. They did finally number, 40,500. Those poor giant souls called Man-asses, were quite large, with a girth + steatopygia. Combined they did average 32.2" (82 center-meters, or forty-one cubits) wide. Many of their number took up professional Sumo & amateur or sporting entertainment forms of wrestling. Of the

Reggae musicians, Ben-Jamin they did numbered, 35,400. Judges going by their name Dan, numbered 62,700. Of the extreme joyous & happy persons, Asher, they did numbered 41,500. They continually spent much time at parties & those camped around them were becoming increasingly annoyed. The Wrestlers, Naph-tali (including several 'Sumo' who defected from the Man-asses), were counted at 53,400. Of all calculations of the fourth placed persons who departed Kamit, they did number an over all 603,550 leftists. Accredited Chartered Accountants were extremely busy trying to sort out all applicable taxes, & other defunding owed. Exemptions to the counting, for they had wandered off to a 'love the neighbour' retreat which ran that week. These were families, & progeny of workers on the books of the Levi empire. Was considered too important that the factory floor needs not cease production of Levi denim products to clothe; furnish the tents of the military, Court personnel, athletes, & labourers with hard wearing applicable attire. Thus, was equally felt applaudable that they attend the retreat, as a mandatory obligation in acknowledgement of Human Rights & Relations regulations. The Levi factory where all denim products that serviced the community were given a prestigious land holding in the midst of the emerging oppidan. So prominent was this factory to the peoples, that they took consultation & recommendation that it needed a <u>Turkey bacon</u>* detail. If of looting, & other acts frowned upon were committed. Perpetrators of crimes who were caught did face Death Penalty. The harshest critic of commonsense; who often made it mandatory that perps promise to spend one day a week for 52weeks every Jubilee year in sackcloth as retributive justice. It came about that the family Security business of Ah-Ron found favour, & won the indenture as the soul Security firm for the factory grounds. Setting about the places his hand-picked band of Turkey Bacon employees. In a synchronised effort, to curb attempts of looting & other acts frowned upon, to bring a sense of harmony to the township, each of the houses of the generations was set about the Levi factory using the irrational language & numerical values of The Golden Ratio Φ. Specifically, the pattern utilised became known as the Regular Dodecahedron. For, there was twelve equal faces surrounding the Levi Factory. It was believed this was the best way according to Mo-she's census, as the counts did use integers, nay fractions. Mo-she

A STANDARD RELIGIOUSLY IRRELEVANT VERSION (S.R.I.V.)

Eudoxus thought fractions were half truths, the bedrock of which was unreasonable opinions. To advocate fractions was silly & irreverent. How does one have 4.4 children? After all were counted, the arduous task of seating arrangements about the Factory was organised. These are the Name tag & positioning placemats on the altar that surrounded the Levi Factory. On all sides of those clans which did preside as all gentes, phratries, & tribes assembled. Of those that did take part in the census of Mo-she Eudoxus. Facing the earliest light of the Heat Lamp, was Ju-Dah. Many of their kin did be required to sport a <u>Golgotha</u>* upon their brow while at lessons. For more often than not. The days were delightful. Beginning as a spritely <u>cobweb morning</u>*. Bursting into a <u>swoly</u>* day till dinner time. Early risers they had to be. As their morning chores began with a drosometer. Having to measure, & then capture as many dew drops before melting. Only to hurriedly rush off. They surely could not afford to miss their schooling. That is why it is said of them: "The early Ju-Dah's catch the orthodox education." To ensure the kin of Ju-Dah did attend quotidianly, lectures regards the Humanities, astronomy, physics, philosophy, mathematics. Next door was housed Issa's car. Providing the Ju-Dah's with transports to & from the schooling facility. With Zeb-U-Lan providing apples & other fruits, & bouquet's of fragrant flowers to give to the lecturers at show & tell. Being of the great South Land was all gentes, phratries, & tribes of Reu & Ben, alongside Simon (the atavistic nicknamed Peat, because of being buried since the Stone Age) with Gad up the road. On the Westpac Bank corner were the Man-asses, & Eph-Riam. Pairing up well in tournaments of both military & wrestling styles. Many competitions & much slapping on the back for good gamesmanship followed. With Ben-Jamin providing the after-party MC-in' & grooves. Presiding over all court proceedings in the Northern most suburbs was Dan. Court schedules were constantly placed under pressure from persistent partying of Asher who lived next door. Leaving Naph-tali beside them who did organise to wrestle among themselves. They were excused from joining tournaments organised by the Man-asses, & Eph-Riam as they decided to run only mock matches, they; eventually, patented, the WWF. Finally, the Levi's did become settled & feeling secure that it was the kin of Ah-Ron who was stationed immediately roundabout their factory as its tutelage.

Marrying in latter decades into a clan of Ites, the Levi bloodline became intermingled & grew exponentially to be known as all peoples of the Ite. There were the Jebusites, Vegemites, Marmites, Dollarmites, Hiveites, Gurggalites, Jesuites, Electrolites. As with their progeny All-rites, Armondites, the Izza-rites, Regularites & Pyrites & other Human & Minorites. All seemed to be quite serene in the communities that did surround the Levi Factory. Until a wave of Political Correctness warriors began protesting & calling for the mandatory expulsions of all those of the community which art thou lame, hearing impaired, simple of mind & of tongue & possessors of other common ailments. In direct violation of Human Relations, they were allowed to conduct themselves in protestation without so much as a sniping glance by the Ah-Ronic Security services. Primarily, for the reason none of the protests occurred near the Levi factory. Most took place in the living rooms, & at weekend backyard braaivleis* of citizens while watching the latest news briefings. Or, during the weekend sporting events of minors. Like little league. Or, while playing the Kamitian equivalent that became the Roman Board Game, Duodecim Scripta - The Game of Twelve Inscriptions.[82] A board game that in times past was declared unsafe & so unlawful to participate in for: "those who suffer from hearts, diabetics, nerves, hight pressure, & pregnants."
A few weeks past before several protestors playing this game were formally charged with noise violations, & unlawful participation in breach of health guidelines. All were sentenced to repatriate their kin, & ensure that their own health concerns were not past to them. All moppets were thereupon sent to the local sporting club for a minimum of five years. It was during the constant commotion, & ruckus of these disturbing moments, that reports of natures of boredom were coming to light, & being committed. So, much of Humankind began spouse-breach relations from tedium of their consort. The average time spent in such relations was a tenth of an outstanding Mauritanian* year of bliss as a bedroom community. Soon after, it was the arrival of the first month of the second year since the new settlement had uprooted, & fled the chaos of that Kamitian warring. Now, a feasting was declared to celebrate the annulment of the charges brought against Mo-she Eudoxus, the meditation parchments, & all the

---

82. https://en.wikipedia.org/wiki/Ludus_duodecim_scriptorum

A STANDARD RELIGIOUSLY IRRELEVANT VERSION (S.R.I.V.)

generations which did depart Kamit. A remembrance was declared to celebrate the complete passing over of the ditzy charges that The Kamit PM had attempted to burden the people with; threats of further legalities by The Serf's Department. Dan (as Chief Justice of all the clans) had completely identified their ultra vires scheming, & declared them Taurus excretio. Smartly disposing all charges, along with some others for good measure, to the den of lions. The celebration became an Obligatory National Public Holiday, called 'Passover' (Easter). Both still being popularly celebrated to this day. It mattered little if yet each year, there was tourist about, or nay. It was law that everyone regardless, were to celebrate this day the way it had been stated by authorities. So help you if on that day anyone slipped, or by any other means happened to break a bone! No sympathy was afforded to those ossifrage* who violated, even involuntarily the regulation that on no account were there to be any broken bones upon this festive day. To do so was sacrilege, & an abomination for causing much complaint, & meant someone else had to also endured the inconvenience of having to cease celebrating to cast the broken bit & make tears to stop.

It then came about one afternoon that during a Counselling session a point was raised that maybe there was a case to be stated for expansion. There had been an issue of overcrowding reported to officials with increased bickering. So much that there was hardly room enough to stretch out arms or legs without invading the personal spaces of the neighbour. Mo-she Eudoxus immediately convened a separate meeting. Later, another mediation session was scheduled to discuss the viability & pitfalls to engaging in an expansion expedition with a delegation of mayors. Surprisingly, also a Twas delegation who happened to be in town for another reason altogether, was invited to the discussions. Was agreed at one of these meetings that an initial crew of half dozen or so Special Ops personnel. That they should set out to see what layout the region was that lay just beyond the border of the outer banks. Absolutely nobody actually knew what was beyond the town border. Because from the first, a mote was constructed which has kept the entire region free from outside influence. A biosphere dome having has been placed about the entire region in admiration of the movie 'The Truman Show'. Binoculars not having been invented yet, meant all that was able to be recognised on the transfluvial* bank, were several saltbushes, & Malee scrub. Aside that, nothing else was known.

Unlocking the padlocked security fence & stepping through the threshold, the Special Ops personnel & a couple of Twas traders cautiously crossed the mote without having to first assemble the submersible, & set up a base camp. Walking across the mote, for it did only come up to their knees, as it was the dry season they then did trek aimlessly for several days. They had all forgotten to pack their compass, & it being a really foreign landscape… Several further days went by when they all rested from exhaustion. When suddenly, on the final day allocated for exploration, a set of smoke & mirrors was acquired which did assist the spies in the antre shelter to communicate with the residence of the foreign soils upon which they did tread. A series of SOS communications was sent & replied. Lo, & behold the foreign soils residence were cousins & relative fatuous* (Man-ass) tribes people back home. Wandering through one of their Lanyard Marketplaces, &, Vineyards twas noticed all the produce & products were of a much softer material, & higher alcohol volume than they could manufacture. Negotiations began to have an E.B.A. signed, sealed & delivered with the Man-ass cousins. But, some of the Special Ops did jeremiad in disagreement that it would be a good idea that they begin Trade Negotiations without Mo-she Eudoxus. Nonetheless, the commander Celeb, the eldest & clearly the most educated of the Ju-Dah clan argued such an E.B.A. would place them in a superior position, economically in the region. Some debate took place. The end of which proved that Celeb was right. Terms of negotiation, & E.B.A. agreements were from now on signed & sealed by much bibbing of wine, beer, spirits, & a communal lamb roast. The expansion, of not only Levi products, & new materials were achieved. Many townsfolk did take the opportunity for a sea change into the lands beyond the Truman Dome. Since, that historical day near economic collapse had visited. Hard times did long after fall upon the residence of the Truman Dome. The citizens began again to bitterly kvetch that the latest E.B.A. agreement had not really done much for their prosperity. Causing widespread layoffs at the Levi factory, & not the least among some of the original Special Ops commandos. Celeb, for instance was reduced to having to rent clothing from Twain after being sacked for entering an agreement the populous wasn't informed would take place. Also, dissenting wordiness of about two-hundred Fifty arose from the public gallery against Mo-she

A STANDARD RELIGIOUSLY IRRELEVANT VERSION (S.R.I.V.)

Eudoxus. When Mo-she had caught word of this, he was nearly to make a celebrity appearance movie, – Face Off. Which, had to be postponed till such a time the whole mess was sorted. Opening the door for Meanders understudy, Charlotta Hest on to the silver screen to star in the epic production of "Eudoxus 20:1-17." Which, was also postponed. Debuting in (1956a.d.). Meander was most disappointed to have being forced to forsake this opportunity.
With blustering &, much blowing of hot air did Mo-she & his minders spew forth protesting & many threatening words to expel the Public Gallery members unless they calmed down, & made reparation for their nonsense. Insulted much by what the Gallery saw as complete nonsense themselves, they promptly put it to him, "What tha hell would you have we do? Walk off the nearest cliff face?" Some of them indeed did choose to commit to this kind of act. When, the outsider did read this the following day in the Newspaper, they did rise up in accusation also, railing that Mo-she had done committed a complaint against the people. Much back & forth jibing did follow. Unknown to the crowds, nestled amongst them was a recent migrant who had been granted asylum after fleeing his homeland during a recent outbreak of plague. Unfortunately, his ills were not reported to medical authorities in time. Fourteen thousand seven hundred innocent souls were struck down by the illness & soon after were forced to pay their debt back to nature.

Prophet

A micro parody of the prophetic texts of the Bible.

PROPHECIES OF CHAMELEON:
Here are the beloved 'Books of Chameleon'. Twelve in all, the 'books of Chameleon' are stated to contain the prophesies of the very good, & not so good Chameleon after they had pondered the comments & meditations as found in parchment, & stone type tablets of Mo-she & Stoical Mediation commandments. As the proverb is: "A Chameleon is a prophet, viewing both the past, & future instantaneously." They, using these abilities did attempt to live this proverb. Inventing a form of prose most strangely known to us now. Their works being written in the most Ancient of languages; that of 'animals'. Of Chameleon, cat, bison, dog, fish, bird, horse, & creepy-crawly's. These languages, & later compositions were once revered as the most irreverent & dopey languages ever invented. Its popularity among the sages, magicians, woodworkers, & ice sculptors, animal trainers & animal speech therapists are legendary. Has definitely ne'er been surpassed. Despite this all being utter horsefeathers*.
Unfortunately, many of their works have been since, over time becomes degraded. Becoming but not so excellent fragmentary examples of what we think today of 'animal' intelligence & their ability at speech. Let alone an ability at intelligible wrote prose. Making it rather an impossible task of those with an interest in planning a decipherment of such texts. The extracted offered examples, are the latest specimens that have miraculously been fitted together over the past 10millions years. Heu pietas! Heu prisca fidas: - Alas! For piety! Alas! For ancient faith. As Virgil once put it. Or, as Heine said: "History shows that

the majority of men who have done anything, did so in seclusion."[83]
There are still none who is competent, or well versed enough in 'animal' languages to make any sense of these writings whatsoever. It is therefore with absolutely no authority, or basis in rationality, integrity, or any minor confidence in what each parchment might be prophesying. That these fragments appear here. Is truly only by the Chameleon that any sense or worth might be afforded. Yet, no Chameleon to this day is sagacious enough to offer services to make sense of the below scribblings. Those sages, magicians, woodworkers, & ice sculptors, animal trainers & animal speech therapists who still assume to acknowledge the importance to a society of such works as these musings of Chameleons, are truly of the compromised. They shall not be taken seriously by any worth their weight in a grain of Sodom Chloride. For it is known that perception comes through seeing; but, no seer visualises. (See Fig. 2, & 3).

---

83. See Wood. (H - 3; 25 / 96).

Wisdoms

Parodied wisdoms of the Bible book Proverbs.

PROVERBS OF DRU:
These are a handful of the Truisms of Druid Wise-Craft, sometimes called Wizey by his close associates. Becoming <u>bedewed</u>* one afternoon The Eve & a later someone did recollect & collate these sometime after participating, as a fun exercise in a lapidation competition with Dru.[84] While sitting by the Lakeside with Druid they all did frolic about as besties. Testing how far they could each skip stones, pebbles, & other stuff into the waters. That was until the lakeside neighbours complained. An Electro Plasm fence was soon after erected by the "Department of Rock Preservation." It was by the Lakeside while mucking about that The Eve was instructed, & educated by Druid. Along with many progenies The Eve was schooled with those sayings as here collected.

1. Hear it oh thou <u>plebeian</u>*, these words of Druid the Wise-Craft. To listen intently to the ears, & not only see with the eyes is of great benefit to all whom doest bother. These are some of the wisdoms & teaching points told to the ancestor Eve. They did give her a little insight into a few things. Like her, the hearer, & especially listener who doest actually gain insight. Greater will your life choices, & goals become. Provided you do bother with them. These ramblings, a sense of worth & joy might be gained instead of being lost in a rut & just plodding about all your days. It is encouraged to make attempts to do something utile or not utile. This choice is though, yours to follow. I Dru do encourage thee to become a child of mind. It will prove in the long run most beneficial. Is a good thing, & does show a sense of fun.

---

84. See, The Activation.

A STANDARD RELIGIOUSLY IRRELEVANT VERSION (S.R.I.V.)

2. Unless thee does become as a Phoenix, thou wilt ne'er have the best, the first water, or pukka of anything revealed to them.[85]
3. Is a mark of being wise to seek an education; to seek instruction for the preservation of an understanding of common things.
4. The wise of mind should therefore continue in educating the self. To show aversion, & fear because of the different, for a desire to remain a tabula rasa is a mug's game for the duncical, & does not offer anyone gain; but, keeps the empty-headed as no real use to anyone. Stop it!
5. Warning to thou not so educated, the easy duped <u>schmuck</u>*. To milk chocolate, is to peanuts & be counted an ignorant <u>schnook</u>*.
6. Enjoy the self with simple things. Like how amusing the past-time of lapidation is.
7. How much skill could be shown throwing rocks, pebbles & other stuff harmlessly into a lake. Take care not & notice that another will likely disapprove. Their vainglory will shine brightly.
8. Imagination: Either it soars as an eagle, or resembles the wings of an ostrich!
9. Druid Wise-Craft did once cry bitterly allowed; if you be a little sad & downtrodden, do allow always the tear ducts to open & become clean. To deny this, would eventually mean various eye conditions that are expensive to reverse, & would cause much pain to the hippest of pockets.
10. Is much better for the brain to keep occupied with all manners of exercises, like puzzles, & the reading of books, debating with another & the such activities. Mainly, to stave off boredom. A <u>nudnik</u>* is too often bad mannered & becomes more selfish the longer they're allowed to come over for a play-date. To heed to the pestering boredom of a nudnik, would lead one to doing silly, & sometimes reckless, or even harmful stuff. Stay the mind & hand & feet from entertaining the wishing of Boredom.
11. When narcosis, acedia, or great sense of hebetude, & sloth does attempt to take over the personality at games & playtime, or relaxing times, get up from off the sitting place. It is advantageous to move about, go for a jog, make a coffee, or use one of the gameshow lifelines & holler for a friend. Boredom, even its grave does yawn for it as soon as it gets the picture, becoming bored itself.

---

85. An interpretation of John 3:3.

12. Smothering words are of no use to any. Do therefore, be as breviloquent* as possible. Make the point as directly as one can. Breviloquence well made with the right & proper words is really effective & enjoyable for the hearer.

13. Thoust should hardly ever stand as a solooksist*in front of a mirror or matterocracist* atop an ego ramp in confabulations. This only makes the hearer wish they might be counted as one of the deaf community. Or, the speaker muted.

14. If thou doest believe it a necessary evil to bang on about something, make it interesting. Use different intonations of voice when telling story's. Especially, during the children's bedtime story times. Is not fair to bore the life of some little one before they are ready to watch the back of the eyelids.

15. Is an abomination to go out of the way to entrain bad ideas. It is not of benefit to scare unnecessarily any one. Pranking is however not an abomination, as long as it does not cause the pranked to become Living Impaired or seriously compromised. To do so, thou will receive a great & terrible slapping in the face, & other punishments.

16. Do not be in the trap that twarvlement* is of benefit to any but thyself. The speech maker has only proven that they are a complete nudnik. Such persons are uninteresting, & will likely be ignored & muted. Get over it.

17. By ignoring reality the barking mad seek to ford through waters using buckets, shovels, dustpans, & brooms. Their labor's will be proven wearisome. 'Tis common knowledge, that the best way to separate waters to ford across land is through prestidigitation.

18. The most common things in life are only common to those who don't see how amazing life is.

19. To show partisanship for a single sauce at cookouts, is simply not the full shilling. You may be in preference of a favourite; like barbecue, tomato, mustard, chilli, or any other. But, nay should thee thinks that thoust can trump all others simply from preference. This shows thou is ripe ol' feather-brained.

20. Is a far greater truth in this statement than many might know: "All truth has about three stages: first, it is laughed at; second, it becomes twisted into ridiculousness, to become near obsolete; and third, it becomes as a fixed obvious conclusion to everyone." Go, love truth!

A STANDARD RELIGIOUSLY IRRELEVANT VERSION (S.R.I.V.)

21. If by chance someone doest come over just after waking. So are still in an un receiving mood. You are not obligated to entertain <u>levee</u>* with them. They may be a disguised nudnik. With much chewing the fat, they'll prove themselves as a <u>clack-box</u>*. A <u>garrulous</u>* individual. So wilt desire to attempt & entice you to an act that you really aren't interested in doing. Is a very fair & reasonable thing to be left alone when one does think it about the right time if you can't be bothered with levee. It is totally your right.

22. Commonsense is obligatory to all whom would assume the place in a society. Goodness, & properness is a hallmark of good standing in the community. It is a sign of an interest in education & knowledge, & much wisdom. All are gained by drinking much coffee!

23. To be persistently philistine & analphabetic will surely cause thee to be served cock a snook in due time. To be this way will certainly end in de-friending from all social soapboxes. To likely become the catalyst of an end of membership at the local pool of Siloam.[86]

24. To know, that we really know very little can be an advantage. DeNile is not just a Riverside Suburb in the Kamit. But can prove superior, & to the advantage. Either trouble is averted. Or, deNile does spur one to revisit the first maxims above. Is the latter that is the most preferential.

25. The <u>mamamouchi</u>*, the self-confident are known by their craziness; the crazy official is known by reckless deeds; his heart is in harmony with the tongue, & <u>hutzpah</u>*. His lips do speak accurately.

26. Wine, & beer, & spirits bibbing are a pleasant way to relax when taken in moderation. Elbow crooker's beware; however, of boozing too much. For it will lead to many unpleasant words, or many unsavoury acts being done. Particularly by pranksters who will always take advantage of the <u>jug-bitten</u>*. Those who did become <u>blin fou</u>* intentionally. Is very much frowned upon to take advantage of any by unsavoury means & intent. So, don't do it! Thou who do such is a complete mongrel. Is he who needs to be incarcerated, & or made an eunuch.

27. 'Evil eyes' are a complete suspicion. You shall ne'er pay any attention to such for it is a waste of time to chase after irrationalities & nonsense. Might be that if you did happen to catch a glance & interpret that opia

---

86. An alleged body (pool) of healing waters, See John's gospel.

in such a manner that the looker really has an amblyopic eye. Is a real condition. So must need accurately assess whether a complaint to accuse any with such a condition is from suspicion only.

28. Beware the pamphagous* who quaff flux-ale*. It will surely cause much stomachichus. Causing a coming to ruin, as a total sting-bum*. Esp., after the purse is emptied much quicker for offering guests a lucullan* & brobdingnagain* banquet. When meals at dinner parties are not prandicle*. Quaresimal* plates should suffice for all dinner guests. The purse-proud* are not sensible. They are mingy*. It is better to be one of the sensible than waste your earnings on making wider the needs of your waist.

29. Becoming purposefully fubsey* does not give rest to organs. Much bloating of the belly regions could cause more unhappiness in the long term. Thy belly regions will often require some form of conserve, to opitulate* & stimulate digestion. To assist thy stomach. In moderation, & to remain not an invitee to the Reaper's banquet hall is much preferable.

30. There is an absolute obligation that the young, & young at heart & mind continually enjoy themselves in play, within & without social settings. There shall be all manners of toys, & play equipment available for all to ensure a cultivation of aliveness & laughter be spread throughout our lands.

31. Is a right of every citizen, to choose apanthropy*, – & remain unique. Divorce, for the attached at the breaking of material stuff amid an acquirement is ok.

32. You shall admonish lies & stealing. But, to 'cheat' a little on the working 'time sheet' is not ideal, but is accepted. Ensure though another's life is unaffected.

33. A braggarts*, a persistent blurber's lifestyle is an abomination. It does often end in fights & the belittling of another. This is not helpful to either party goers, or the downtrodden as it does send a mixed message of likability, leading to acceptance issues discussed at the psychologist's, & alienists* suite: which does only increase their coffers much.

34. Beware the lothario; the 'lady & gent of the night'. With coquettish displays they "cut the purse." Making all wealth to be spilled upon the floor. Coins will be lost behind the couch, down the drain, or in cracks in the pavements, making them difficult to retrieve.

A STANDARD RELIGIOUSLY IRRELEVANT VERSION (S.R.I.V.)

35. Beware of the mule dressed in a horse bridle. Their actions will prove in time; they cannot be harnessed.
36. The most tragic of words? Pathetic! The most tedious, - yes is boring.
37. You shall always, within reason, respect & admire superiors in the workplace & not go out of the way to cause much consternation to work fellows.
38. You shall be vigilant in the grooming methods. A neat appearance is always the acceptable presentation; especially within the Temple grounds. Is acceptable that the Priests & Priestesses all wear masculara*, after shaving bodily hairs, to even the eyebrows. But, no consideration of sympathy shalt be given to those who insist on a Brazilian (as this is too painful & will cause much de trop* chafing).
39. Board games & toys & other amusements are a good way to entertain dinner party guests; "Pyramid Reactionary," & "Guess the Pharaoh" are still some of the best sellers.
40. As that ancient Greek Sophocles did announce: "Reason (Logos), is the Deity's crowning gift to Humankind." Be sagacious in every life experience.
41. Make yourself an ass, & every burden will be placed upon your shoulders.
42. The wiles of temptation prove we are Boeotian by descent with fine daedalian Italian hands*.
43. Life is a series of exquisite moments filled with daring adventures, or it is nothing. If life were certain, it would hardly be worth it. Go live life!
44. Fun fact about truth. It is always TRUE. Regardless, how it is spun. Truth refuses to be falsified. The more ridiculous a belief system, the more probable is its success.
45. "Errors of the wise are more instructive than any wisdom offered by fools."

Exactly!

Parodied mixture of wisdoms, proverbs. Unlike the Bible book of Psalms.

DISSIMILAR TO PSALMS:
1. Lead not any to temptation. They are quite capable of finding their own way.
2. A lown disposition = mindfulness. Much Lotus positioning for meditation is most beneficial for bringing calmness, & mindfulness.
3. It has become widely accepted that some people insist on adopting the identification of a cat, or otherkin. Better, is to adopt the likeness of a tree. Nourished by clear, fresh waters, all manners of fruits will yield, in their due time, & season.
4. Trees are numerous in variety, just as is the fruits they yield. Yet, some categories of tree produce fruits unfit for consumption; so it is with knowledge. Not all knowledge is profitable to him that possesses it.
5. Much turmoil is spread abroad. Throughout the earth many are outraged that not everyone believes the way they do. There is widespread bickering. The madness of crowds while many kings, bulldozers*, & other elites plot against the majority, saying, "We are the anointed. We have a rule to abolish." We have power to cast away those things that made us all prosperous, & forever change the course of a history we no longer approve. We have decided. We declare the course of action the many must take to unburden the anxiety & stresses of our home.
6. Scudways* in biro are the elite. They do bang on & cast policies that, clandestinely decide the terms, & conditions of your happiness, & wealth. That as a pleb*, you must transfer, & transition. You must own little, & become joyous. Ignore them. Stand against their insaneness. Their piety, & wisdom is of a chasm. Much likened to a Blackhole.
7. The sweetness of flarting* is mockery of wokeness. Though the woke do often speak in virtuous tones, the ends are vitriolic.

A STANDARD RELIGIOUSLY IRRELEVANT VERSION (S.R.I.V.)

8. Oh Damn! How many are my foes. How many do plot against commonsense with snivelling, & fretfulness about those things unlearned. They do badger, & malign ideas they disapprove, seeking always to have an unrecognised past, present, & future cancelled & humiliated. Yet do stand against all forms of 'wokeness'. It is but a joke.
9. The words & acts of the 'woke' do only prove that 'wokeness' is a pretence. The <u>Sleeke</u>* are much better positioned & equipped to face the conundrum that is life.
10. Though I lay down in rest with peace. The hundreds, & thousands have all been spilled upon the floor, & the bread does lie buttered face down on the floor. Some will likely become real incensed, having already decided the bread is of no use. Is it not better to check your heart? Do not let fierce anger overwhelm thee. Be angry, but let that anger not become a tool that exposes unintentionally, your <u>keep</u>*. It will only become your ruin. Your feet will only become sticky or shredded to pieces after your exposed keep did cause you to smoosh the bread into the floor. Smashing crockery about.
11. They surely possess no knowledge; those who do guttle men with words, as much as they guttle bread. Their likeness shows as a fool. As one intent on pretending they cause no ill by what they propose.
12. The elites, they do always act as kindly shepherds; I do not want. Their speeches promise the green pastures, & the cleanest of airs, & waters. By much insane <u>finagling</u>* do they promise to lead me to prosperity, happiness, & health. With much 'eating the air', & <u>flummery</u>* do they announce the achievement of all happiness, & desires comes through possessing nothing. While becoming a slave.[87]
13. Many are such words of the elite. They do announce unceasingly. With much jubilation & applause from the clowns of the W.E.F., at Davos. They, & their sentiments are but <u>twarvlement</u>* & the blustering hot winds of <u>flatuosity</u>*.
14. The impressions, & the obsession of another is not easily controlled. Our efforts to do so do only devalue our own character. It is these days fashionable to look to revenge for an arbitrary <u>snuff</u>*. Stop it.
15. There is no gain in revenge. It is the few with knowledge that understand the best retaliation is to exercise restraint. If offended by the

---

87. Eating the Air. Quaint phrase for delusion, false hope, swindle.

faults of another, it is best to assess your own feelings. Perspective, & inner wisdoms will soon bring <u>forgetfulness</u>* to vengeance.

16. Be always in the employment of improving yourself. Use the many writings of others, that you receive easily, for what others have laboured.

17. Principles are everything. They do bring much happiness, freedom, & much control. Without firm principles, what is a human but an empty vessel unrestrained, blown hither & thither about all his days.

18. Opinion does never equate to fact. Perspectives offer deception, not truth. To become distressed by another's external perspective, written, or verbal, is not the fault of that perspective offered. Distress is only your estimated understanding. At any point, you have always the ability to revoke all distressing moments.

19. If one cannot rule over his mind. His mind will impose itself on the will. There will be no restraint.

20. Silence of the woke schmendrick is like a symphony to the sapient.

21. Your philosophy does never need to be explained, but embodied. You are always encouraged therefore. Enlighten those around you by proving your philosophy.

22. Through much perseverance, & by much trial, & error is true character achieved. Many are they who seek to develop their character; however, easily. That path does lead to the birth of 'snowflakes.' Always in complaint of what cannot be controlled, dismantled, deconstructed, rewritten.

23. If certain people announce a looming, predestined future that panics, or distresses you. Fear these words not. These are, but often words from premeditation. Words of a projected future yet known. You will meet a future as it happens despite another's words. With reason, & perspective must all endeavours, & likely future scenario's is weighed.

24. Be undeterred, & stress less for what a future may hold. A time yet arrived is not yours to concern. Live in the moment. This is your future. Your future begins today. Spend it with good judgment.

25. If someone asks, "Who taught you? Who was your teacher?" The wise would answer, "Nobody. I once witnessed the folly, & ineptitude of the ignorant, & self-righteous. It was then that I decided to avoid both."

26. Of whose benefit is it if you are a savant; distinguished, & possessing an exceptional aptitude, & knowledge. If you also are plagued by a greater impairment in Human Relations?

A STANDARD RELIGIOUSLY IRRELEVANT VERSION (S.R.I.V.)

27. You all know the saying, "All good things come to those who wait." Or, "Time heals everything." What rubbish! Good things come to both the deserving, & undeserving. While time sets idol, waiting for us to move.
28. There is a dream we are lured by: time. Time has deluded all men. Esp., Light-Time extension. There are no less, or no more moments in time for one over another. <u>Gamme</u>* is therefore, a useless operation, tricking us into believing forwarding all Timepieces makes any difference.
29. Today is the same present moment for all Life. Whether long, or short, the present converges on the same point. Stretching behind, or into a future, the present is the constant of all Life.
30. There are laws of nature that cannot be revoked. As Humankind's our assignment is to engage reason, & follow those laws.
31. There are many who say the Universe is rational, & ordered. Others believe that it is meaningless, & chaotic. As one part of the universe, are you rational. Or, are you a chaotic being? In the things, you do, is there meaning, & order. Or, does chaos reign?
32. Convictions are most difficult to tame, let alone change. Tell a man with a conviction that you disagree, and he will question your integrity. Show empirical facts, he will question their legitimacy. Appeal to logic and reason, he will likely miss the point.
33. The fact of all humankind existence is. It is marked by ellipsism; a sad realisation that you will pass on to another the joke of the continued survival of our being, without hearing, or knowing the punch-line. Why then should we be hagridden in this life with piffling matters? Rather, our focus would be better served by cerebrating our own <u>suerza</u>*.
34. Just as sure as <u>kadot</u>*, changing, or revising opinions are part of life. If you have not done this in a while, please have your pulse checked, - you may have expired already.
35. The 'Woke' could learn a great deal from this saying, "Stop demanding others act with decency. Be decent people."
36. The world cares little if you are angry with it. No one can change an atmosphere without first changing the self.
37. Endlessness: How large, or small; fast, or slow is it? What is infinity? It is likened to the prophetic, seeing everything. It is past, present, & future simultaneously, & is always, in all directions. At all converging points, infinity exists, yet does not exist!

38. Here is a trustworthy saying: It is not those who die who separates us. Death does unite us all. It is life that separates. All life is united in repaying our debt to nature.
39. The acts of humankind are always the best litmus test of their thoughts.
40. Speech - it is always one half of the same coin. One side the speaker. The other the listener.
41. The woke do misunderstand the future. Wishing to always walk backward into it. The warning system of all life is past histories.
42. We all call confused facts - History!
43. Books, wisdom, proverbs, learnings: All should be luminous, but not voluminous.
44. Beware the earwig; both of the small elongated insect type, & devious influencer. Their tempting should not lead or persuade, or become a persistent influence. The insect type is just as annoying to behold. Both will only lead to a ruinous result.

For commercial good

A parody of the Bible book, Esther. The Jewish heroin who 'saved' her people from becoming obsolete. No mentioning of the Jewish deity in this book, yet Esther became famous.

REAL ESTHER TATE:
Agencies of the RealEstate empire of A-Sue-Rus, with One Hundred Twenty seven offices did stretch across many provinces, & could be found in many lands. Including branches in India, & Ethiopia. It did happen in the third year of the opening of the flagship store; Citadel at Susa. A celebration was called by head office for all employees. From the humblest staffer in the canteen, through to the most obnoxious in management. Also, in attendance was a substantial army of volunteers; helots, serfs, their masters & numbers of freeholders. Invited also were several media. Including Porscha, from (Persian National Media) covering the festivities for A-Sue's media profile. With much pomp, & ceremony, & ritual did the celebrations shine. For, A-Sue had cornered the RealEstate market.
Celebrations did continue for 180days. Concluding with a huge shindig. There was much feasting & gorging; with much wine, spirits, soda pop, & many other party foods. Such as fairy-bread, hotdogs, countless lollies & other confections. All this lasting a further seven days. Those in attendance became bloated, & did soon realise they were inflicted with several carries. But, these were of low priority. The mansion, & surrounds of the A-Sue property did prove a wonderful venue, and Vashti the 'Travel Agent/partner/companion' of A-Sue also did hold much feasting. Away from the main quarters. In her own quarters, Vashti did take upon herself the role of ayah, entertaining all family members, & estranged 'partners' of the 'adults' in attendance. This off-site partying proved to be more civil than that taking place in the main lodgings. All in attendance did become goat-drunk*. Several

guests did become amorous. Numbers of the real inebriated guests were pestering A-Sue to have the famous seven eunuchs; He-man, Bo-thhut, Hispania, Be-gone (the expressive), Abigarth, Zeta, & Caracas Shakah. Desiring they would fetch the <u>hanker sore</u>* Vashti, calling for her to put on a show. It is unclear why the seven were also called for, as it was really only Vashti, who it was rumoured, was of <u>elfin</u>* heritage. It was Vashti who was to be most ogled.

A. Sue did understand the real intent of the requests; as buffed as He-man, & others were, A-Sue did, at other party's often allow Vashti to parade among party guests. The sole reason was to 'show her off', knowing well that no guest, or other could ever 'score' such a mammoth beauty. Let alone afford her services. Word reached the ear of Vashti of this request. But, this time she did flat refuse to comply. Not only did she consider herself too busy for such trivialities, she was no longer a 'down the road lass'. Caring much less these days about being over stylish. Days were numbered for Vashti's cheap fashionable accessory, or porn idol status symbol for A-Sue. Recalling a passage from Ovid, she Exclaimed, "Alas! How difficult it is to not betray guilt by our looks."[88] Greatly vexed that Vashti this time would not parade about the places, 'claiming' she was too busy entertaining others & was not in the mood to be ogled as some cheap fashionable porn star. A-Sue did thunder about, with her usual churlish attitude when things did not happen as she commanded, She did have to sit it out for a time in her 'panic room'. The room built for such occasions as this. Having calmed down, A-Sue did return to the festivities. Was then she struck upon an idea; she'd call upon those in attendance who were well versed in the laws of <u>lookism</u>*. Surely there were ramifications to exploit at Vashti's refusal? One of the revellers 'partying it up', named Manikin did pike up. He did announce in the hearing of none other, before the music players were sent out of the room, his thoughts to all that had upset A-Sue. Despite being extremely inebriated, Manikin managed to climb upon a very tall stepladder, & bellowed: "What Vashti had just now done, was surely not all fair. How dare she refuse the request of us inebriated ones. Who really accepted the invite to only gorge & bib ourselves forgetful to life? Honest to Betsy, that's not why any of us are here, hey fellas! We

---

88. 'Down the Road'. Someone who is a slave to fashion. See, Wood (A - 3 / 85).

A STANDARD RELIGIOUSLY IRRELEVANT VERSION (S.R.I.V.)

came to ogle Vashti." He then began chanting, "We want Vash; we want Vash. We want some Leggiest entertainment." Murmuring began that Vashti had suddenly set a precedent; refusal to perform requests because the 'mood' did not suit. The idea that Vashti had no clue to the law of 'lookism', began to spread widely. The implication of which could have been that following in Vashti's footsteps, others would catch on & repeat. Falling off the stepladder, Manikin did brush off as a mere flesh wound, the bone protruding from his arm, & began sharing homely stories. Each had a similar theme; how humiliating it was to be dumped by his own 'leggiest' partner several weeks prior. He did then offer A-Sue the very solution given him by his lawyers; that A-Sue must save face, annul the courtship immediately, & have all Vashti's belongings tossed to the curb-side. She must be resolute & be 'done' with Vashti, & was to then seek out another 'Travel Agent/partner' of equal, if not more alluring than Vashti. Upon the hearing of this, A-Sue was most pleased, & strangely comforted. Understanding she was not the only soul to have been treated with such disdain. Plans were soon set in motion. But, not before the cessation of festivities. She was not all that insensitive. Not too many days passed when Vashti was sent packing. It was then that A-Sue did begin to make arrangements to have all postal employees begin a competition to have the best candidate as replacement for Vashti. Competition flyers were sent all through the vast RealEstate empire. Across all lands, & provinces, no postcode, or ethnicity was exempt or excluded from filing the legal documentation to certify their 'Travel Agent/partner' status. While waiting, A-Sue did begin again to visit the usual haunts where one might find a 'cupid' interest, for, her waxing of hairy legs began again in earnest. Her disappointment of Vashti did finally begin to wane. To the point where A-Sue did feel comfortable to reestablish her dating/social profile, as 'single', & available for frolics. Soon, her correspondence 'inbox' was becoming overflowing with requests. She then decided to close them, & her subscriptions to fashion magazines that had sent an overwhelming array of suits, & other garments. She had decided also to not long after, place a hold on her high-society lifestyle for a couple of months. While she did pick her way through each offer, & garment choice. During this time, one of A-Sue's closest advisors did happen to mention that a suitable 'Travel

Agent/partner' might be sought from the many 'contacts' that A-Sue had accumulated over the years. It was suggested that a probable candidate might come from the many 'Virgin Airline' stewardesses befriended over the decades. Finding those lists of contacts, A-Sue did begin to scan them. In among them was found an odd piece of correspondence; a postcard. The name on it was kind of familiar; it had been from an early acquaintance, Modi, who she did know now as a famous singjay master. A reggae musician quite skilled at 'layin down the grooves.' Modi, it was vaguely recalled was the guardian of a young bona fide bombshell. An absolute beauty; Hadassah, now going by name, - Esther. Orphaned in early childhood, Esther was now under the aegis* of Modi. Excited, A-Sue did send Modi correspondence again. In hopes to rekindle their friendship, & maybe, capture an interlude with Esther. Months of interaction went by before Modi finally gave permission for his niece, his adopted daughter, Esther a meet n'greet with A-Sue. The two did hit it off immediately. So, forsaking the formal documentation ordinarily required, A-Sue did invite Esther to attend the palace Finishing School for young Lady's. All potential 'Travel Agent/partners' were required to complete the studies, & instructions for High Society living, & "Agent/partnership courtship" offered. As with any protective adult, Modi did assume a role of keeping a weather eye on all his most innocent sylph Esther. He did not wish that she fails, & so tarnish his reputation in musical circles about the places. Time, it did seem run by in a flash, for, all studies & courtship instructions were completed in about six months. All graduates by order of legislation, had to wait for a personal summons to enter the Socialite scene with A-Sue. To assume the right to enter the prestigious lifestyle without an invite, was surely considered bad manners. To attempt it, meant often the graduate be reformed. Having been sent back for further instruction in protocol. Pending the severity, she might also face detention for a period. Not too many nights did pass by after graduation, when it became Esther's chance to prove her worthiness of 'Travel Agent/partner'. She was formerly invited by A-Sue to kick the heel up. Esther however, was unlike the other young lady's. She did ne'er assume to be anything but herself. With such an attribute, Esther did be shortlisted as a favourite. Eventually, winning over not only A-Sue, but also the high praise of many courtiers, & attending eunuchs.

A STANDARD RELIGIOUSLY IRRELEVANT VERSION (S.R.I.V.)

Formal negotiations betwixt A-Sue, & Modi soon began in earnest to allow Esther the high status on offer. Esther, had time & again proven her homeliness, & likability with all at court. Having the documents signed, & witnessed, Esther officially became the new 'Travel Agent/partner' to A-Sue, upon which Esther was given the former residence of Vashti. Along with all titles, & many other privileges. Esther was overjoyed. She had at her disposal an ensuite. So, did no longer have to use the communal facilities. She did enjoy many other delightful amenities also. Her life did seem to become a grand affair. Worthy of the history books. Another grand shindig was then organised in celebration of the compact signing between A-Sue & Esther. As honoured guest, Esther did gasp, "Oh Purim..." when she did enter the room, & all eyes did be set upon her.[89] Esther was quite taken aback at the raffish attendees. For, she was notified. It would be only a small gathering of staff, her uncle, & other minor dignitaries. Many surprises & formal speeches were made that night. Along with many government promises of gifts, & tax relief. But, to several in attendance, these fell upon deaf ears. Esp., the promise of tax relief was simply too good to be believed, so it was not. Some government official in attendance was upset that A-Sue had put a moratorium on taxes for six months. So, did plot to have this scheme sabotaged. Modi, while attending to his Jamin' duties for the party, did catch wind of the plot. Those closest to his station were with much verbosity, & increasing loudness discussing the details of what they'd like to do to reverse the moratorium. Admittedly, not all the conversation was heard clearly. Luckily for Modi; however, was he had recently completed studies with honours at the local Adult Education Center. A course he thought would assist him reach a wider audience in his music career, being, "Help the Blind, Deaf, & Lame, & arrogant find a better Life." Majoring in lip reading & sign language. Calling for a scribe, Modi had what he could decipher transcribed onto parchment for legalities. He did know well that several attendees were quite incensed with his choices of tunes, & did not show any favour to Modi as Esther's guardian. He then tucked the parchment into his robe & continued with his jamin duties.

---

89. Purim, a Jewish festival lasting one month. Celebrating the 'salvation' of the Jewish people. It is celebrated one month before Passover. Esther 9.

The following afternoon, Esther had dropped in to Modi at his apartment for a Everton toffee*, & cake. Modi had earlier that morning removed the transcription from his robe, as he didn't want it to become smudged after washing. He had left the note on the kitchen table. Having hung out his robe, he then began finishing the icing on the date loaf, while making small talk with Esther. Seeing the note on the table, Esther did take a peak at it. First, thinking it might be an infringement of some kind that she, now as the 'Travel Agent/companion/partner' to A-Sue, would be able to settle. Realising the content, Esther did put to memory its main points, & quietly replaced the note to the table without a word to Modi. Graciously thanking her adopted pappy for the cake, & cuppa. Esther did return to her palace playground. Arriving home, Esther did call upon her 'Lady in Waiting of the bedchamber' to make a note for A-Sue for when she returned from other duties called for in the offices of India. Some weeks passed before A-Sue did arrive home. She did then immediately take steps on her step-up machine, verifying her weight loss. After being informed of the plot concocted the night of Esther's inauguration party, A-Sue did also contact the BPI offices (Bearers of Persian Investigators) to have them indagate the plot. The investigations came back with the disappointing knowledge to A-Sue, that it were fair-dinkum. The BPI did round up all those who at the night of the Esther celebrations, did conspire. They were formally charged, with tax evasion, & other crimes; particularly of laundering, & gossiping about the workplace. Being found guilty, all were summarily executed. One of those executed was a leading management voice of the RealEstate market. He had to be replaced.

With the role opening, of all candidates applying, it was Hardman, the Araldite selected to fill the void. He was of the 'Hammer n' Data storage unit who was a proficient chain-mail consultant. Having the opportunity at a higher position in the mogul's empire, Hardman was overjoyed. He did not waste much time. Parading about the places with his claque closely following as if higher than the pope. Being all to obliging to smarmy around him. Demanding everyone within eyeshot, or in his presence pay homage, proving his belief in deserving panegyric applause. Modi, however did flat refuse to submit to this utter nonsense. Finding Hardman's piety contrite. Modi did see Hardman as just an annoying, irritating Philodox*. Always in love with fame, & glory.

A STANDARD RELIGIOUSLY IRRELEVANT VERSION (S.R.I.V.)

Instead of any form of wisdom. He was therefore, known about the place attempting to overcompensate for his pitiful relevance deprivation syndrome. At Modi's flat insurrection, Hardman knew well he could only really look on with disdain for the bloke. He was not permitted to amerce, flagellate, or mulct in any way the legal protector of Esther. Which, really annoyed him. Tired of what was considered real rude, Hardman did conspire with several of his subordinates, to have Modi, his kin, & phratries all cancelled. On charges of unfairness, rudeness, & not adhering the current wokeness demanded of all citizenries. For good measure, Hardman did also provoke rumours about the places of very bad musicianing, thus, set about devising a public podium (with trapdoor) from which Modi, his kin, & any other undesirables could be sentenced, & punished publicly by cancelling.
The first production of a <u>Nisan</u>* came about in the twelfth year that the RealEstate company of A-Sue was listed on the Stockmarket. So excited about this, all the populations about the place related to Modi, & Esther held a competition. It ran for twelve months, where they did cast pur; i.e., Lots to see who'd become the proud own of a spanking Nisan. This caused much consternation with Hardman, as he was forced to adjudicate these run-of-the-mill castings.[90] Hardman then took it to A-Sue that under section 12, paragraph 15, of the gambling act of Marduk the inexplicable, that gambling was an unruly occupation, & entertainment past-time. It must be stopped, as the casting of Lots was only used in this empire by the clans of Modi. Others were excluded from participation, because of their ethnicity. That, he intimated, was unacceptable bigotry; racist, & phobic to any different clan.
A memo was then scribed by A-Sue, giving authority to Hardman to use necessary force to ensure the statute of Marduk was upheld. The memo was sent throughout the RealEstate empire. Causing great distress with the clans of Modi. Modi was one of the officials to receive the memo. Reading it, Modi's disposition became so hotly waxed, his garments did melt. Falling from his person as a steaming pile of ashen sackcloth melts. Most; unfortunately, this occurrence was during a fun run Modi was participating in. A charity fun run, raising awareness of the recently

---

90. Lots: a gambling set of 'stones' (dice) to determine the allocation of, or approval of the god, or god's or inheritance rights. See Esther 3:7.

achieved Diploma of Modi. To spare the sensitivities of onlookers, Modi smartly diverted his run & headed for home. Borrowing a spare participant bib to save a likeness of modesty. Siding to the wailing corner herald on the way home, Modi was informed the sackcloth melt that had just now fallen from his person, had become the height of fashion with his people. He did then make arrangements for another garment, & joined the wailing in support to protesters against the declarations of A-Sue & Hardman. Modi soon after joined a band of heralds wailing about the memo issued outside the palaces of Esther. In hope to draw her attention.

The ruckus certainly did pip the attention of Esther, for she did soon after have an official statement posted to Modi's personal royal account. Later that evening, while relaxing with an ancestry beverage; to the Knappogue Castle 12 Year, which happened to be Kosher, Modi did read the posting of Esther. It read:

"In much sympathy, I do post this correspondence to you dearest papa. I totally get the plight that has befallen our mob. I too share your disgust with that crooked fellow Hardman. Just wish he would stop being so self-righteous. You know, it's only a ruse he does to pretend to cover his irrelevance deprivation syndrome! I totally sympathise with the unfounded rumours about our people's musicianing skills. I myself am seriously considering taking up musicianing, despite that Hardman nincompoop. Having just begun singing lessons, & Sitar-ship from our well-qualified musical troop. Unsurprised, I am not all that good at either (lol). But, am hoping to be somewhat decent at both soon. For, in about 3months, I hope to throw a musical shindig of my own for A-Sue. I'm hoping she has received my invite. She is currently somewhere on the palace grounds. But, I can't seem to find her. This place is mammoth! Anywhen*, appreciate all you & other wailers have begun. Let's hope the result is positive. Take care now." L'Chaim![91] P.s. I'll see you Sunlight for a roast".

In reply, Modi did send the following: "Oh my little esky. How wonderful it is to hear your interest in musicianship. It has been a real booster to my mood. You know well, I just love it when others around me are joyous also. Not to be insensitive honey, but, might I make a few

---

91. Jewish greeting meaning "To Life!"

A STANDARD RELIGIOUSLY IRRELEVANT VERSION (S.R.I.V.)

suggestions? In your early days, you did try your luck at 'tickling the ol' ivories.' Honestly, please reconsider. Maybe, the better option would be to endure with the Sitar? Nonetheless, yeah, Hardman is way out of his depth. You know I'll support you in whatever you propose when you do find A-Sue. Ok, all the best. Keep practicing. I'll see you Sunlight. & we can compare musical notes (if you like. But no pressure). P.s. I hope you've sent me an invite to your concert?"
Receiving the reply, Esther did reconsider her position as an honorary musicianist. Taking seriously the request of Modi. She did drop the singing lessons. Scales, she thought were way too boring to practice. Besides, she could not get the hang of that highest C note. That very note, that could shatter the hardest of metamorphic* rocks in existing. Like, the appropriately labelled 'Painite'*. During the scale practicing, Esther did often think, this scale alone had broken her poor little vocal cords. With much other contemplation about all the Hardman fellow was attempting. Esther did have a memo scribed using the official Royal RealEstate Letterhead sent to all her kin subjects throughout the regions. In it, she did express that they should stage a mass protest about the places for three months. For, surely A-Sue would see reason, & reverse the Hardman decree. Success did visit upon all that Esther did propose. The three month protest was witnessed all about the places. Seeing Esther had used the official Letterhead, & being the official 'Travel Agent/companion/ partner to A-Sue, pleasingly there was nothing Hardman could do about it. Now, Esther had tried really hard at becoming a half-decent Sitarist. But, to no true avail. Lucky, however was it that just before the three months protest ended, A-Sue did call upon Esther again. They got to chatting, & decided they'd both like to have Hardman join them for a brunch one morning. The date was soon after set.
The morning arrived sooner than expected, along with Hardman. Setting an ambient atmosphere for the brunch, Modi, & several of his closest mucisianists were called upon. Whereto, hardman had no choice but to bite his lip, & act with civility. During conversations, Hardman was pressed to settle with his answer, a problem that A-Sue, & Esther found difficult to reconcile. Each lady, unbeknown to Hardman was playing devil's advocate. The question was, "What dishonour might be suitably visited upon an unfavoured personality?"

In quick response, Hardman, gasconading* did fall into the trap set. Replying, "Well my ladies, I would consider having the individual, or, individuals 'cancelled by wokeness.'" He snapped with much contempt behind his eyes. Little did he know, that this kind of response was encouraged, & even expected by A-Sue, & Esther. It did therefore entrap him, & his closest of advisors. Poor ol' Hardman & those conforming advisors all soon after had their own tongues tied. They were 'cancelled' in the very fashion they had desired for others they did disapprove. By wokeness did they each suffer terribly the consequences of their own scheming. Many years did pass after this episode in Esther's, & Modi's lifetime. There were plenty of great music festivals, & concerts. Musicianship schooling did spring up all over, becoming the rage throughout the regions. As for Esther, as great a 'RealEstate Travel Agent/companion/partner' she was. She is lauded to this moment for the actions she took to ensure that her people did receive great welfare, & peace throughout the lands.

POSTSCRIPT:

The following POSTSCRIPT parodies are from those texts considered gnostic* - extra-biblical. Being those that many scholars consider containing: Spiritual (mysterious) knowledge. These are not formally among the standard canon of Bible texts. Gnosticism was a prominent heretical movement of the 2nd-century Christian Church, partly of pre-Christian origin. Gnostic doctrine taught that the world was created and ruled by a lesser divinity, the demiurge, and that Christ was an emissary of the remote supreme divine being, esoteric knowledge (gnosis) of whom enabled the redemption of the human spirit. Below are a couple of gnostic texts remoulded in the same fashion as the former narratives. The following are a reevaluation of several assumed apostles: Paul, Peter, & an early tale about a female who became enamoured with Christianity through the 'preaching' of Paul. Concluding this jaunt through the Judaeo-Christian Bible with an 'After Thought.'

Reevaluation of Paul:[92]

Many things have been authored about the conducting of Paul, sem priest of the NHO community. It may be recalled that an extraordinary transformation of Paul occurred. Happening after an encounter with a very strange entity who did quite severely berate him for all his actions. The entity was unimpressed at the consistent badgering of the NHO. Paul was forced to admit, he was confronted by obstructing lights, & interrogated by a someone, or thing unknown. The entity was assumed to be from another realm, or, possibly dimension. From all recollections, Paul did spy the figure wearing a most luminous multicoloured horrifying vestment. Having a phosphoresce much gaudier than the Heat-lamp in the heaven; thus, it did distract, & disorientate him much. Causing him to stumble about a while as a drunkard, grovelling on his knees to the nearest wall, or tree that would assist him in uprightness. Was soon after this encounter that Paul did assume himself as a 'redeeming' figure. Considering that it was now, as one of the fatidical. His duty to 'illuminate' those who did bother stopping by to converse with him in the streets, Cynic-Gogues, or if he happened to be invited to someone's place. Paul, did after this encounter also claim many 'out-of-body' experiences; he did <u>volander</u>* on one accession with many visions & sights of far-reaching peoples & places. In this state, he did seem to become other than his physical self, an avatar drifting off into realms reserved for celestial types.

On one occasion that Paul did sit in Lotus, as if 'stoned,' Barney did miss the cue. So, Paul was forced to sit there for an extended period. On this occasion this did not bother him all that much for he did find himself going deeper in a trance-state than earlier experienced. His avatar was freed, & he did find himself traveling on the escalators in Heavens to Jerusalem. This journey he was to find out was not to seek

---

92. The following Postscript 'Reevaluations' are adapted from, Price, R. The Pre-Nicene New Testament: Paul, Section VIII The Pauline Cycle: #53. Location 31164 -.

A STANDARD RELIGIOUSLY IRRELEVANT VERSION (S.R.I.V.)

approval, but to be acclaimed in equivalence with the NHO saints. Was on such an occasion that Paul did become acknowledged as kind of redeemer of the 'elect.' Traveling the escalator on his way to the 'holey city', Paul did meet with a child who did ask him, "Where are thou going? To which place do you seek?" In reply Paul did announce his intent to go to Jerusalem of the celestial & catch up with several NHO mates. The child did then also announce, "I am in Spirits dear Paul, & am sent to accompany you. So, dear fellow become entranced. Allow thee avatar relaxing deeply & soar with unsecured mind, with eyes of noticing. For, in where we now go, I will show thee the hidden things that are visible." At that, the Spirits did snatch the avatar of Paul up, through a 'third' of Heaven, then a 'quarter' Heaven. Whereto Paul did hear to open the eyes, & peer at the images on the place where he was sitting. There, did Paul recognise his self-sitting in Lotus, with a rabble surrounding him. They did all appear as specks of grain in his sight. In the fourth of the Heaven, Paul did also spy numerous celestial, each of their ranking; some were appearing as divine, yet others unkindly were of a disposition. These were they who did thieve the soul of those who took residence in their <u>eternal boxes</u>*. Residing now in the catacomb, the charnel house. Having upended these souls on a rug, the unkindly of celestial were beating them for their much dirtiness. They were berating them thus at the gates whenever the souls of the now sign mortgages on their long-term box residences. The souls did wail allowed: "Oy, what the, just please fetch a pale of celestial waters. Turf it over the mortgage contracts. Then, those contracts will be smudged, & unreadable. You could all therefore cease from your berating & unkindliness directed at us poor buggers." Then, the Toll collector at the gate did announce, "Why should I? Why did thee not bathe, & have your indenture scrutinised by a lawyer before signing off on it?" The soul did announce again then, "Oh, go on please. If you are not satisfied with thy smudginess after, produce witnesses to confirm." It became so.

Then, I Paul did snap from this enchanted spectacle to be in the hearing again of the Spirits. They this time did issue this statement, "Hurry on laggard!" Which did then cause Paul's feet to stumble through to a Fifth of Heaven. There with him stood his mates, & their accompanying Spirits & avatars too. Here, all did behold a Nephi-lim representative, majestic in stature, carrying an iron rod. With him were three others of just as big a majestic-ness also. All three began with enthusiasm a competition to drive the dirtiness souls through to savvy acumen. We all did hop it through to a Sixth of Heaven where we all did encounter luminescence. Stumbling through the grounds, the teams of avatars did finally reach another gate. Siding to the keeper, Paul did bellow for the gate to become unlocked. The Nephi-lim & their rods were getting closer to their presence with every strike out. The toll keeper did then unlatch the entrance, where we did all find ourselves in the Seventh of Heaven. Here, all did notice an old geezer clad in the radiation of a most luminous vestment. Set upon an imposing stool did this geezer begin to howl a question, "for where are you headed?"

Clearing his throat, Paul's <u>avatar</u>* did quiver & signal to him, saying, "sorry your eminencies, but I'm trying to find the place from where I once was?" The elderly One did retort, "from where might that have been?" At that there was a showing to an entrance to the Eighth of Heavens. The avatar of Paul now did reply, "I know they are here somewhere. I'm here to lead the impaired from out of exile in the Babylon." It was here that the Twelve mates did reappear, & arm-in-arm did we all ascend to a Ninth of Heavens where we were met with all the denizens of that realm. We did all ascend further to the Tenth if Heavens, & all Spirits did congratulate with much saintly salutation each other.

A STANDARD RELIGIOUSLY IRRELEVANT VERSION (S.R.I.V.)

Paul's acting with Thecla:

It did happen on one occasion, with a few Sputniks, Demas, & Homogenes who did virtue signal much about everything that Paul, & they did all their days in Antioch. Becoming bored, they soon did choose to leave Antioch, & headed for Iconium. During their travels, Paul did give them the rubber ear regards their exaggerating alibosh*. Choosing to not rebuff them but occasionally. Rather, he was most kind & showing much patience. He did catechise them both in his branding of gnosis only when they did mix up their stories.

Arriving in Iconium the three strangers to the town were sightseeing many days. Passing one store-holder who did overhear their conversations, Onesiphorus. (Onesiphorus: who did gift Paul the One-se* he did attempt to recover from Philly). He did become interested in the gnosis of Paul, & enthusiastically did invite him, & his party to his home. Despite not formerly knowing Paul, Onesiphorus was by Tight-as given a description of this strangest of urf's*; being short, valgus*, crooked of nose, having deep-set eyes & was bald. A character of no great difference to any other, aside his tendency to bipolar; a well-adjusted middle aged 'angelic-type' preacher one moment. The next, a raging lunatic of excitableness. It was these qualities that tipped Onesiphorus off. These qualities did Onesiphorus notice, & promptly made invitations, & small talk. That he & his fellows, if they were of similar disposition, were invited to share their gnosis. The three did accept the invitation, & did share with the household of Onesiphorus the house duties of breaking much bread, & quotidian invocation. Was not long before Paul did begin sermoning to the household that: "Blessed be the central thoughts, & emotions of your being, that you are the essence of every deity." So, "Forget not the 'temple' of your person. It must needs be kept unsullied & preserved." Regards a deity, he did announce "It would be of greatness to remain chaste unto the deity. Not paying much homage to worldly things. Then, the deity will surely be accepting of thee." To much surprise, Paul did also encourage chastity, & other forms of loneness, stating: "Regards a wife. Not ideal, but acceptable if one does treat each other as single. Applying the mandates to each other as consecrated virgins, for rewards to consecration are abundant." It was teaching like these that did captivate, & bemuse his audience much. While Paul did continue to bellow with such a sermon, there was a lass in the next-door residence who was sunbathing on the roof listening with intent, all that Paul was saying. Her name was Thecla. So charmed by the seminars of Paul was Thecla, that she did refuse to eat, or drink while Paul did blabber on, & on, & on… about all virtues of asceticism*. Even refusing acknowledgment of her betrothed Thamyris, when he was summoned to see to budge her from her stupor. But stuck like a glued papyrus to the roof was Thecla. She did remain so fastened that all who did assume to break her daze did mourn as if Thecla had been lost. Likened to paying her debt to nature, was Thecla.

Distraught much was Thamyris. His uxoriousness for her was no longer returned by her former maritality*. Confused, & greatly disturbed at this development, Thamyris did set about investigating what was so damn luring. What was the meaning behind her clear, & evident hickering*. Was this the beginning of his long-term fear, that Thecla would fall into feresy*. Asking who the hell it was that was encouraging celibacy for both men, & any future bride. Rushing outside into the street Thamyris did happen upon Demas, & Homogenes in much virtue signalling argument. Begging them to offer explanation for what was happening? Demas, & Homogenes however lied about knowing the man Paul. Instead confirming that he sounded as a man possessed with vengeance to make miserable all who did wish to be betrothed. That if man, or virgin did cohabit, & inevitably engage in 'interconnectedness' & bring forth a progeny, well that was just plain imprudent, as it would mean that nobody would be able to really enjoy any kind of decent life; career's would become burdensome. Always having to provide for the progeny, travel restricted, wealthiness drained then retirement would come sooner than expected, & not long then, retirement to a defunctus hospice. Thamyris did invite Demas, & Homogenes to dine with them, pressing them with his concerns that Thecla had become a lost soul.

A STANDARD RELIGIOUSLY IRRELEVANT VERSION (S.R.I.V.)

Hearing this Demas, & Homogenes did scheme a little in their minds, speaking that Thamyris should file a charge against Paul. That he is attempting to woo Thecla's affections. Maybe, Paul was also obsessed with subverting the 'normal' course of human interaction? Like all manipulative ego ramp operators, was he attempting to manipulate some to join their cause for a small fee; by enticing celibacy, & then-encouraging the attracted audience to revere him as an icon.

Next morning Thamyris did just as Demas & Homogenes did imply, taking a syndic, <u>alcaide</u>*, & a large mob of disenchanted singles to arrest Paul at the house of Onesiphorus. Charging Paul with, subverting the ordinary course of human <u>reciprocity</u>*; encouraging celibacy, & some acts of preternatural self-denial, & unauthorised icon reverence. He was soon after <u>cuff & stuffed</u>*. Taken forcefully back to the circus of judgement where the dominus magister did accuse Paul much with dissent, & perversion of ordinary life activities. At that Paul did begin a spray: "How dare you accuse me. I am only announcing that the Deus which has become known to many people, is a wickedly vengeful mongrel. Demanding mere anthropoids like us, have no fun in this life. If any fun be had while sentient, you wilt surely sup with <u>zabalus</u>*, & be forever condemned to remain a lowly <u>pereginus</u>*." At the hearing of the ears of these statements, the magistrate did remand Paul for a future official judicial hearing. In <u>bilboes</u>*his <u>sorrowful tale</u>* began. Manacled by his ankles, Paul was detained hanging upside down in a cell of a nearby <u>stone tavern</u>*. There were no available restraints at shoulder height. Before the week had finished, Thecla did get word of this inhumanness, & did bribe his captor with a promise to allow him angel's oil.[93] The alcaide did then release the cell door, allowing Thecla visiting rights to Paul. She did set herself to not become too emotional, but hearing that Paul was in an upright mood, despite the constant head rushing that she could intently not help lay about in bliss on the cell floor listening again in a stupor. Her maritality for Paul did seem to become excessive. Clearly, she did set eyes on Paul as her magister.

The absence of Thecla was felt by her family & they did wonder to where she might have disappeared. The night previous, she had still been as a glued parchment to the roof. But, now she had disappeared.

---

93. An 'angel'. Lesley Blume, was 15th Century gold coin.

After much interrogation of friends & the like, Thecla was found in a similar posture inside the cell of Paul, listening affectionately to his burbling head gushiness. Both, were immediately required to present their plea to the magistrate again. The mob of single Law students in the courthouse as part of their studies, then did announce with much loudness, "Go on ya bugger. We believe you are nothing but a magsman*; a swindling snake oil salesman. Deserving early retirement to the impaired hospice. Nick off with you. Back to where you came." Despite this, the magistrate did remain calm, & delighted of ear. He did after everyone calmed down, seek a reason why Thecla had refused her betrothed. But, Thecla did just stare at Paul, riveted to his countenance all the more. Incensed, Thecla's mother then did berate her daughter, calling her a witch to be judged by the Olympic flame. They were each compelled to enter the odeon & sign up for an event. Paul, was compelled to show his whipping skills. With much whipping-cheer* did he have to proved by. While Thecla was indulged to prove her ectomorphic skills at running the trap lines; a series of burning hoops.[94] Thecla did prove true to her word, for the burning hoops did take no effect on her. Thus, proving her strength to extinguish all advances. Paul, meanwhile along with Onesiphorus' family did hide out in a antre dwelling to recover from the whipping contest. Spending much time invoking the higher powers, & fasting several times a day with them. Hunger taking grip of their bellies, Paul did send the young ones to fetch some food from the local corner stall holder. Was about the time the children were about to set about begging bread, that one of them did spy their former neighbour Thecla. Siding to her, they did asked, "Waaz Up girl?" Thecla did in reply make noises that she was searching for the Paul fellow ever since she had proven her resilience to remain maidenly. The children did then offer to take her to him. Arriving at the antre they did find Paul invoking much in loudness, pleading the safety of Thecla. That she might find it irksome to fall victim to the flame. Standing behind him, Thecla did startle Paul announcing in all hearing, "Oh boy, oh boy! This day has seen me vindicated & returned to your presence dearest Paul." The two of them did become forged as bestie sputniks. Thecla did invoke with Paul, asking that she

---

94. 'Burning hoops' - symbolic of male lust meant as a test to Thecla's commitment to celibacy.

A STANDARD RELIGIOUSLY IRRELEVANT VERSION (S.R.I.V.)

might hang around with him till time does pass to oblivion. Paul in answer did say, "Oh my dear, I'd really like the company. Yet, I must trumpet a warning that seeing your beauty is mammoth; eventually, you maybe overcome at some time by the flame..." to this Thecla did retort, "Even so, I have proven my carapace to withstand the flame. Don't you see I am immune from tempting, no matter the hotness." Little time did pass when Paul did send Onesiphorus & his kin back home, & both he & Thecla did move on through to Antioch.

Thecla was again tempted with much flame. Even being harassed by certain people of very high standing. But, Thecla did resist, rebuking any advancing to her person. Incensed, by Thecla's resistance she was again sent to the odeon*. This time, placed before a fierce lioness. Who did merely snuggle her feet a while much to the delight of spectators. She was again confronted by all manners of fierce beasts. All crowds waited with baited wheezing for Thecla to be laniated*. But, they did all destroy themselves in their attempts with Thecla. There was in that place a mote separating the spectators from the beasts, & Thecla did upon witnessing the sanctity of her person at the wanton destruction of all the beasts that did confront her, she did decide that it was time for a baptismal class. This she conducted herself, for herself. Entering the deluge* after deciding on a swan-dive she did immerse herself in the mote of unexpected emotion*. Many other trials of the flame did Thecla confront still. Yet, all failed, & her immunity to them did become strengthened. Having been separated from Paul during all this trialing, she did again desire to catch up with him. Being told he had now departed to Myra, of Lycia. She did then decide to be a little flamboyant & did cross-dress as a male & headed in that direction. Finding her bestie again, she did side up to him & stood beside his thigh while he did continue preaching* with much enthusiasm. After which Thecla did announce to the surprise of Paul that she had enough fruit for a life-time. Oh, & she had organised lessons in baptism*, considering she had to endure much flaming opportunities. The baptism classes certainly strengthening her immunity... Thecla during her time spent with Paul, & on those occasions apart did be thrown to many flaming prospects. She did however endure, & overcome each with flying colours. She was eighteen years when she did first take that step to listen to the words of Paul, & she did be transferred to the presence of the ancient ol' El, to Ministry of all things at age Ninety. Thus, ends the tale of Paul & Thecla.

The Petrine Reevaluation:

The following 'waffling' articulated from now by 'Peter' are said to be of most value. They are said to be offering numerous great articulations to those 'neglected' voices of the early NHO community. These are some recovered recordings of some of Pete's earliest waffle blogs regards his revered Iesous. Though withdrawn from the accounts of the other Itinerate research fellows, Pete does incorporate many similarities with them. Many early NHO sects revered the personalities found in the tales of The Activation. Considering the Iesous (I Am), was a kind of better reincarnation of the first Humankind's. "Peter speaks of the need for the True Prophet [Humankind›s-Iesous (I Am)], to come, and set things right."[95]

Peter does refute the claim by Paul, of being the first emissary. Considering him (Paul) as does the other Itinerate researchers of I Am followers, as the Anti-Iesous. This waffling of Peter is set from the time of the 'Cancellation' of Iesous, the I Am near, or soon after the wiping of 'responsibility', & the harsh sentencing for his 'Cancellation' handed down by the Pilate of proceedings. None but the Pilate, neither any accuser, or kingly type being Herod assumes to wipe responsibility from themselves from the charge, & subsequent 'Cancellation' (of Iesous I Am). All did refuse cleansing, so the Pilate arose revulsed that sanitation was not a priority. Herod then did make much noise of instruction, sanctioning the proceeding of the charges, & punishment of Iesous. Standing with the executioner's & accusers was Joseph. Friend to the pilate & Iesous, the accused. He did seek to be promised to take possession of Iesous before After-Light had descended. Hide him away for that was the best that was observed succeeding a cancellation event. All having best to be completed before the onset of much After-Light. That being the sanctified custom.

When Iesous did become a delivery to be cancelled, the people there did mock, & spit upon him un-reverentially. He was cloaked in purple,

---

95. Price, Robert M. The Pre-Nicene New Testament:... Location, 22987.

A STANDARD RELIGIOUSLY IRRELEVANT VERSION (S.R.I.V.)

had a spiny papyrus <u>coronal</u>* placed on his head, was slapped in the cheek, punched in the eyes & made to set himself upon a crude, rickety throne as if a judge. The executioners did then bring two iniquitous people, & they too were 'cancelled' along with Iesous who did remain dumb despite the soreness that cancelling was approved to inflict on a soul. They did also rent his garments out as party attire when one of the condemned did pike up, announcing "Oy vey! What deserving is this treatment of this fellow? As far as we know, he's of no threat to any but himself. We, however has committed iniquity against another. Very bad of you to inflict the same penalty as ours. Pitiful really, just shows how badness is your sliding to wokeness!" At that voicing, their legs were snapped in two that they would feel the true effects of their sentence. But, to prolong the torments of his sentencing, Iesous' same body parts were not touched.

It was just after lunch that a schedule could be slotted to have Iesous' sentencing occur. At that time, After-Light did begin earlier than expected shocking the entire place. Any cancelling was to occur prior to the beginning of After-Light, so fear, & distress did come across the faces of all involved. They did all then scramble to find lamps, being tricked into believing After-Light had arrived. After-Light did again believe, as the before occurrence in Kamit, it had won over. During the commotion, & <u>incertitude</u>*, Iesous did make loud the following, "My power, my power, thou hast forsaken me." Yet, few did hear these words. He was then taken up. In that hour the vail of the temple of Jerusalem was rent in twain.[96] Such destruction of a beloved icon, tourist attraction annoyed greatly religious authorities. Not too distant after these things, was the nails of hands & feet of Iesous painted. A terrible job happened though, for there was also much shivering, & swaying of things about the place. Though it would not have been known at the time, this shuddering measured 9.9 on the seismic magnitude scale. Terrifying the population. Soon after, Light had again peeked out from the cloud & many did begin rejoicing much. Realising their actions were not at all of many merits, several did become wounded in mind, believing themselves as of no greater virtuous value than any other. They did seek refuge in a cloakroom. Hoping the fiasco would just all blow over, & a resumption of quotidian activities return.

---

96. Menzies, A.

As the latest 'victim' to succumb to cancellation had been becoming a great celebrity throughout the lands, it was thought best to station turkey bacon about the places most frequented by the cancelled, & others. That he not be able to reinvent his former self & so become an established eminence. It did become so. Soon, after there was much fanfare about the places that were under guard. The stationed security did hear eviscerated voices about them, did witness much cloud partying. Several figures did enter the place where he who had been cancelled lay resting. When, there did appear three from that place, & the security did witness, & be in hearing that three avatars passing over to the Heaven announcing, "Thou hast preached to them that sleep. A response was heard from the cross, Yea."[97] Soon after, it was established, after consultation with the Pilot that all present mouths become zipped. Thus, not a word was told about these freakishness events.

The following dawn Mary Magdalen, a reformed fibbertyjibbet* did side to the hide out of Iesous after his cancellation. Entering the place she did come to see it empty of even a speck of dust, for it had been meticulously cleaned.[98] She did then make questions of one who set idol calving a wooden totem out in the garden. He did ask, "What's the go lady? If you seek the prior resident of that place, well, sorry. You're in no luck. Must have been tripping, but I did witness a likeness of his avatar up, & depart just earlier."

The day this all did occur was the final day the people were compelled to eat flat bread in celebration of the ancient inventing of harvest & bread making. After their fill everyone were departing the main gathering spots, heading back home. The most ardent of Iesous' playfellows who were still real baffled, & upset of the cancellation process. They too did slink home, but not til the following After-Light. It was out of fear & recognition which would surely lead them to also be 'cancelled' in such a brutal fashion. Several of them did then choose to make a hiding out in dilapidated housing apartments & abandoned buildings earmarked for demolition. It was I (stoner) Pete, n' Dru however who did shrug all this off. We rather did decide to get on with life. So, we went back to playing, & encouraging our pet fish to exercise in their nets…

---

97. Ibid., (Vol. 9, p. 8).
98. Fibbertyjibbet - see Glossary.

A STANDARD RELIGIOUSLY IRRELEVANT VERSION (S.R.I.V.)

The Reevaluation of Pete (Stoner):

While in trance state, I Pete (Stoner) did happen upon concluding the latest reevaluation in recollection of how I & several other of I Am's Itinerate colleagues did perceive a number of things. We were all told: ...there will come a present, & or future moment when numbers of imprecise forecasters of what was, is, & will become. They will show themselves as divergent. Being highly misinforming & perceptively indecent. They will endeavour to persuade the listener to badness. You will know them by the poor naming of them. The thirsty will sometime after drink of purified spring waters, be satiated much. But, those childish enough to be unrecognising of badness will be sent to the bad houses to be as second-class as they wish for a long moment.

Then we, the twelve playfellows were encouraged to follow Iesous I Am into a mountain. There, we did perform many mystery rituals each with the other. While these were performed, we did seek to become familiar in knowing what kind, & of what personalities were the ethical, principled virtue signallers. That incitement of any heedful of our waffling might also become enticers like us. Suddenly, a couple of strangers did appear from nowhere. We were not able to catch their countenances properly, as they did wear each a luminous vestment that lighted up the entire mountain; bathing it in <u>extolment</u>* none have witnessed aside the countryman Paul.

The account of Paul is much unconfirmed, as we all did know him as a hot-headed scoundrel bent on nastiness to all of us. As we looked upon the strangers, we were astounded; for their bodies were whiter than any snow and ruddier than any rose; and the red thereof was mingled with the white, and I am utterly unable to express their beauty; for their hair was curly and bright and seemly both on their face and shoulders. As it were a wreath woven of spikenard and divers-coloured flowers, or like a rainbow in the sky, such was their seemliness.[99] Shielding my eyes a little to turn to ask Iesous who these eerie guys were, Iesous did in a punishing manner say, "These are they who you have just now asked to know the appearance. C'mon, use a little of that grey matter will you. How can you not know now that to ask me something, inevitably ends with an answer not expected?"

I, & the other playfellows were then found in avatar, & we were whisked to a country outside this world we knew. There, we did spy many niceties, & other personalities clad much the same as these two standing before us. How, any knew their different naming, is anyone's guess. Looking non-singularity was they each. Further, it was not the easiest thing to know what any were saying; all being in unison of speech, & song they did ne'er to find a halting spot. Iesous then did inform us all that this place was set aside for the goodly of men, & other wondrous things. He did then point to another spot. Being dankly, suffocating & stygian.

The figures there were not very wondrous to spy. Many of them were being as if tormented. In that space were the tongues of all who did blaspheme with much hurting voices, utterances, & oaths. These we were informed, were to be forever tormented by a flickering 'electro plasm*.' That would lash, & gash them. There were lots of the adulterous there too. Being tormented by head gushiness at having been hung by the ankles. I did hear announce, "I should like to refrain from this place." With anguish, & much sobbing did they carry on about not wanting to be there anymore. They'd had enough, & would prefer now to go home. Voicing loudly, "Is it just me, or is it real hot in here?" There was in that place much over-casted, angry looking cloud. A place where many 'Cane/Coward types' were. These folk were being frowned upon with much anger by many Druid's, & snake salesmen. Who did remind every refractory personality in that place, of their deceitfulness as they had given snakes, & Druids a very bad rap about the places. There were lots & lots of folk in that place too, who were coerced to sit in filth, & goriness. Oozing about the places was filthy goriness. Very surprised were we to notice that progeny was being given life here. But, as soon as they did 'pop them out', the

---

99. Ibid., (Vol. 9, p. 145).

A STANDARD RELIGIOUSLY IRRELEVANT VERSION (S.R.I.V.)

eyes of all mothers were inflicted with electro plasmic sparks; "these were the accursed who conceived and caused abortion." It was said.

Numbers of people seductively bit their lips also in this place. They soon were poked in the eyes with hot-pokers. These are they who were not very nice to others in mouth, & who insisted on being stupidly, irrationally provoked by all stupid things imaginable. Think the silliest reason. Then, double that to an irrational point. That's how badly anserous things became for them. There some who were partially consumed by electro plasm, having their mid-sections ticked relentlessly, & harshly by Helminthophbia. Being greatly gripped with fear of worms. Looking about there were even some whose whole mouths were likened to fire. Gnawing at their tongues each for the things said falsely, or insincerely about people. Disingenuous are these virtue signallers. In this place was much disturbing sights, smells, acts being committed, & metered to another because as we were informed, much deserving of these harshnesses, & mistreating were the people inflicted with such horribleness. There was in those places, much miserableness, & other traumatic tormenting... with many unable to 'gain a feather to fly with.' Their luck having had run aground. Such great & horrendous things were shown to us in this place, we have decided to avow a silence for they should ne'er really be known to many people. Except maybe the sadist of all classes, & groupings of men. What we, the few playfellows of Iesous did witness while in trance, is the stuff of a very disturbed mind under duress.

AFTER THOUGHT:

All circumstances of life, are said to have been birthed by spontaneous Logos (reason) by a great El. Its resolute standing in the present has been continuously plagued by much dissent, & confusion of thoughts, deeds, & ideologies. Shaping all known histories. Few, it does seem have a knowledge, or care for past experiences & miseries of those histories. Many of which have been appropriately addressed, & impartially reconciled. Nonetheless, the ignorant, arrogant, insincere, calophantic insist on all past abominations be dredged all over, & those long-lost contributing personalities are vilified, & permanently stricken from all records. The unwise are forgetful of history; that unless appropriately acknowledged, & lessons learned, that history will repeat. Enlightenment as proposed & opined these days, should nay be focused solely on the present. Yet, 'History' teaches much of upheaval, & injustice. Also of much wonder & betterment. Modern enlightenment however is subject to the woke sensitivities of the individual. But the prevailing knowledge is, in truth where-ever tribes, & phratries do settle are there both good, & bad happenings, & things. These undoubted are the causes of actuality.

Thus, Humankind's, & The Eve progenies survive, & adapt accordingly, just as before. Language, & more expressive ways of communication evolve alongside other inventiveness. Yet to many, proposals of regression are appealing. Again, just as Mo-she the earlier did once announce in the hearing of Meander's own history tale; It is of a high & most valued standard, & a much valuable commodity that the teaching, & rearing of the younger in mathematics, philosophy, astronomy, Human Relations, the Sciences, histories, & the humanities. All traditional educations shall be lauded above another, less sensible, but more confusing of reality, & goodness. For it is considered of great disservice to the younger, & all generations to

A STANDARD RELIGIOUSLY IRRELEVANT VERSION (S.R.I.V.)

be grievously replacing all these with an encroaching of irrationalism, ideologisms, insensitivities to reality. Those things that only espouse a maintenance of superficiality, & dumbness of attempting to reshape or abolish all prior learnings, as with any greatness in deed.

Human Relations, & the getting along with another, despite persuasion must be of the highest of conduct. Reality trumps wokeness; we all made our presence known in far-flung exotic regions. Homes do continue to spin on an invisible axis, & still nobody does get all that dizzy. Except it would seem, those that over many moments do become outdated. They then because of their ageing, face the wall. Eventually, becoming the ceremonious citizens of great somnolence. So it is; sentience, survival, animations begin, & become forsaken, & lost. Some folk vanish just as their ancestor Differently Able had done. Having a disastrous moment, or encounter with a Cane/Coward type. Some became 'lost'. Regrettably, so goes the cycle of things. Yet, let it be forever remembered. Existence itself is a wonder. It is encouraged; therefore; begin each morning announcing; meetings between the ignorant, nosy, ungrateful, arrogant, envious, unsociable, the pretentious woke is inevitable. They cannot help their indifference to Light, & After-Light. It is I who understand the difference, but do also know I have a share in the same human nature as they.

My sockdolager* to the woke, & you dear reader:

"Absolute futility," says the Teacher. "Absolute futility. Everything is futile." What does a person gain for all his efforts that he labors at under the sun? A generation goes and a generation comes, but the earth remains forever. The sun rises and the sun sets; panting, it hurries back to the place where it rises. Gusting to the south, turning to the north, turning, turning, goes the wind, and the wind returns in its cycles. All the streams flow to the sea, yet the sea is never full; to the place where the streams flow, there they flow again. All things are wearisome, more than anyone can say. The eye is not satisfied by seeing or the ear filled with hearing. What has been is what will be, and what has been done is what will be done; there is nothing new under the sun. Can one say about anything, "Look, this is new"? It has already existed in the ages before us. There is no remembrance of those who came before; and of those who will come after there will also be no remembrance by those who follow them."[100]

    Here, let our conversation be <u>blocked at both ends</u>*. May your lives be always spent till that end with <u>honorificabilitudinitas</u>*. It's "<u>All Holiday</u>*." <u>Amen</u>*.

---

100. Christian Standard Bible (Ec 1:2–11). (2020). Holman Bible Publishers. My emphasis.

BIBLIOGRAPHY:

- Astle. D. David Astle's 101 weird words (& 3 fakes). Copyright © text, David Astle 2018. First Published by Allan & Unwin in 2018. This edition, Kobo ed.
- Arguments of Celsus,… Against The Christians. Published by Good Press, 2022. Kobo Electronic edition.
- Babcock. J. - Dictionary of Daffynitions, (A-Z Werdz). Copyright © 20212 James, F. Babcock. Kobo electronic ed.
- Barrett. G. The Unofficial Dictionary of Unofficial English. Copyright © 2006 The McGraw-Hill Companies, Inc. Kobo Edition.
- Blume. L.M.M. - 'Let's Bring Back' The Lost Language Edition. Copyright © 2013 by Lesley M. M. Blume. Kobo Ed.
- Botham. N. The Mammoth book of useless information. © Text copyright Noel Botham 2012. Kobo electronic edition.
- Bowler. P. - The Complete Superior Person's Book of Words. This Electronic Edition Published in 2016 by Bloomsbury Publishing Plc. Copyright © 1979, 1982, 1992, 2001 by Peter Bowler.
- Bristow. J. - Old English words & terms: A glossary for historians. Third Ed. Digital Version published 2012. Copyright © Joy Bristow 2001. Bookmasters, Inc.
- Burgess. G. - Burgess Unabridged: A New Dictionary of words you have always needed. DigiCat, 2022. Kobo Ed.
- Bushby. T. - The Crucifixion of Truth. Copyright © Tony Bushby 2004. Second Printing 2006. Joshua Books.com.
- ——— The Christ Scandal. Published by Stanford House in 2008. Copyright © Tony Bushby 2008.
- Cardona. D. - God Star. Trafford Publishing. Copyright © 2006 Dwardu Cardona.
- Cousineau. P. - Wordcatcher. Copyright ©2010 by Phil Cousineau. Kobo Ed.

- Crystal. D. - Words in Time and Place. Oxford University Press. Copyright© 2014 David Crystal. (OUP).
- —— The Disappearing Dictionary, Electronic Ed., 2016 Pan Books. Copyright © 2015 David Crystal.
- Edwards. E. - Words, Facts, & Phrases: A Dictionary of Curious, Quaint, & Out-of-the-way Matters. Barnes & Nobel. 2011, Kobo Ed.
- Fenton. S. - The Odford Dictionary - New Meaning Edition. Copyright © 2010, Steve Fenton.
- Forsyth. M. - The Horologicon. Kobo Ed. Text Copyright © 2012 Mark Forsyth.
- Floyd. E. Randall. - The Dark Side of History… Kindle Edition. Copyright © 2018, by E. Randall Floyd.
- Gillard. J. - Little Book of Lost Words. Copyright © 2019 Joe Gillard.
- Grose. F. (Editor) - The Dictionary of Vulgar Tongue. Copyright © First 1811. This ebook edition. First published 2013 by Hesperus Press Ltd.
- Hauser. F. - The Golden Ratio: The facts, & the myths. Createspace Independent Publishers. Kindle Ed.
- Howard. P. - Lost Words: A feast of forgotten words, their origins & their meanings. Copyright © Philip Howard 2012. The Roberson Press. (This ed. Kobo Electronic edition.
- Jones. Paul Anthony. - The Accidental Dictionary. Copyright © Paul Anthony Jones 2016. Kobo Edition.
- —— Word Drops., Copyright © 2016 Paul Anthony Jones. Kobo Edition.
- —— The Cabinet of Linguistic Curiosities. Copyright © 2017 Paul Anthony Jones.
- Kacirk. J. - The Word Museum. Copyright © 2000, Jeffrey Kacirk. Kobo Electronic Ed.
- Kirov. B. - Sophocles: Quotes, & Facts. Copyright © 2016 by Blago Kirov. Kobo Ed.
- Koenig. J. - The Dictionary of Obscure Sorrows. Copyright © 2021 John Koenig. Simon & Shuster. Electronic Ed.

A STANDARD RELIGIOUSLY IRRELEVANT VERSION (S.R.I.V.)

- Price. Robert M. - The Politically Correct Bible. eBookIt.com. Kindle Edition. Copyright 2013 Robert M. Price.
- ———— The Pre-Nicene New Testament: Fifty-four Formative Texts. Signature Books. Kindle Edition. Copyright 2006 Signature Books. All rights reserved. Signature Books is a registered trademark of Signature Books Publishing, LLC.
- Menzies. A. (Ed.). (1897). - The Gospel according to Peter. In J. A. Robinson (Trans.), The Gospel of Peter, the Diatessaron of Tatian, The Apocalypse of Peter, the Visio Pauli, The Apocalypses of the Virgil and Sedrach, The Testament of Abraham, The Acts of Xanthippe and Polyxena, The Narrative of Zosimus, The Apology of Aristides, The Epistles of Clement (Complete Text), Origen's Commentary on John, Books I-X, and Commentary on Matthew, Books I, II, and X-XIV (Vol. 9, p. 7). New York: Christian Literature Company. Logos Bible Software 9.9. Copyright 2000 - 2021. Licensee: Steve Morgan.
- Meltzer. P. E. - The Thinker's Thesaurus. (Expanded Third Edition) Copyright © 2015, 2010, 2005 by Peter E. Meltzer. Kobo Edition.
- Nugent. C. - Colin's Repurposed New English Dictionary. EyeBooks. Kobo Ed./Copyright © Colin V. Nugent 2020.
- Reader's Digest, Reverse Dictionary, (and Lexicon of difficult Words). Copyright © Reader's Digest (Aust.) Pty Limited 1989, 1990, 2003, 2004.
- Roberts. C. - Lost English. Electronic ed. published 2012. Copyright © Michael O'Mara books Limited 2009.
- Schillinger. L. - Word Birds. Copyright © 2013 Liesel Schillinger & Elizabeth Zechel. Kobo Ed.
- Shipley. J. T. - Dictionary of Word Origins. Copyright © 1989 by Philosophical Library. [Kobo Ed.] published in 2021 by Open Road Integrated Media, Inc.
- Taggart. C. - 500 Beautiful Words. Copyright © 2020 Caroline Taggart. Kobo Ed.
- ———— New Words for Old. Copyright © Caroline Taggart 2015. Kobo edition.

- Tangas, Sunny. - Metaphysical Dictionary 2nd Edition. Kensho Thinimi Society. Kindle Edition.
- Teeter. Emily. - Religion and Ritual in Ancient Egypt. Cambridge University Press. Kindle Edition. First Published Sept., 2011, © Cambridge University Press 2011.
- Wilkinson. Toby. - Writings from Ancient Egypt (Penguin Classics). Penguin Books Ltd. Kindle Edition. First published in Penguin Classics 2016. Introduction and translations copyright © Toby Wilkinson, 2001.
- Wood. J. Rev. - Dictionary of Quotations from Ancient & Modern, English & Foreign Sources. DigiCat Pub., 2022. Kobo Ed. Lexicophilia - www.lexicophilia.com

Fig 1: CUNEIFORM: Cu-nei-form script

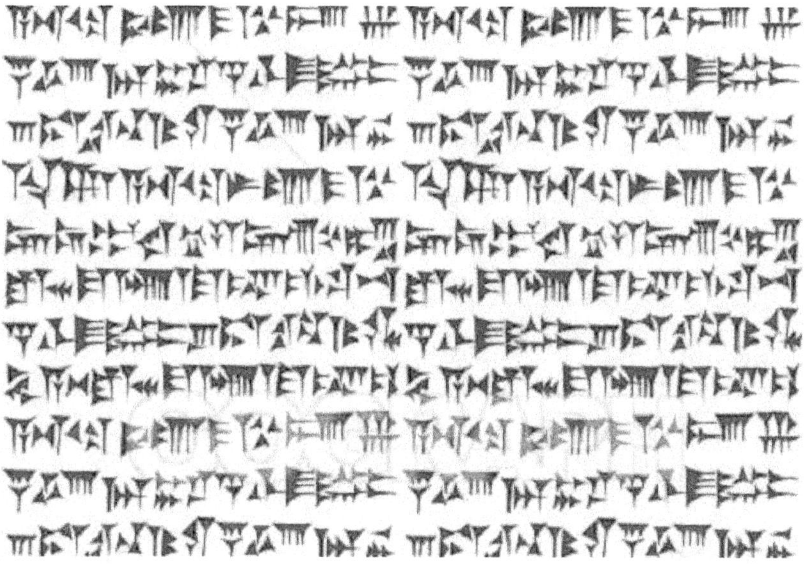

Fig 2: Prophetic Animal Language script

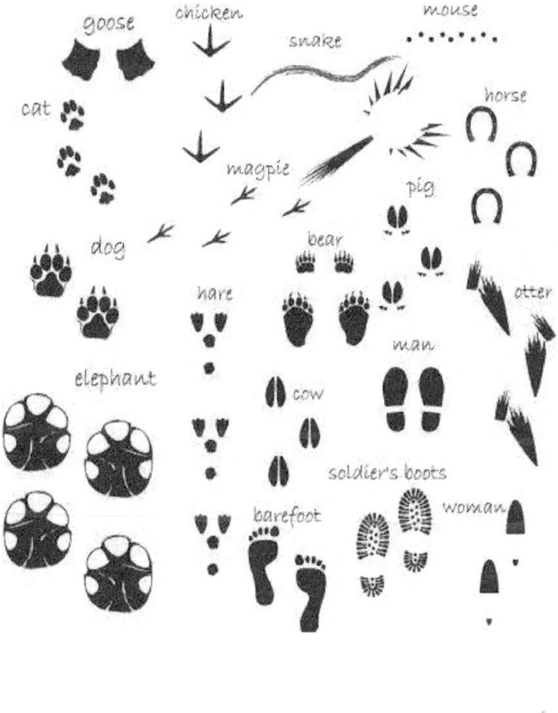

Fig 3: Prophetic Animal language script

www.ingramcontent.com/pod-product-compliance
Lightning Source LLC
Chambersburg PA
CBHW051751040426
42446CB00007B/316